The Narratives of Caroline Norton

The Narratives of Caroline Norton

Randall Craig

palgrave
macmillan

THE NARRATIVES OF CAROLINE NORTON

First published in 2009 by PALGRAVE MACMILLAN® in the United States - a division of St. Martin's Press LLC, 175 Fifth Avenue, New York, NY 10010.

Where this book is distributed in the UK, Europe and the rest of the world, this is by Palgrave Macmillan, a division of Macmillan Publishers Limited, registered in England, company number 785998, of Houndmills, Basingstoke, Hampshire RG21 6XS.

Palgrave Macmillan is the global academic imprint of the above companies and has companies and representatives throughout the world.

ISBN-13: 978–0–230–61217–4
ISBN-10: 0–230–61217–2

Library of Congress Cataloging-in-Publication Data is available from the Library of Congress.

Craig, Randall, 1951–
The narratives of Caroline Norton / Randall Craig.
p. cm.
Includes bibliographical references.
ISBN 0–230–61217–2 (alk. paper)
1. Norton, Caroline Sheridan, 1808–1877—Criticism and interpretation. 2. Norton, Caroline Sheridan, 1808–1877—Political and social views. 3. Norton, Caroline Sheridan, 1808–1877—Influence. 4. Women and literature—England—History—19th century. 5. Women—Legal status, laws, etc.—England—History—19th century. 6. Women in politics—Great Britain—History—19th century. 7. Feminism—England—History—19th century. I. Title.
PR5112.N5Z64 2009
828′.809—dc22 2008035829

Design by Integra Software Services

First edition: April 2009

10 9 8 7 6 5 4 3 2 1

Printed in the United States of America

FOR JANE
A RING OF WORDS
WELL WORN, WELL, WORN WELL

Contents

Acknowledgments

This project was supported by grants from the University at Albany and United University Professions. I am grateful to both. The research was conducted with the able and generous help of the Houghton Library, the Beinecke Rare Book and Manuscript Library, the British Library, and the Morgan Library. I would like especially to thank Sandra Stelts of the Pennsylvania State University Library and Nancy Moore of the Cornell Law Library for their willing and generous assistance. The University at Albany librarians have received my numerous requests with patience and pursued them with tenacity, and particular gratitude is owed to Peter Bae, Mary Casserly, Regina Conboy, Timothy Jackson, Winifred Kutchukian, and Roger Lipera. The administrative and secretarial staff of the Department of English have consistently and with incredible good nature eased the challenges—small and great—of professional life at UAlbany. I am pleased to be able to thank Liz Lauenstein, Regina Klym, Brenda Miller, and Connie Barrett. I would also like to express my appreciation to Farideh Koohi-Kamali, Kristy Lilas, and Brigitte Shull at Palgrave Macmillan, who have made the process of publication such a pleasure.

I would like to express my appreciation to David Craig and Jeffrey Berman for reading early versions of the manuscript and for commenting patiently and thoroughly on what could only with considerable optimism have been labeled a work in progress. That it did progress owes much to them. Thanks also to Richard M. Goldman for his careful review of the manuscript. Later versions of the book were proofread by Jane Craig, who has devoted a great deal of time to saving me from myself. In that—and many other ways—she is co-author of this book.

And while this project took many hours away from my family, it could not have been written without their continual presence in my mind and heart and their constant support and love in all aspects of my life. So, many, many thanks to my wife, Jane, and my son, Graham; also to David, to Jennifer and Ellen and their families, and to my mother, Cheryl; and to the Pattersons, who have so graciously and warmly made me a part of their family: Eleanor K. Patterson, Bob and Mary Kay Patterson, Julie and Jonathan Griffitts, Dan Patterson, John and Darla Patterson, and Lolly Patterson Cummiskey.

Two people have been important to me during this project and throughout our parallel paths: from the intellectual awakenings of our undergraduate years, through various courses of graduate study, to the pursuit of careers in different branches of education, Joseph Ciancaglini and Dennis Sheehan have served, perhaps unwittingly, as models and mentors—and invariably as admired friends.

Foreword
The Cassandra Dilemma

Have I missed the mark, or, like true archer, do I strike my quarry? Or am I prophet of lies, a babbler from door to door?[1]

Aeschylus, Agamemnon

Nineteenth-century writings by and about Caroline Norton demonstrate a recurring concern with society, law, and politics—all filtered through the lens of gender. Narratives about these interests and from this perspective constitute the subject and establish the organizing principle of this study. Whether as silver fork author, legal reformer, or political hostess, Norton was defined—and often confined—by gender, and doubly so. Her celebrated beauty and expressive demeanor on the one hand, and her status as female scion of a literary family, the Sheridans, on the other, contributed to a persona never entirely free of the aura of theatricality, therefore, never without the connotation of meretriciousness. As Nina Auerbach has observed, "Reverent Victorians shunned theatricality as the ultimate, deceitful mobility. It connotes not only lies, but a fluidity of character that decomposes the uniform integrity of the self."[2] During her lifetime, Norton was associated with numerous female archetypes, suggesting not only protean performativity on her part but also an ongoing effort by others to interpret and symbolically to control this provocative public figure.

Norton herself occasionally turned to iconic women to represent the conflict between private expectation and public constraint experienced by many nineteenth-century women. As a writer, she identified with Sappho, for whom the sorrows of private life and love outweighed the fame garnered through poetry. As a victim of inequitable marriage laws, she invoked the example of Hagar, although others insinuated that her circumstances were closer to those of Mary Magdalene. Because a lifelong interest in politics was frustrated by exclusion from public office, she turned to the example of Aspasia—as

George Meredith would to that of Egeria—to lament the limited civic role open to women. Through each of these associations runs a common theme of one woman's effort to speak truthfully about the condition of women, with the result of being discounted, if not decried, and ultimately disbelieved. For this reason, Cassandra, a figure blessed with foresight but cursed with incredibility, perhaps best represents Norton's maddening circumstances. Although an audience entrenched in convention, fortified by conservatism, and reinforced by complacency was often impervious to her barbed narratives, contemporary readers recognize the voice of someone quite other than "a prophet of lies, a babbler from door to door" in her tales of women in society and her pamphlets about women and law.

Beyond the fate of disbelief, Norton is linked to Cassandra by the themes of beauty and sexuality, politics and power. When Benjamin Robert Haydon asked her to sit for a painting of Cassandra in 1833, noting her "Sybil eyes lustrous and shining," he could not have foreseen the ironic aptness of the model to the subject.[3] While her Sybilline countenance and Grecian beauty were often remarked, it was not until 1836 and the prime minister's trial for adultery that Norton became an infamous public figure, whose subsequent analyses of English law would be dismissed as the hysterical jeremiads of a "she-devil."[4] By following pictorial convention and depicting Cassandra as a madwoman—signified by frenetic gestures and swirling lines—Haydon unwittingly predicted, albeit hyperbolically, Norton's tempestuous future. She herself offered a more prosaic—though hardly a less pessimistic—assessment of her fate, commenting to Mary Shelley that both possessed "a *sauvagerie*, a feeling of not being able to amalgamate with other and new associates."[5]

Exceptional as her experience was in so many ways, Norton insisted upon the ordinariness of her situation. She could laugh at the inherent tendency of mythological comparisons to aggrandize. For example, when writing to cancel a session with Haydon because "my face is swelled, & my eyes are so red that the Spirit of Prophecy would be ashamed to look out of them," she refers not to wild-eyed insanity but to the effects of the common cold.[6] The prosaic is not inevitably fatal to the prophetic, but Norton often felt that the voice of the suffering wife and mother was more suasive than that of the allegorical effigies she herself encouraged. When asked on another occasion to sit for a portrait, she urged the artist to remember "the fatal truth that my face is not so regular as the artists *expect* who have casually seen me—and that I am anxious to meet some painter who will be matter of fact enough, and sufficiently resigned to the will of Heaven, to copy what they see."[7] A tension between the allegorical and the realistic, the heroic and the ordinary, is a common theme in the narratives of Caroline Norton.

The beauty that led to numerous requests for portraits was an equivocal blessing for the author. Pulchritude and poetry, combined with a famous family name, might seem a foolproof formula for success in the fashionable literary world; however, early reviewers, while acknowledging the power of Norton's emerging poetic voice, muffled its impact through a variety of contradictory discursive stratagems, including superimposing the image of a Siren upon the Sibyl—a preoccupation with the author's beauty that implicitly demeaned her work. The introduction to this study, " 'The Caudine Forks' and the Optics of Authorship," considers these efforts and concludes with a brief analysis of "crossways," the trope arrived at by George Meredith to express the antinomies of Norton's character and career.

Some aspects of that career are not considered here, for example, her fame as a composer of popular songs. Similarly, no attempt is made to deal comprehensively with her poetry and fiction; rather, the book is divided into sections (each consisting of two chapters) dedicated to authorship, law, and politics. Chapter 1 analyzes Norton's post-Regency writing, which manifests opposed impulses of satire and sentiment and expresses ambivalent feelings toward fashionable society. From *The Dandies' Rout* (1820), written at age 11—to *Love in 'the World'*, begun before her marriage in 1827 but never published—to her first novel, *The Wife and Woman's Reward* (1835), her subject matter, themes, and style anticipate those of Thackeray, who freely drew upon her example in his own silver fork fiction, *Vanity Fair*. Chapter 2 argues that Norton's late narratives present familiar themes in a mode more consistent with the sensationalism of the sixties than the sentimentality of the thirties. The continuity of topoi throughout her career is documented by reading *Lost and Saved* (1863) in relation to her first long poem, "The Sorrows of Rosalie" (1829). To the preoccupations of a lifetime, the final narratives add sensational subplots as well as sexual and racial content that reflect the social tensions emerging in mid-Victorian England.

Chapter 3 shifts the focus from literature to law and the tenor from melodrama to comedy. The criminal conversation trial of Lord Melbourne, Norton's alleged paramour, elicited considerable courtroom comedy. This humor was a significant factor in securing a verdict for the defendant—indirectly, therefore, for Norton as well—but it invoked stereotypical narratives of gender that did little to remove the aura of sexual license surrounding her and women in general. *Norton* v. *Melbourne* inspired both farcical imitations (*The Pickwick Papers* and *Trial by Jury*) that reinforced and satiric redactions (*The Newcomes* and *Diana of the Crossways*) that critiqued these stereotypes. Though widely divergent, these adaptations provide an additional perspective upon the social and sexual narratives to which Norton was subjected throughout her life. Chapter 4 concerns the serious rather than the humorous side of the law. An unhappy marriage and the protracted legal battles over children and money led Norton to a realistic portrayal of domestic and legal violence in *Stuart of Dunleath* (1851). This novel, like those by Thackeray and Meredith based on the Nortons' history, depicts the unfortunate consequences of marrying spousal discord to legal action.

Part III turns to the question of women in politics and to Norton's critique of marriage law. Chapter 5 examines the role of the political hostess. The Sheridan family legend—notably the personal and political flamboyance of her grandfather—and increasing literary prominence prepared Norton for the role of salonnière and established her as a rival to silver fork authors and reputed bluestockings such as Lady Morgan, Lady Blessington, and Letitia Landon. Although scandal ended her public affiliation with Melbourne, continued literary success and public attention made Norton's invitations attractive to writers and rising politicians alike, notably Sidney Herbert. This relationship inspired several fictional parallels, including Lady Laura Kennedy in Trollope's *Phineas Finn*, Lady Berengaria Montfort in Disraeli's *Endymion*, and Meredith's eponymous Diana. Chapter 6 shifts to Norton's campaigns for reform of child custody and married women's property laws. Although her status as a blue was debated in her day, she proved a worthy successor to Mary Wollstonecraft, whose unfinished novel *Maria* coincidentally anticipated the opinions and experiences of Norton herself. Unlike her forebear, however, Norton did not endorse sexual equality, preferring to enlist conservative social narratives about saintly mothers and dependent wives in order to secure concrete advances in laws pertaining to married women.

The "Afterword" returns to the figure of the author and to a final instantiation of Meredith's trope of the writer at the crossroads. The focus here, as throughout, is neither upon the spectral private self underlying the spectacular and shifting public images, nor upon the welter of contradictory images of Norton found in Victorian diaries, periodicals, and fiction. These protean personae function as mirrors rather than lamps, and it is precisely this mirroring—the process, not the subject, of signification—that accounts for the title, *The Narratives of Caroline Norton*. The question explored here is not "Who was Caroline Norton?" but "What do the versions of her story say about the crossroads at which women of the period were poised?"

Abbreviations

"AM"	"A Mother"
BH	*Bleak House*
CI	*The Child of the Islands: A Poem*
D	*The Dream and Other Poems*
DC	*Diana of the Crossways*
DD	*Daniel Deronda*
DR	*The Dandies' Rout*
E	*Endymion*
ELW	*English Laws for Women*
FDS	*Fisher's Drawing Room Scrap-Book*
"I"	"The Invalid"
K	*The Keepsake*
KB	*Kate Bouverie and Other Tales and Sketches in Prose and Verse*
L	*Letters, etc. third and fourth correspondence with summary of facts*
LCN	*The Letters of Caroline Norton to Lord Melbourne*
LLG	*The Lady of La Garaye*
LM	*Letters to the Mob*
LQ	*A Letter to the Queen on Lord Chancellor Cranworth's Marriage and Divorce Bill*
LS	*Lost and Saved*
LW	*Love in "the World"*
M	*Maria*
MF	*The Mill on the Floss*
N	*The Newcomes*
"OLF"	"One of Our Legal Fictions"
OSD	*Old Sir Douglas*
P	*The Princess*
PF	*Phineas Finn*
PL	*A Plain Letter to the Lord Chancellor on the Infant Custody Bill*
PM	*The Prime Minister*

PP	*The Pickwick Papers*
PR	*Phineas Redux*
SD	*Stuart of Dunleath*
SMC	*The Separation of Mother and Child by the Law of "Custody of Infants," Considered*
SR	*The Sorrows of Rosalie, a Tale with Other Poems*
T	*Taxation. By an Irresponsible Taxpayer*
TJ	*Trial by Jury*
"TT"	"Leaves of a Life; or, the Templar's Tale"
UO	*The Undying One and Other Poems*
VF	*Vanity Fair*
VFF	*A Voice from the Factories*
WWR	*The Wife and Woman's Reward*

Introduction

"The Caudine Forks" and the Optics of Authorship

[A] baronet of large fortune... spoke with enthusiasm of her kind-heartedness as well as her beauty and talents; he, of course, passed under the Caudine Forks, beneath which all men encountering her had to bow and throw down their arms.[1]

Fanny Kemble, *Records of a Girlhood*

Fair Mrs. Norton! Beautiful Bhouddist, as Balaam Bulwer baptizes you, whom can we better choose for a beginning of our illustrious literary portraits, when diverging from the inferior sex, our pencil dares to portray the angels of the craft.[2]

William Maginn, "Mrs. Norton"

Caroline Norton was one of the most "visible" women of her day. She was a cynosure of public attention for nearly half a century following her formal introduction to fashionable society during the London season of 1826. Recognition and influence might never have been more than the result of physical beauty nor have extended beyond Almack's and its immediate environs had she not also been a prolific author of the sentimental verse and melodramatic tales popular with fashionable readers. Her initial literary impact, in turn, might never have been felt beyond the world of ton and its aspirants had she not, in 1831, attracted the attention of a man soon to become prime minister. Her relationship with Lord Melbourne led to a sensational scandal after which she would never be in the position to benefit from the wisdom of her own aperçu: "Obscurity is a thicker shield than virtue."[3] Even though her husband's charge of adultery was not proven, Norton was left with a maculate reputation in a marital no-woman's-land. In a relatively short period and well before the age of 30, her public persona had changed dramatically: from one of the beautiful Sheridan sisters, whose literary precocity established her as a worthy successor to her grandfather, Richard Brinsley Sheridan, to a scandalous woman separated from her husband and excluded from the drawing rooms of polite society.

After the humiliation of a public accusation of adultery and the outrage of having no chance to defend herself, Norton presented yet another face to the public, that of feminist reformer. When her husband denied access to their three children, she mounted a successful campaign to change child custody laws; when he provided intermittent and insufficient financial support, she lobbied in favor of married women's right to property. These efforts returned her to the public spotlight in a different guise and subjected her anew to personal attack. All the while, she supported herself (and her children) with a steady output of poetry and fiction. For more than 50 years, then, as a central figure in one of the century's most infamous scandals, as a political activist and feminist, and as a prolific author and editor of popular literature, Norton remained squarely—and controversially—in the public eye.

The crossway of gender and authorship was vexed for nineteenth-century women. Victorian Cassandras may not have been invariably disbelieved, but they did occupy a compromised situation. Perhaps intuiting Robert Southey's infamous advice to Charlotte Brontë that "[l]iterature cannot be the business of a woman's life: and it ought not to be," Norton published her first collection of poetry anonymously. She quickly learned, however, to capitalize on the persona intimated by her compatriot Thomas Moore: "I again fell in love with Mrs. N last night at Almack's. . . . The blood of old Brinsley!"[4] Her next collection, *The Undying One and Other Poems* (1830), appeared under her own name, and a reviewer commented that the "transmission of talent from generation to generation in the Sheridans is really wonderful."[5] That this essay dedicates more time to her grandfather's life than to her poetry, however, demonstrates that this form of literary attention obscured rather than illuminated her accomplishment.

Linda M. Shires notes that male writers like Byron recognized the value of "being seen—seen at certain places, with certain people, and in particular outfits or poses."[6] A woman author wishing to make her way in the world of Regency publishing had similarly to cultivate a public image, even though the effort contravened gendered standards of modesty and decorum. Norton did assiduously court literary attention, opening her modest home to fashionable authors of the day, among them Samuel Rogers, Edward Trelawny, Edward Bulwer Lytton, and Benjamin Disraeli. Numbered among "the Regency blues," she was associated with women such as Mary Shelley, Lady Blessington, L. E. L, and Lady Morgan, whose questionable personal reputations enhanced their literary standing in certain quarters—typically fashionable and male—at the expense of others.[7]

Ultimately, Norton's reputation seemed to fall somewhere between that of Byron and George Sand. With the publication of *The Dream and Other Poems* in 1840, she was, in fact, hailed by Hartley Coleridge as the "Byron of modern poetesses"—a comparison that increasingly assumed the pejorative connotation of self-promotion at the expense of poetic accomplishment.[8] Only four years later, for instance, R. H. Horne noted the Byronic association and asserted that Norton's poetry was tinged with "morbid despondency taking the tone of complaint and the amplification of private griefs."[9] By 1883, her reputation as "the female Byron" had become entirely negative:

> In all her poems we are constantly reminded of herself—a very interesting person to be reminded of, and we do not judge her harshly for the fault. Fault it was, however; and had she not been so caressed by society, and personally so worthy of the world's admiration, the continual suggestion of her own sufferings and sorrows abounding in her verse would be nothing short of an impertinence.[10]

Thus over the course of the nineteenth century, Norton's work was discounted in two ways: the Sheridan heritage militated against recognition in her own right and the Byronic association accentuated biography at the expense of art.

Two other factors in Norton's equivocal visibility can be symbolically traced not to her grandfather but to his wife, the accomplished actress and celebrated beauty Elizabeth Linley. Her profession did nothing to diminish the slightly louche reputation of the Sheridans. If authoresses were "liable to be looked on with prejudice," actresses were literally looked on, therefore, regarded as beyond the pale of proper society.[11] Norton, however, delighted in the connection, telling Fanny Kemble that "she . . . would give anything to try the stage herself. I thought, as I looked at her wonderful, beautiful face, 'Oh, if you should, what would become of me!' "[12] Although never acting professionally, she enthusiastically participated in private theatricals. Haydon, for instance, recalls "a delightful evening . . . [of] charades—written and acted by that extraordinary creature for beauty & Genius, Caroline Norton."[13]

Her social manner in general was demonstrative, a trait many, including Mary Shelley, attributed to her "eloquent blood."[14] Among the more staid matrons of fashionable society, this demeanor elicited censure. Lady Cowper wrote that Norton and her sisters were

> strange girls, [who] swear and say all sorts of odd things to make the men laugh. I am surprised so sensible a Woman as Mrs. Sheridan should let them go on so. I suppose she cannot stop the old blood coming out. They are remarkably good looking . . . and certainly clever.[15]

Norton suggested the burden of such social judgments in her tale "Kate Bouverie." Gertrude, the middle of three sisters (like Norton), is

> beautiful in person; harsh in manner; fearless by nature; she said everything, and did everything that came into her head, and the consequence was as might be expected. She was flattered by those she amused; courted by those to whom her notice gave a sort of notoriety; admired by many; and abused by the whole of her acquaintance.
>
> (*KB* 1:29–30)

Norton's public demeanor exhibited similar traits. The abuse was not limited to those who knew her following *Norton* v. *Melbourne*, in which she had been depicted as "a sort of strolling actress at a fair" (*L* 3:30). Anonymity would then have been welcome: "I am worse off than another woman might be, because my name, my family, & something in myself, makes me an object of attention & curiosity—and turn all that was a flattery into insult" (*LCN* 155).

The other Linley trait, striking beauty, was prepossessing to the point of obscuring all other qualities of mind and character. The Sheridan sisters were collectively known as "the Three Graces," and Norton commented: "People whose beauty is a familiar thing to their ears from childhood, might as well be vain of it as of being able to read and write" (*LCN* 53). She understatedly told Kemble, "Yes, we are rather good-looking people," and deadpanned to Disraeli, "Yes, I shall be beautiful even in my coffin."[16] Too sensuously beautiful, too self-dramatizing and self-promoting, Norton found herself cloaked in narratives whose effect was to reverse the victory at Caudine Forks. Late in life, she wrote to longtime friend and legal advisor, Abraham Hayward, wondering "whether a hundred years hence (when it can do me no good) people will be reading 'Hayward's biography of that remarkable woman,' and going to look at the turn-pike-gate on the road from Guildford to Shalford on the scene of inspiration for the story of 'Rosalie.' "[17] That biography was never written, and Norton's Surrey rivals neither the Brontës' moors nor Hardy's Wessex as a destination for literary tourists. The next century did see the publication of three biographies, but the anxiety revealed to Hayward would have changed to anger at the title of the most recent, which is not "that remarkable woman" but *A Scandalous Woman*.[18]

PORTRAITS OF THE AUTHOR I: THE WOMAN FEMINIZED, THE WRITER DOMESTICATED

The reading public's first glimpses of Norton occurred in February 1831, when she was featured in the *New Monthly* series "Living Literary Characters," and in *Fraser's* "The Gallery of Illustrious Literary Characters" the following month. Engraved portraits by John Hayter and Daniel Maclise, respectively, accompanied brief essays introducing the author whose name in a few years would be immediately recognizable to fashionable and unfashionable audiences alike.

The *New Monthly* praised Norton for "thinking before she writes"; however, the credit for this quality is given less to her than to the combined effect of heredity and instruction, both represented in masculine guises. It is noted that she is a "Sheridan by descent . . . and one, consequently, of the rich cluster of genius and talent which is wreathed round the name she inherits."[19] No mention is made of her mother (whose novel *Carwell* also appeared in 1831) except as a force trying to suppress her daughter's "*furor scribendi*."[20] Credit for her literary blossoming is awarded to "the masculine teaching" of her tutor and of her uncle.[21] Hayter's illustration (Fig. 1) may be intended to illustrate the thinking that precedes writing—the subject holds a book and stares into the distance—but it accentuates the corporeal at the expense of the intellectual. The portrait belies the claim that the Sheridan birthright is evident in what "phrenology would abundantly establish by the ample development of certain cerebral organs."[22] Whatever the physiognomic evidence of cerebral organs might be, the salient feature of this portrait is the subject's elaborate coiffure. Long, dark tresses sweep over the eye and are gathered on top of her head. Norton is shown in nearly full profile, looking to her right and slightly upward; her face is meticulously drawn and shaded. Her body, by contrast, is quickly sketched from a frontal perspective. The neck and shoulders are bare; a dark boa offsets her hair and thick eyebrows, framing the bodice of a gown that she appears less to be wearing than posing behind. One has only to look at Hayter's portrait to understand Sydney Smith's description of his friend as

Figure 1 John Hayter, "The Honorable Mrs. Norton," *New Monthly Magazine*, February, 1831

Source: Reproduced with the permission of Rare Books and Manuscripts, Special Collections Library, the Pennsylvania State University Libraries.

"a superb lump of flesh."[23] Apart from the iconic book, which is suggested rather than represented, the image does little to emphasize the article's claim of serious intelligence; indeed, the entire impression is of "*other accomplishments.*"

Figure 2 Daniel Maclise, "The Author of 'The Undying One,'" *Fraser's Magazine*, March, 1831
Source: Courtesy of the University at Albany Libraries, State University of New York.

The next month *Fraser's* took a gibe at Hayter: "A caricature of this lady appeared in a rival publication. . . . There her characteristic features were lost in a nonsensical straining after effect. What has a lady, the head of a household, to do with staring at the stars or any other wondrous body stuck over head?"[24] Mrs. Norton may be one of "the angels of the craft," but only because she is "[h]eiress of a race to whom genius his constant boon has given, through long descended lines to bloom in wit of earth or strains of Heaven!"[25] Maginn's commentary and Maclise's drawing (Fig. 2) return the subject to earth, defining "her characteristic features" in terms of the "beauties of that symmetrical form" (a reference to her person, not her poetry) and the duties of a married woman.[26] Norton contentedly superintends the homely ritual of tea, looking demurely downward rather than up either to the portrait of her grandfather or into the heavens.[27] The head and face, meticulously rendered by Hayter, are not drawn in detail and appear to be disproportionately small in relation to the portrait on the wall behind her. Greater attention is given to dress, which is matronly, and to setting, which is domestic, than to any indication of authorship—a net bag, apparently of books, hangs over the back of the chair and is partially obscured by the bustle of her gown.[28] The scene illustrates that Norton has not succumbed to the danger cited by Maginn:

> Authoresses are liable to many rubs. Mrs. Norton, it would appear by her picture, at breakfast, has escaped some. . . . And her look, as depicted in the sketch before us, is enough to shew that she has not passed the night in any sublunary matters; but in the contemplation of that divine philosophy and sublime poetry which is best indulged in without intrusion. The consequences are upon her countenance.[29]

This praise is at best backhanded: literature is relegated to nocturnal hours, and "sublunary matters," such as matutinal tea and "the comfort and convenience of her husband," take precedence.[30] Indeed, even when praising her verse, Maginn reduces its virtues to those of the national beverage: it is "as fluent, as clear, as lucid, and as warm as the liquid distilling from the urn."[31] True Irish genius, he implies, such as that possessed by her grandfather—shown "rubicund in the nasal feature"—demands stronger and more manly beverages.[32]

Not yet tainted by scandal, Norton is implicitly contrasted to other fashionable female writers: "Spent in elegant retirement, the grace of her private circle, or blazing forth the ornament of brilliant society;

there is no unfeminine display about her which can supply matter for the anecdote monger."[33] Maginn sounds a warning, however, in his closing line: "a lady ought to be treated, even by Reviewers, with the utmost deference—except she writes politics, which is an enormity equal to wearing breeches."[34] The critic's condescension further diminishes the woman writer, who has already been confined to "elegant" and "brilliant" quarters. She is now excluded from politics as well. While readers would be unlikely either to confuse the elaborate gown of Maclise's domestic goddess with bloomers or to suspect its wearer of being a bluestocking, Norton's familial ties to the Whigs and early support for the Reform Bill may have elicited this preemptive admonition. Maginn's relative—and uncharacteristic—mildness may indicate that Irish loyalty outweighed Tory sympathies, but William Bates offers a different and now familiar explanation: "The terrible 'Doctor' is in his softer mood . . . he has for the nonce divested himself of tooth and claw, like the amorous lion of Babrius, and is prostrate before the throne of beauty."[35]

PORTRAITS OF THE AUTHOR II: THE WRITER ETHEREALIZED, THE WOMAN MASCULINIZED

Her literary presence well established by the mid-1830s, Norton encountered a different set of critical responses in the next decade, although the tendency to personal notice remained constant. Separation from her husband dispelled the domestic narrative of *Fraser's* but did nothing to quell admiration of her "symmetrical form." Norton aroused grand passions in figures like Haydon and Trelawny and elicited tawdry sexual innuendo from fellow writers like Dickens and Thackeray.[36] For example, underlying Dickens's declaration that Norton "was a sight for the Gods" were some decidedly carnal thoughts, and Thackeray's recollection of Norton's sitting "bodkin in her own brougham," prompted his remark: "indeed there are very few more beautiful bodkins in the world."[37]

Comments of that order, along with the frontispiece to Norton's third volume of poetry, *The Dream and Other Poems* (1840), suggest that little had changed in the decade since her first collection. Edward Landseer's drawing (Fig. 3) emphasizes the bare "bodkin" prompting Thackeray's questionable compliment. From the exposed shoulders framed by dark hair and trimming on her gown to the disregarded book, Landseer very nearly copies Hayter. His portrait would not seem to be what Hartley Coleridge had in mind when he hypothesized that English society had evolved beyond the "sensual philosophy"

Figure 3 Edward Landseer, "Caroline Elizabeth Sheridan Norton," *The Dream and Other Poems* (1840)
Source: Courtesy of the University at Albany Libraries, State University of New York.

that kept women modestly veiled in the background. Women writers, he claimed, were no longer equivocally situated: "A different tone prevails in society upon this subject; the peculiar talents of women are acknowledged, and the powers common to them and men are, in particular instances of exhibition, fairly appreciated."[38] However progressive this view might appear, Coleridge had more in common with predecessors like Maginn than he might have realized. Seemingly liberal sentiments are belied by the trope of the impotent pen with which his essay begins:

It is easy to be critical of men; but when we venture to lift a pen against women, straightway *apparent facies*; the weapon drops pointless on the marked passage; and whilst the mind is bent on praise or censure of the poem, the eye swims too deep in tears and mist over the poetess herself in the frontispiece, to let it see its way to either. Edwin Landseer's drawing must be removed, or we shall hold our court, like the Areopagites, in the dark.[39]

Critics, "fitter for the distaff than the spear" in the words of Winthrop Mackworth Praed (who coincidently acknowledged "a look from Miss Sheridan's eyes" in his poem "Good-night to the Season"), are helpless before poetic Phrynes, whose sexual power robs them of all reason.[40] Frances A. Gerard corroborated his century's assessment of Norton's "singular power of fascination," commenting in 1897

Sweet Caroline Norton what a singular power of fascination you possessed! Even the coldest of reviewers fell under your influence, and had a kind word for your literary efforts, and were nearly always in your favour. Some of them, indeed, wrote of her in terms that would affront more than gratify writers who would rather be judged by the merit of their work than their personal attractions. Still, after, all, a reviewer is but a man.[41]

While Areopagitical darkness might be one defense against "personal attractions," a more common tactic involved etherealizing epithets like Trelawny's "the divine Mrs. Norton." Disraeli referred to her as "Starry Night," and Meredith's fictional Norton is both "the Duchess of Stars" and "the starry she" (*DC* 1:222, 2:46).[42] Empyrean epithets reconfigured a corporeal being as a sidereal voice—cool, remote, and unapproachable. When Bulwer Lytton's adulatory poem "The Honorable Mrs. Norton" apotheosized her as the "Queenly Spirit of a Star" (*FDS 47*:83), Thackeray objected to the mythologizing. He labeled the poem so much "flimsy, mystical, namby-pamby" and rejected its "attitudes, platitudes, beatitudes": "Isn't a woman good enough for you that inherits Sheridan's genius and sweet Cecilia's eyes and voice, but you must assume an inspired air, and declare she is a stray angel?"[43] Even allowing for his long-standing animus against Bulwer Lytton, Thackeray seems to protest too much. That he so adamantly and "fearlessly assert[s] Mrs. Norton to be only a woman, and always a woman" suggests that he, too, has passed under the Caudine Forks and must avenge the defeat by returning the angelic author to a womanly sphere.[44] Like the reviewers of a decade

Figure 4 Thomas Carrick, "Caroline Norton," *Fisher's Drawing Room Scrap-Book, 1847* (1846)
Source: Courtesy of the University at Albany Libraries, State University of New York.

earlier, Thackeray cannot resist a comment on the poet's appearance. His apology to Norton for having done so is far from heartfelt: "Instead of praising the Drawing Room Scrap book for instance, I find I have made remarks on the Editor's ... personal appearance of w^{h} to speak favorably seems on my part to be a *balourdise* and impertinence—but I couldn't help it."[45] The reviewer is, after all, "but a man"—and one evidently more interested in "beautiful bodkins" than "stray angels."

Thomas Carrick's drawing of Norton (Fig. 4), which served as the frontispiece of the volume in which Bulwer's poem appeared, resists allegory and avoids Landseer's sensuality. A matronly Norton is frontally portrayed, with hair pulled demurely back. She wears a modest dress with a ruffled collar that cloaks her neck and shoulders. Noting the "black velvet band round her forehead, and buttons on her dress," Thackeray asserted that Norton was "not a spirit of a Star, but a woman in black with buttons. . . . Fancy an angel in buttons! No! no!"[46] Nonetheless, he unwittingly reinscribed Bulwer's idealization by suggesting that "Mr. Carrick's picture no more represents her magnificent beauty than Mr. Joseph Hume resembles Apollo. To have seen it is to have seen something in history."[47] After invoking the names of legendary beauties, such as Helen and Cleopatra, he asked if readers would like to have seen "that sweet ancestor of Mrs. Norton's own, who smiles on Reynolds's canvas with such ravishing, delicious purity—the charming, charming Lindley [sic]."[48] Thackeray thus succumbs to the very mythologizing impetus of which he is so critical. Like so many other critics, his preoccupation with the person occludes the author and discounts her work. After insisting that Mrs. Norton is only a woman, he subsequently returns her to the constellation of legendary beauties as the reincarnation of her "ravishing" and "delicious" grandmother.[49]

In "Miss E. B. Barrett and Mrs. Norton," R. H. Horne expressed weariness of the entire subject of Norton's beauty—an ironic dismissal insofar as it paraliptically introduced the subject into an essay that otherwise concentrated on poetry not poetesses:

> We cannot admit that any picture, engraving, or other portrait of Mrs. Norton with which the public has been favoured does full justice to the original; nevertheless they may be considered as likenesses, to a certain extent, and by reason of these, and her popular position as an authoress, any introductory remarks on the present occasion would be needless.[50]

Norton must also have wearied of the subject, and she obtained a portion of good-natured revenge on critics and portraitists alike in "The Beautycultural Society." The poem imagines an organization that establishes codes of beauty and awards medals for such things as perfect eyebrows and complexions. Disputed decisions are adjudicated by "a Court of last Appeal" composed of artists because "it really is *their* interest, it cannot be denied, / To keep down the spread of Ugliness, which threats on every side" (*FDS 49*:6). Among the judges are several Norton portraitists: "Eastlake and Etty,—Landseer,—Maclise, and others, came / And volunteered, most handsomely, each to put down his name" (*FDS 49*:6). Their generosity, of course, is suspect given the evidence to be paraded before them:

> For several great ladies, whose names, of course, I spare,
> Have all been lately fined, my dear, for dressing much too bare:
> Such an expanse of shoulders that were not fit to show!
> "*Ma foi! Mais ça commence trop tard,—et ça finit trop tôt,*"
> As Talleyrand, the famous wit, said, when he first looked down
> On a desperate abridgement of a "low-dress" evening gown.
> (*FDS 49*:6–7)

Even if the fault were less a matter of "dressing much too bare" than of possessing "shoulders that were not fit to show," the jury nonetheless is not insensible to the evidence presented to them:

> The Artists flinched a little, when the half-dressed ladies came;
> Etty, (who's used to models nude,) acquitted them of blame,—
> Eastlake, with pure and gentle eyes, looked shyly on each dress,
> And said, "perhaps the milliner had made a stupid guess,"—
> Maclise, who (being an Irishman) meant kindly, I'll engage,
> Said, "Bedad, dress did'nt signify, after a certain age."
> Landseer spoke Delphian oracles, whose meaning yet may dawn,—
> "That the fronts of such fine palaces deserved *a little lawn*."
> (*FDS 49*:7)

The satire good-naturedly returns the gaze that Norton experienced when sitting for the portraits that both adorned and masked her poetry.

The inclination to return the male gaze, the refusal to cast eyes demurely downward under male inspection, suggests another reaction to Norton's personal and poetic presence. Rather than construct her as female exotic, domestic exemplar, or ethereal muse, some dismissed her character—and her writing—as masculine. On one occasion, her exuberant behavior shocked the Earl of Malmesbury: "Mrs. Norton came to Mme. Sebastiani's party, wishing, I suppose to feel the world. She talked in a most extraordinary manner, and kicked Lord Melbourne's hat over her head. The whole *corps diplomatique* were amazed."[51] The impression of the evening never faded. More than a dozen years later, Malmesbury remarked of Norton's stay with his family: "We found her very agreeable and amusing, but her beauty, her manners, and her conversation are all of the most masculine character—and the latter is often coarser than even a man should use."[52]

The kicking of Melbourne's hat is an instance of life imitating art. In "Kate Bouverie," the beautiful but tomboyish protagonist is engaged to her cousin, who is embarrassed by "that anomalous being they intend for my wife" (*KB* 1:22). Harry's discomfort is expressed in a dream: "Suddenly, he thought she turned and kicked him, and the little well-turned, firmly-knit anckle was unaccountably transformed into Selim's hoof" (*KB* 1:21). The horse's name is an inside joke. After Melbourne had offered to give her a horse, Norton mocked her husband's assessment of "the comparative dangers to my moral character & physical strength, of rides on Carthugh's kicking horse Selim, or frequent caracoles on your [Melbourne's] mare in the Park" (*LCN* 47). Her comment reveals a failure to attend to the niceties of female decorum that also characterizes the eponymous heroine. Both fastidious and fearful, Harry transmogrifies his formidable fiancée into a physical and social grotesque. Kate's improper sexuality, suggested by the exposed ankle, is expressed by her invasion of a male bastion—the military barracks. This "anomalous being"—the centaurian Selim—possesses equine energy and exhibits mannish behavior. Norton represents in Kate, as she had in Gertrude, aspects of her own "*sauvagerie.*"

Confronted with the woman writer who refused enshrinement either before the tea service or upon the empyrean heights, reviewers employed a strategy similar to Harry's. To reverse Praed's formulation: Norton was imagined to be "fitter for the spear than the distaff." Recognition as "the Byron of our modern poetesses" necessarily invoked a male standard and compromised the woman writer. The praise is further qualified insofar as it connotes personal scandal and the "flashy literary talent," leading critics like Harold Nicholson to discount her as the author of "volume after volume of Byronic verse."[53] Coleridge identified the Byronic elements of Norton's poetry as "intense personal passion . . ., beautiful intervals of tenderness, . . . strong practical thought, and . . . forceful expression."[54] He compared her passionate outpourings to "javelins hurled by an Amazon" and her calmer expressions to islands "amidst the arrowy rushing of her passion."[55] By transforming the author into an amazon who launches javelins and arrows, critics wield a double-edged sword of their own: the woman writer is praised in terms that simultaneously discredit her. Norton's pointed "forceful expression" is necessarily a failure in "purity and correctness of diction."[56]

Percy Fitzgerald refers to Coleridge in making virtually the same objection many years later:

> there is a breadth and finish in her work which is almost masculine. We cannot, however, go so far as the enthusiastic Quarterly Reviewer . . . who pronounced that she was "a female Byron;" but there is certainly a strong Byronic tinge in her effusions. . . . What strikes us in her poetry is the earnestness of feeling, the masculine cast of thought, and the mode in which her own personality is made to furnish dramatic colour and action.[57]

With "the blood of old Brinsley," perhaps it was inevitable that his formidable granddaughter would be represented as an anomalously gendered entity. Indeed, Norton was repeatedly situated at the intersection, not simply of gender, but of other competing social and cultural forces in mid-Victorian England—a dilemma recognized by Meredith, whose Diana Merion ably expresses the contradictions of the women after whom she is modeled.

CAROLINE AT THE CROSSWAYS

Diana of the Crossways appeared eight years after Norton's death. "Crossways" is the protagonist's ancestral home, symbolizing both her identity and her independence. The house figures literally in the plot when it becomes a point of contention in the Warwicks' marital dispute. The name derives from its proximity to a rural intersection—in the local dialect, a "crassways for four roads . . . and a post in the middle" (*DC* 1:111). Whatever the ironies evoked by the provincial pronunciation, "crossways" resonates with figurative meaning, suggesting among other things the decisions to be made on life's highway. Meredith repeatedly places his heroine in situations in which she must select from mutually exclusive, sometimes irreversible directions—and do so without the benefit of signposts. Paradoxically both a residence and a road, and rife with literal and symbolic significance, "crossways" is an apposite term for the fictional heroine and her real-life model.

As a common rather than a proper noun, "crossway" denotes an impediment as well as an intersection. It can also imply a period of inaction or indecision prior to determining a future direction. To be at a crossway can mean to encounter either enabling, if confusing, alternatives or insurmountable obstacles. The former sense is apparent when Diana flees to the Crossways after her husband initiates a criminal conversation action against Lord Dannisburgh. From here she must decide whether to escape to the Continent, leaving scandal behind, or return to London, defying opprobrium and avowing her innocence. In this instance, her choice is literally made at the Crossways: she retraces her steps, defies her detractors, and begins a career as a writer. The latter sense, implying an impediment or complication, is evident from Diana's account of her marriage to Augustus Warwick: they "walked a dozen steps in stupefied union, and hit upon crossways" (*DC* 1:178). The collision culminates in a failed divorce action, which places the couple in legal limbo and renders Diana "a wife and no wife" (*DC* 1:217). Crossways may be exacerbated by law, as in this case, but Meredith further implies that they are existential and not merely situational. Both by nature and as a woman in Victorian society, Diana is "actuated contrariously" (*DC* 2:230). As a result, her journeys into marriage—"The Anti-Climax Expedition, as she called it" (*DC* 2:220), or in the narrator's terms, the "Final Struggle for Liberty and Run into Harness" (*DC* 2:248)—are anything but smooth.

"Caroline at the Crossways" would be an appropriate title for a study of a conflicted character and the narratives that both explained and constrained her life. Norton entered the public sphere—socially, professionally, politically—at a time when English society itself was at a crossroads, poised between an inaccessible past and an unknowable future: in Arnold's famous formulation, "[w]andering between two worlds, one dead, / The other powerless to be born."[58] Bulwer Lytton expresses this sense of existing neither here nor there in *England and the English* (1833):

> We live in an age of visible transition—an age of disquietude and doubt—of the removal of time-worn landmarks, and the breaking up of the hereditary elements of society—old opinions, feelings—ancestral customs and institutions are crumbling away, and both the spiritual and temporal worlds are darkened by the shadow of change.[59]

Norton lived in the midst of this "visible transition." While the reign of William IV may have seen the last vestiges of British romanticism, no particular light illuminated "the shadow of change." It would be some time before any notion of what it meant to be a "Victorian" would develop, and when it did, its significance was not congenial to an iconoclastic woman and "the Byron of modern poetesses."

The "age of disquietude and doubt" made it difficult for writers in general to establish a clear voice and a receptive audience. Norton in particular seemed vexed by the shifting boundaries between the public and private spheres. Her writing, literary and political, was motivated by and infused with her own experience. If the pathos of her poetry and the force of her political rhetoric were partially due to this fact, then it was no less true that writing from and of the self led to critical devaluation of her works and angry opposition to the legislative reforms she advocated. As a poet, she was encouraged to "break through the narrow circle of personal and domestic feelings, and adventure herself upon a theme of greater variety and less morbid interest."[60] Similarly, her political tracts were dismissed as the expression of merely private grievances. In the midst of the debate of child custody law, for example, John Kemble sneeringly remarked:

> If the friends and relatives of that lady think it a proof of good taste to be continually appealing to the public about her private affairs, they may continue, for us, to think so; but at all events we must beg to remind them, that if the sympathies and passions of honourable members and the public are to be excited, it ought to be done for a legitimate object.[61]

Norton's politics, like her poetry, were too personal, too passionate, too public; hence she was repeatedly upbraided for her crass ways.

The persistent tendency to read Norton's writing solely by the glaring light of biography has dimmed the insight of contemporary critics no less than that of their predecessors. A broader focus—a more diffuse critical light—reveals not only the crossway of style and genre that occurs within her writing but also the elements of art that made her a subject of interest to writers like Meredith. A counterpoint to the tendency to see her work primarily in terms of biography is Mary Poovey's pioneering discussion of the political writing, which, she argues, must be read in terms of its assimilation of literary modes, especially the vision and method of melodrama. She suggests that Norton negotiates Victorian standards of gender and privacy by splitting herself "into two persons: the long-suffering victim of social injustice and the vindicating polemical writer," the former "female and the latter male."[62] This strategy is explicitly dramatized in *Diana of the Crossways.* The bifurcation of self into narrator and narrated results in a proliferation of voices and modes that defies convention. This approach, extended to her poetry and fiction, allows us to recognize that the shadow of change detected by Bulwer Lytton in *England and the English* can also be seen in Norton's "contrariously actuated" forms and voices.

Meredith's recognition that Norton inhabited a Victorian crossroads establishes the foundation of this study of narratives by and about her. Poised at the meeting point of divergent social forces, Norton cannot be read simply or singly. Her contemporary, Lady Granville, astutely noted with regard to Norton's early work: "How excellent, how beautiful I think some of her writing; but somehow or other she does not fit into her own frame, she is not in keeping with her own opinions and feelings, and it is impossible to bind her up with her own stories"—or, I would emphasize, to bind the stories up with her.[63] Norton "does not fit into her own frame," and in a sense Horne was right: no portrait can do justice to her. Certainly neither a static picture nor a univocal interpretation can capture her protean career, her contradictory personae. Whatever the public identity—the witty socialite and silver fork writer/editor, the unhappy wife but devoted mother, the feminist and legal reformer—Norton was impelled in contrary directions but kept more or less in the same place. She is, therefore, a figure for her times: an author seeking a voice in the wake of the Romantic past, a citizen of the Regency seeking an identity and place in a Victorian world in the making, and a woman struggling to emerge from the social and legal constraints of the nineteenth century.

Part I

Authorship

Chapter 1

"The World" and "The (Sm)all Great": Silver Fork Narratives

Oh!—depend on it, there is no treadmill like the life of a "Woman of the World," and you see it in the expression of the face. It is not late hours *that bring the jaded, anxious, restless look; on the contrary, I believe you might sit up till morning, singing till the lark interrupted you, and be none the worse. It is the perpetual struggle to* be *and to* do, *and the internal and continual dissatisfaction with all one* is *and* does, *that eats away the freshness of one's life.*[1]

Caroline Norton, Letter to Mary Shelley

The Duke of Devonshire called on me the other day if you please, and I am going to his house tonight. I don't care a straw for the great people I find: only knowing them makes me a little more impatient of the airs of the (sm)all great.[2]

William Makepeace Thackeray, Letter to Mrs. Carmichael-Smyth

Placed in quotation marks, "the world" shrinks in size but expands in significance—at least in the eyes of its autochthonous denizens, whose names might be gleaned by scanning invitations to Almack's and membership lists of select clubs like White's and Boodle's.[3] Its borders are easily circumnavigated, since they enclose the few fashionable districts of London that are the center of social activity during "the season." In late spring and early summer when Parliament is in session, the aristocracy congregate for rituals of driving, dining, and dancing; as Dickens noted in *Bleak House*, "The fashionable world—tremendous orb, nearly five miles round—is in full swing, and the solar system works respectfully at its appointed distances" (*BH* 572). The objective of all this motion is less "to *be* and to *do*," in Norton's words, than to be *seen*. As courtship rituals run their course, the heat of the London summer brings the estival diaspora.[4] The fashionable disperse to the comparative quiet and coolness of country estates—the successful to celebrate advantageous matches, the unsuccessful to rethink strategies for the next season.

In 1826 Norton was poised to "come out," hoping to enter the very society that she had mocked in the juvenile parody *The Dandies' Rout* (1820). Numbered among the "civilized gipsies" residing at Hampton Court, the Sheridan sisters sought a place in a world to which neither birth nor wealth promised entry:

> the glittering, feverish London of the 1820s . . . was ruled by wealth and fashion, and characterised by reckless extravagance. In this world there was one magical quality which shed an ineffable glow on its possessors, and whose acquirement was the cause of the most ruthless, and indeed, fanatical struggle on the part of the uninitiated. This quality was summed up in one short and pregnant word—Ton.[5]

As "Hampton Court Bohemians" and never more than on the fringes of the beau monde, "the Three Graces" depended upon their extravagant beauty to succeed in the "match-making nation" described by Bulwer Lytton:

> We boast that in our country, young people not being affianced to each other by their parents, there are more marriages in which the heart is engaged than there are abroad. Very possibly; but in good society, the heart is remarkably prudent, and seldom falls violently in love without a sufficient settlement.[6]

In a society "(b)red in tooth and claw," prudence is indistinguishable from rapacity. The polished veneer of this glittering but superficial world obscured the harsh commercial reality that shaped Norton's experiences in the late 1820s as debutante, wife, and fledgling author.

THE EQUIVOCAL VALUE OF VISIBILITY I: AT ALMACK'S AND IN PRINT

Accounts of this endogamous society, such as those found in "the lively novels of Mrs. Gore," had become so common by 1827 that William Hazlitt deridingly referred to the "Dandy School" of literature.[7] Bulwer might have as easily said "living" as "lively," since these novels typically featured thinly disguised portraits of actual people. Self-representation confirmed the values of "the world" and allowed outsiders a glimpse of its clubs, customs, rituals, and even its leading "characters."[8] To be visible may have been the chief desideratum among the denizens of "the world," but to be "seen" in a novel was a particular badge of success. It was not inconceivable, for instance, that Norton might have appeared in *Almack's*, a highly successful roman à clef published in the year of her debut at this exclusive institution, and she did appear briefly in Lady Blessington's first novel, *The Repealers* (1833).[9]

Marriage to George Norton—second son of Lord Grantley, Tory MP, and nonpracticing attorney—did little to advance her standing in fashionable society. Union with an undistinguished, unambitious, and unartistic man was widely perceived as a waste of beauty and talent. After her husband lost his seat in the 1830 election, Norton turned to Lord Melbourne, admirer of her grandfather and friend of her father, to request a patronage position for her husband. The ensuing friendship provided social capital but did little to alleviate the family's financial strain and nothing at all to improve her already unhappy marriage. She wrote to Melbourne in 1831: "I have not, in spite of the change of opinion among my friends on the score of my looks, obtained what I wished—perhaps I should say what I *expected* when I first began to look in the glass with satisfaction" (*LCN* 53). Her next letter, whose date (August 26) occasions a pun on Melbourne's high status, seems no more ingenuous than Thackeray's claim to have become "impatient of the airs of the (sm)all great." She writes, "On the point of replying to that part of your august epistle which relates to my regretting *that I had not done as well as I might have done*... I would not give a fillip to be a Duke's wife tomorrow" (*LCN* 59).

Professing to reject "mere position in the world," Norton nonetheless actively pursues one, and her success, insofar as it involved Melbourne, is registered by a tableau recorded by Fanny Kemble:

> I sat for some time opposite a large, crimson-covered ottoman, on which Lord Melbourne reclined, surrounded by those three enchanting Sheridan

sisters. . . . A more remarkable collection of comely creatures, I think, could hardly be seen . . . taking into consideration the high rank, eminent position, and intellectual distinction of the four persons who formed that beautiful group.[10]

Family, intellect, and beauty gained Norton a place on that ottoman and in "the world," but only at the exclusion of her husband. Literally not in the picture, he initiated an action for adultery against Melbourne that expelled his wife from the tableau and placed her, figuratively speaking, in a mud-spattered pillory.

The early 1830s marked a coming out of another kind for Norton: her entry into the world of fashionable literature, facilitated, as we have seen, by appearances in "Living Literary Characters" and the "Gallery of Illustrious Literary Characters." These series, according to Judith L. Fisher, document "the burgeoning profession of writer and a non-Byronic, proto-Victorian celebrity-dom."[11] With increased recognition also came invitations to edit annuals, those "gorgeous watered-silk publication[s]" that in George Eliot's ironic account "marked modern progress at that time."[12] In *Lives of the Sheridans*, Fitzgerald attributes the keepsake "to a curious phase of literary taste . . . which originated in an ingenious publisher's idea of utilizing the vanity of 'persons of quality' for purposes of trade."[13] Henry Colburn, exactly a publisher of this sort, advised Norton to "devote her talents to the fashionable vices of the day and he would pay her what she chose—not romances or imaginative things."[14] Although not rigidly adhering to this advice, Norton characterized the "light serial literature [that] was the express fashion of the day" as "ephemeral" (*ELW* 25) and occasionally spoke disparagingly of her own keepsake productions.[15] While the work of editing and writing for annuals was tiresome and not invariably conducive to literary excellence, it was remunerative, as Colburn's comment suggests, and she continued this work until mid-century.[16]

Some of the pieces that Norton wrote for consumption by those whom Hazlitt described as "eat[ing] their fish with a silver fork" were collected in *Kate Bouverie, and Other Tales and Sketches, in Prose and Verse* (1835).[17] The work is of interest for several reasons, not the least of which is its reflection of changing social and literary values. Winifred Hughes observes, "the silver fork novel, however self-consciously ephemeral, evidently touched a popular nerve in its open preoccupation with shifting class boundaries and insecurities. Its fixation on the elegantly scandalous mores of the Regency evoked both nostalgia and disapproval in its not quite Victorian readers."[18]

In a transitional period—one that Norton herself characterized as "an age of 'progress,' when every one is tossing, struggling, wrecking, and foundering on a sea of commercial speculation or political adventure"—it is not surprising that shifting boundaries typify literary genres as well as social classes.[19] As Hughes further notes, "silver fork novels were marked by a radical instability of tone: they could be, and were, read both as celebrations of the aristocratic ascendancy and as devastating satires."[20] Norton's writing reflects these contradictory attitudes, and she seems both to desire and to deride the "glittering, feverish London of the 1820s."

SILVER FORK SATIRE

An early indication of Norton's ironic temperament is her youthful jeu d'esprit, *The Dandies' Rout* (1820), a comic look at society fops, each "[d]etermined the Dandy of Dandies to be," and their ladies, the "Dandizettes so mild and sweet."[21] The brief poem, 32 couplets accompanied by 14 of her own illustrations, chronicles the preparations for a fancy ball by various guests. For example, M'Carey, "a Dandy full of grace" (*DR*), must be laced into his evening wear by his valet. At age 11, Norton possessed limited direct experience of this world, and her poem reflects the prejudices and preoccupations of "the gipsies of gentility." Included among the broad ethnic stereotypes are an aspiring Jewish dandy (unnamed), Mr Pink, and a turbaned Turk (Hal Dandyso). Pink, who relies on false whiskers and padded calves to disguise his limitations, is depicted in dress-like underclothing, washing his shirt for the rout—an act that, were it to become known, would indelibly stain his reputation. The juvenile humor and craft of *The Dandies' Rout* anticipate the keen sense of the ridiculous and the great delight in exposing social foibles and pretensions that is found in her later work. Tellingly, the child's focus reflects Norton's own circumstances: it falls upon neither the haves nor the have-nots but those in the middle, the dandy wannabes.

"Recollections of a Faded Beauty" (1840) similarly relies on cultural and literary stereotypes and employs rhymed couplets. It demonstrates, however, more sophisticated language and broader knowledge of society's "prodigious littlenesses, etiquettes, ceremonials, sham moralities."[22] The child's delight in the ridiculous is heard, for instance, in the aging speaker's remark upon her asymmetrical visage: "They called me Chloë for they said my grace / Was nymph-like; as was also half my face" (*UO* 229). The poem is an ironic lament by a comic coquette, Diana, who "didn't marry, . . . / But I had handsome lovers by the score; / Alas! alas! I always sighed for more" (*UO* 229–30). The tragedy of the formerly flirtatious, now faded beauty is muted by the farcical list of past lovers and by her blasé good humor. Content to celebrate past conquests, she describes a cast of characters straight out of *The Dandies' Rout*—a cross-eyed soldier, a dairyman, a Scotsman, "a certain Irishman," and a Byronic poet—all of whose valedictory speeches are reproduced. The last of these, Frederic Mortimer de Veaux, bids adieu in words that comically recall Norton's reputation as "the Byron of modern poetesses":

> Allah hu! Shall I ever behold thee again,
> Sweet cause of my transport—dear cause of my pain?
> Al, hamdu il Illah! what place can be fair,
> My Rose of the Desert, if thou art not there?
> Yet I go—for stern duty compels me to do so—
> From the world where my heart is, like far-banished Crusoe.
> Gul's gardens invite me, but Fate says, depart,
> Bismillah! Farewell, young Haidee of my heart!
>
> (*UO* 231)

While Diana is never more than a farcical figure, an intimation of tragicomedy concludes the poem. She sits alone, regretting Captain Popkins most of all: "but some curst power / Bade me nip off his young Hope's budding flower: / I did not even answer that sweet letter, / Because I thought, perhaps, I'd get a better" (*UO* 233). Diana's life has not been characterized by dramatic event; she does not appear to have suffered any particular hardship; but after a career of flirtation and social superficiality, she is left with little more than bemused discontent.[23]

Another example of Norton's later satiric poetry, "The Princess of Hohenlöhe Langenbourg" (1847), relies less on comic stereotypes and anatomizes more comprehensively the means by which the fashionable establish themselves as a special order of being. Over time, artificial distinctions come to be seen as a part of a divine scheme: "God made them quite of a different race, from other young ladies,—who know their place" (*FDS 47*:57). To know one's place is, in effect, to know the places from which one is excluded. Admission to such venues brings exemption from accepted standards of conduct: "If it were Mrs. Tomkins of Stroud, instead of the Countess Bustle or Loud, / They would call her a vulgar noisy woman;—but such a decision were superhuman, / When the lady on whom they pass an opinion, is queen of a part of Fashion's dominion" (*FDS 47*:57). The poem concludes with a ruined Medici statue and this comment on time and human vanity: "Yet this is the end of pomp and state;—/The march of Time is a pauseless march; the chipped arms fall from the broken arch;/And of all the glory, and all the power, what remains in the final hour?" (*FDS 47*:57). The fashionable might control "the world"; time, however, is another matter.

In describing the social scene awaiting the youthful princess, Norton returns to the rituals that had caught her imagination in girlhood. Intervening events such as the Eglinton Tournament and the Powder Ball (both mentioned in the poem) had proven the child's imagination to be remarkably prescient. Latter-day Mr. Pinks "bid their tailors not work by halves, but, making their tights, add in the calves" (*FDS 47*:56). The princess may be too young to run society's gauntlet, but the mature author has a sober view of what awaits her: "Far away be the bitter hour, that shall wither, for her, life's blooming flower;/Glad be her heart for many a year, though her smile must lose part of its radiance clear,/And that floating hair must be twisted and curled, before she is fit for Fashion's world!" (*FDS 47*:55). Delight in the ridiculous is now accompanied by the note of enervation heard in Norton's letter to Shelley. The narrator remarks:

> But the life of the people of fashion I've known, seemed more
> laborious far than my own.
> Toiling, racketing, visiting, shopping—in and out of their carriages
> popping—. . .
> Going to parties, breakfasts, and balls, —holding bazaars with charity-
> stalls,—
> Writing small *billets* all day long, to beg for a pattern, or copy a song;
> Quarrelling, sneering, struggling, and fretting,—plotting, contriving,
> racing, and betting,—
> Sowing the whirlwind, reaping the storm,—and going to church on
> Sundays, for form.
> (*FDS 47*:55)

The participial profusion expresses not so much hard as harried labor. Directionless activity and endless effort leave no one fulfilled and nothing accomplished. This point is further intimated by passing references to the exhausting duties of the domestics who sustain this frenetic life. Although the theme is not developed in this poem, references to tailors and a "languishing lady's maid," who is told that her sacrifices are "all for the good of trade" (*FDS 47*:56), indicate that Norton will not be content to limit her voice to witty satires on "the School of Fashion."

"The Dandies' Rout," "Recollections of a Faded Beauty," and "The Princess of Hohenlöhe Langenbourg" show Norton to have been a witty girl and an observant woman whose interest in "the world" remained constant as her poetic skills matured and she became interested in a wider range of subjects. Another poem, "Marriage and Love" (1829), falls somewhere between the farcical "Recollections" and the more somber "Princess," and it illustrates Norton's tendency to incorporate contrasting modes within a single work. The title reverses the expected courtship sequence, and the poem demonstrates that if marriage comes first, love does not inevitably follow. The protagonist Laura is "lightsome, gay, and free from guile" (*SR* 114) until she reaches a marriageable age, when "the world filled with cares her little breast / Taught her to fear all dowagers and mothers, / Smile on gay lords, and cut their younger brothers" (*SR* 114). The last is a lesson learned too late by Norton herself. The melodic rhythm and rhyming couplets of "Marriage and Love" convey a "lightsome, gay, and free" atmosphere that is at odds with the business-like manner in which matrimony is arranged. Laura is led into marriage with "a lordling" by her mother, who advises her malleable daughter:

> What put it in your head
> That it was needful?—you are asked to *wed*—
> Romantic love is all a childish folly,
> So marry, dear! And don't look melancholy
> Besides, you cannot always live at home—
> Another year your sister's turn will come—
> And you will be *so* rich!—where shall we go?
> Let us begin to think of your *trousseau*!
> (*SR* 115)

Although the comic tone is sustained throughout the poem, increasingly somber and eventually tragic events belie the light-heartedness. The odd juxtaposition of light tone and sad subject emphasizes the cruel combination of filial innocence and complaisance, on the one hand, and maternal pragmatism and insouciance, on the other.

An unloving union to "one too cold to love, too mean to hate" (*SR* 116-17) produces a weary life for Laura and leads her to elope with her lover Francis—an unthinking action that ironically repeats her mother's short-sighted pragmatism. An immediate objective is gained at the cost of ill-considered consequences. Francis naively underestimates the effect of voluntary exile: "My love! My life! What, if we flee? / The world!—the world!—what is that world to *me*? / Thou art *my* world—I, thine—" (*SR* 119). His remapping of "the world" is fleeting, and his love is unequal to the circumstances in which it must be sustained. Isolated and ashamed, Francis comes to embody the very social judgment that he initially scorned in running away with his cousin's wife: "Francis, all his passion o'er, / Grieved she had fallen to rise again no more— / Grieved that harsh scorn should hail her blighted name, / Grieved that she felt and saw *he* felt her shame" (*SR* 120). Although elopement violates an essential principle of the beau monde, the woman bears the brunt of the punishment.[24] Laura dies, and Francis marries "a gentle bride / With gay light heart, and pure and placid brow, / Unused to grief, and impotent to chide" (*SR* 120).[25]

THE DANDY SCHOOL: THE GEOGRAPHY OF VANITY AND THE MATHEMATICS OF MARRIAGE

The two short novels published together as *The Wife and Woman's Reward* (1835) exemplify the preoccupations of silver fork fiction. *The Wife* opens on the occasion of "a great fête . . . at Richmond" sometime near "the close of the London season of 18—, while masquerades were still the fashion, Ranelagh a favourite resort, George the Fourth the handsomest man of his day, and the power of the patronesses of Almacks undreamt of, and unprophecied" (*WWR* 3:46). The protagonist is absent from the party due to the death of her mother, which has no effect at all upon the conviviality that proceeds without her:

> Nothing is more curious than the utter indifference with which in the crowded and over-peopled city of London, we receive the news of the decease of those who have lately joined in the same amusements, listened to the same tunes, smiled at the same jests, as ourselves. The most sudden, the most unexpected death has scarcely the power to sober us for a moment— . . . all this is nothing—is worse than nothing—a theme for idle tongues—an hour's excitement for weary and surfeited hearts.
>
> (*WWR* 3:52)

Bereft and impoverished, possessing beauty but little else, Susan Dalrymple agrees to marry a Scottish lord, "reproaching herself for not loving Glenalton, praying for the power to love him" (*WWR* 3:185), and hoping to enjoy the salutary effect of a simple country life.

Lord Glenalton, however, is not eager to lead the "regular 'Scotch Laird's life' " (*WWR* 3:189) and to isolate himself among the Highland lochs: "He resolved to do as others did, and live in London all the season; making a lengthened visit to the castle during the shooting months" (*WWR* 3:190). Jealous by nature, Glenalton nevertheless uses his attractive wife to curry favor in London society, especially with the Prince Regent. While the fastidious Scots lord could never admit the sentiments, his more realistic friend Carrie Clinton baldly names them: "Glenalton is too sensible not to see, that . . . it gives him great eclât and facility on his entrance into society to have a lovely wife, and to be friends with a prince of the blood royal" (*WWR* 3:236). In this regard, if in few others, Glenalton resembles George Norton (and Rawdon Crawley): each condones the attentions given his wife so long as it remains in his interest to do so.[26] Glenalton intervenes only when the behavior he has encouraged crosses an unmarked boundary of private jealousy or enters the public territory of open rumor.

Susan turns to flirtation in order to forget "in some measure the disappointments at home" and to satisfy "the all-absorbing passion of vanity" (*WWR* 3:201). The attention of the Prince Regent, who has declared "her to be the handsomest woman at a very full opera" (*WWR* 3:201), constitutes her crowning glory. On the very evening that the "royal wooer" (*WWR* 3:234) accepts her invitation to dinner, another of Susan's admirers, Lord Frederick Osborne, declares his passion. She cannot help feeling "flattered, *fetéed*, caressed; it was an evening of triumph" (*WWR* 3:250). Yet it is a "false and unnatural excitement, where nothing is good, nothing noble, nothing lasting . . . —there is no consciousness of energies exerted to a useful or praiseworthy purpose, to support us while in action, or give the feeling of satisfied repose afterwards" (*WWR* 3:255). The combined experience of elation and emptiness yields confusion and paralysis: "those wild bright eyes were still bright, but there was no joyousness of curiosity in their expression . . . a physiognomist could have read in that glance (in spite of the smooth cheek and youthful brow and slight figure) that girlhood's hope and expectation had passed away" (*WWR* 3:238). Anticipating Thackeray, Norton concludes that Susan has crossed the threshold into the "theatre of vanity and display, 'the world' " (*WWR* 3:76).

"London" as the epitome of Regency fashion illustrates a trope in which the whole refers to one of its parts. Hence there is the "London girl," as in, "No, when *I* marry, it shall not be to a London girl" (*WWR* 3:83); the "London bride," as in, "the interest taken in a bride in London . . . is not sympathy . . . it is not even curiosity; but a hard unindulgent speculation as to what . . . will eventually be her conduct" (*WWR* 3:96); and even the "London lady," as in Mary Shelley's account of Norton herself, who "is, despite all her talents and sweetness, a London lady."[27] Men are not exempt from this usage, and the narrator observes that in London "the *habits* of a man's life, and not his actions or intentions, are the subject of censure or approbation" (*WWR* 3:76). "London" and "the world" designate the same discrete universe, and whether the trope is metropolitan or global, the ton remain sui generis:

> "London men" are proverbially callous and selfish. "London women" heartless and coquettish. What! Is there then a separate race of human beings created to dwell in that town, while Manchester and Birmingham remain virtuously peopled? Or does driving through the gates of Hyde Park, in a traveling carriage, alter suddenly the whole heart and mind? No! but the demon of gossip dwells in a dense and idle crowd—falsifying the medium through which each gazes on the other, making merits of vices, and ridicules of merits, till there is no trust or faith, or good feeling between man and man; no confidence, or devotion, or respect between man and woman.
>
> (*WWR* 3:84–85)

Londoners may not, in fact, be a race apart, but they act as if they were, which provides Norton with the central conceit of one of her most successful comic stories, "Curious Customs in the County of Middlesex."

While silver fork literature assumed that the reading public at large was interested in the narrow circle of the ton, denizens of "the world" exhibited little interest in life outside "the County of Middlesex." Hazlitt decried the fashionable writer who treated the working and professional classes "as of a different species instead of members of the same family, loads them with obloquy and insult, and laughs at the very ideal of any fellow feeling with or consideration towards them, as the height of bad taste, weakness, and vulgarity."[28] In "Curious Customs in the County of Middlesex," Norton reverses perspective, placing the story in the mouth of a country squire named Carleton, who reports on London society as if he were an "enthusiastic entomologist, occupied with a new species of ephemera" (*KB* 1:165). Well-educated but distinctly uninterested in topics that stray too far from the immediate concerns of a gentleman farmer, Carleton tells his audience that he has nothing to say on rarefied subjects such as "the inhabitants of Loo-Choo," "ladies' slippers at Aleppo," or "the 'ways' of the upper and lower orders of the Irish" (*KB* 1:142–43). Having "never been out of Old England . . . [or] traveled farther than from London to Edinburgh," Carleton turns to "the 'manners and customs' of the other moiety" (*KB* 1:143–44), i.e., Londoners. The tale inverts for ironic effect the customary expectations of travel narratives in which exotic places and barbaric customs are contrasted with the stately homes and staid manners of England. The narrator is a dispassionate ethnologist who, after "years of patient research," reports on the bizarre practices of a culture whose "existence is a mystery" to half "the population of England and Scotland" (*KB* 1:143).

"The first singularity" that he documents "is the invisibility of London husbands" (*KB* 1:144)—a point corroborated by Kemble's recollection of the "Three Graces," all married, seated on a crimson ottoman with Lord Melbourne, and not a single spouse in sight. In country marriages, by contrast, "man and wife are *one* to a certain degree; they have one home, one set of apartments, and are generally to be found in each other's society" (*KB* 1:144). Carleton's observation is confirmed by Jane Austen, who notes that the admirable couple Admiral and Mrs Croft preserve the "country habit of being almost always together."[29] In "*good society*" (*KB* 1:144)—that is, in the County of Middlesex—the husband and wife are seldom in one another's company. The modern husband is "a visiter in the drawing-room of his own house; is seldom admitted into the 'boudoir;' and has no more right to a corner of his wife's opera box, or a place in her carriage than any other gentleman of her acquaintance—indeed less" (*KB* 1:147). Carleton notes the phenomenon of "the unhappy husband . . . who heartily wishes himself unmarried again, that he might obtain a little more of his wife's notice" (*KB* 1:149)—sentiments echoed by Susan Glenalton with respect to her husband (*WWR* 3:261–62). Both narratives illustrate "how easily those who are made *one* in St. George's church, can contrive afterwards to live as *two*" (*WWR* 3:68). Fashionable marriages free spouses from, rather than commit them to, each other: "they mutually rejoice in the law that allows them mutual liberty; the man to visit his mistress or his club, the woman to flirt behind a little red curtain crossed with gilt wires, with a man perfectly indifferent to her, or guiltily loved" (*KB* 1:152). The primary lesson of the Dandy School would seem to be that two become one in the eyes of the law, but one becomes a fortiori two in the eyes of society.

A similar ethnography and geography are employed in "The Beautycultural Society," whose speaker is a young girl from Northumberland (Miss Letitia Bellamont) on a visit to her cousin in London for the season. After mistakenly receiving an invitation to a ball, Letitia is advised that she had better send

> the card back;
> . . . *town* folks have notions of etiquette, which *country* folks seem to lack.
> And the Marchioness only wishes to add,—and don't care who may hear,—

> That she thinks the Bellamonts better not step out of their proper
> sphere.
>
> (*FDS 49*:62)

The letter convinces Letitia that fashionable life in London is "slavery," and she tells her urban relative: "I would'nt lead the life *you* lead—or bear the slights *you* bear / Not for all the unpawned jewels the Paramount loves to wear" (*FDS 49*:62).

Despite her critique, Letitia does not believe that "the world" can be reduced to "the spangled booths of Vanity Fair" (*FDS 49*:61). The youthful narrator complicates the binary geography of vanity and the short-sightedness of its critics. After two decades of exposure to the British upper classes, Norton recognizes that they are not invariably self-interested snobs. Letitia focuses on the puppet figures of "the world"—Lady Kingcob, Lady Gooseberry, Lady Clack, Magnolia Loud—but this satire is accompanied by praise of the English nobility "who feel their means have been an aid: / A talent lent from Heaven's own hand, and not a trust betrayed. / . . . These are among our noblest names—the others, like a blot, / Fall blurring on the peerage page—stain—but efface them not" (*FDS 49*:63). Letitia counsels her country friend not to be like those who "only see the spangled booths,—and not the better homes" (*FDS 49*:63). Those booths may be the predominant structure in Norton's Vanity Fair, whether it is called London, Middlesex County, or "the world," yet the perspective of an uncorrupted outsider reminds readers that the satirist's lessons in geography and mathematics are an important but only a partial education in the manners and mores of the British aristocracy.

THE DOUBLE PLOT OF COQUETRY

Dualities of theme and mode find a structural correlative in the double plots of tales dealing with a mainstay of silver fork fiction, the coquette. These narratives reverse the conventional marriage plot, as suggested by the title "Marriage and Love." In the initial plot, courtship culminates in matrimony, but love, at least for one's betrothed, is not part of the equation. In the second and main plot, spouses woo each other, ideally but not inevitably achieving the happy union that brings closure to the tale. In several stories, the starting point is a triangle in which a woman rejects or is rejected by the man she loves and in turn marries an aristocrat, whom she does not love. The plot permutations vary, but one of the most common is that the unloved/unloving wife finds solace in flirtation. "The Coquette," for instance, reprises Laura's story in prose and in a consistently serious tone. Bessie Ashton sells "[her]self for a coronet" (*KB* 2:10) and invests herself in flirtation. A cousin, who stifles his own unrequited love for her, serves as the voice of conscience, condemning Bessie for "encourag[ing] every one around you—to traffic for compliments—to barter looks for words, and words for feelings—and to make him [her husband] miserable for the gratification of your vanity" (*KB* 2:12). Unwilling to accept the harsh truth, Bessie garners accolades in "the theatre of the gay world, as an admired bride" (*KB* 2:18) and an unhappy woman.

"The Coquette" is not simply an exemplary tale of the curious calculus of fashionable marriage in which 2 = 1 = 2-with-a-vengeance. Norton also subtly explores the psychology of the social actress. This tale illustrates the dynamic of female power described by Michael Levenson and Karen Chase: "The coquette . . . is an emanation of women's strength immediately condemned to fatal corrosion."[30] The salient consequence of a career in flirtation is the emotional strain of continually performing in compromised circumstances. In a destructive spiral, the reputation for coquetry leads others to expect seductive displays; this expectation, in turn, encourages more theatrical behavior and an increasingly rapid sequence of short-term reward and ultimate rejection. Bessie experiences in extreme form the dilemma described by Norton to Mary Shelley: "though I believe you have some doubts of my general sincerity, in spite of my conviction that living in the world only alters the *manner* and not the feelings. I wish to God it *did* the latter, and perhaps I should not be so wretched just now."[31] In the figure of the coquette, Norton maps an emotional crossway—that no-woman's-land between booth and home—in which private feeling and public demeanor clash.

Bessie, like Norton, wishes "not to be thought ill of" (*KB* 2:32), but the behavior expected of young women of "the world" varies from strict rectitude, to sanctioned insincerity, to actions considered even by some in "the world"—and all outside of it—to be unethical. Noting that "our feelings do not become more simple as we mix with society," the narrator lists the adverse circumstances that transform a woman's life from glittering expectation to embittered fulfillment:

> The positive necessity of sometimes concealing what we do feel; the policy of affecting what we do not; the defiance produced by the consciousness of being disliked without a cause, and abused as a topic for conversation; the contempt excited by the cringing servility of those who flatter for services to be performed, and follow for notice to be obtained; the repeated wreck of hopes that seemed reasonable; the betrayal of confidence which appeared

> natural; the rivalry, disappointment, mortification, and feverish struggling, which beset us in the whirlpool of life, and carry us round whether we will or not,—these are causes which the noblest and the purest natures have difficulty in resisting, and which had their full effect on a mind like Bessie's, naturally vain and eager, and warped by circumstances to something worse.
>
> (*KB* 2:18–19)

These proclivities are exacerbated by comparative youth: she is "not quite a woman, yet but half a child" (*KB* 2:19).

Bessie's immaturity manifests itself in a Wildean insouciance to marital orthodoxy. She thinks to herself, "there was no reason why she could *not* love Glenallan;—except that it would be so exceedingly ridiculous to fall in love with one's husband; it would look as if nobody else thought it worth his while to pay her any attention" (*KB* 2:22). Her flirtations eventually lead her spouse to become "not openly jealous—no, he was too fashionable a husband for that—but coldly displeased, and distant at times" (*KB* 2:24–25). To "the world," she appears to have everything: "all the men run after you—all the women are jealous of you—you've not children—no lapdogs—no sisters-in-law—none of the torments of married life. You are as rich as Crœsus" (*KB* 2:33). Yet even without the bother of children, pets, and in-laws and even with the balm of money, Bessie is "listless and weary" (*KB* 2:31), and unequal to "the feverish struggling."

The brevity of the tale precludes full development of the double plot. A melodramatic death on the dance floor shocks Bessie into awareness of her callous behavior. Skipping several years and the second courtship plot, the narrator concludes with Lord Glenallan "pressing his little daughter's silken curls against her mother's cheek" and bidding his wife to "guide and guard her well, lest she too should be a Coquette" (*KB* 2:39). While his words suggest that the couple have openly acknowledged Bessie's culpability, his gesture demonstrates that one of "the torments of married life"—children—is now experienced as a blessing. Bessie seemingly has learned that it is not "so exceedingly ridiculous to fall in love with one's husband." The mother dispatches the coquette, whose specter nonetheless hovers above the "silken curls" of her daughter.

Longer, but still comparatively short, *The Wife* devotes more time to the second stage of the plot. Susan Glenalton is guilty of marrying without love but not of flirting—not, that is, until after her marriage. Although she no longer loves Henry Egerton, she maintains a connection with him, provoking her husband's jealousy. When Susan resolves to reverse their mutual alienation, Glenalton, acclimated to the ways of the world, "appeared sometimes puzzled, sometimes saddened" (*WWR* 3:269). Her discovery of his emotional intimacy with another woman forces the couple to confront their mutual misbehavior and catalyzes the revival of their moribund marriage. With a formulaic "Years rolled away," the narrator closes the story and assures readers that Susan is "a happy and contented wife" (*WWR* 3:293). The comparatively abrupt conclusions of "The Coquette" and *The Wife* demonstrate that Norton is not primarily interested in the slow processes of interpersonal growth; rather, she emphasizes the woman's agonized unhappiness and emotional isolation. Whatever their flaws, the protagonists learn that the protocols of fashionable society gradually transform foibles into faults with fatal consequences for character and happiness. Norton's reliance upon dramatic events to bring about a newly companionable marriage forecloses consideration of matrimonial maturation and adds a strong element of wish fulfillment to these narratives.

Woman's Reward, a much longer tale, introduces readers to another type of coquette in the minor character Lady Clarice Lyle, a silly woman who flourishes when petted and pouts when not. Among her casual conquests is Altamont Percy, a good-natured but feckless individual known to his public school cronies as Sopsy. The foppish Percy provides Norton with the chance to anatomize the male version of the coquette. In the guise of a comparative mythologist reminiscent of Carleton, the narrator apostrophizes the goddess of love: "give me a name for the species, dear Venus":

> Among rational and talking beings he [Percy] was a cipher; among the active and high-spirited of his "set" at Melton he was a good-humoured bore; among chaperons and mothers he was a dangerous detrimental; and among their daughters and gayer portion of London wives, he was . . . the sort of man for whom all the women try—about whom they all quarrel and are jealous among themselves—and who nevertheless *can* do the unmarried ones no good, and will probably do the reputation of the married ones a great deal of harm. They are as regular and distinct a race, as if Noah had preserved a pair of human beings on purpose to continue it. They are all handsome, or nearly so; all pennyless, or nearly so; all accomplished, or nearly so; and are remarkable for the neatness of their *chaussure*, and the care with which they trim their whiskers. They wear well-chosen and tasteful waistcoats, belong to Crockford's, are very idle, invent improvements in cabs, and eat small portions of excellent dinners with eagerness and satisfaction. They are mostly good-natured, and in some of them the heart is apparent and visible.
>
> (*WWR* 2:249–50)

This passage exemplifies Norton's talent for social taxonomy. Percy, descended from Regency dandies, is the forebear of characters ranging from Thackeray's Rawdon Crawley and Jack Belsize to Ford's Edward Ashburnham.

Norton's early work offers a thorough classification of coquetry. Although scientific tropes generally do not find their way into these texts, a botanical allusion in *Woman's Reward* demonstrates that she is less interested in taxonomy per se than in understanding "the world" and its effects upon those who inhabit it. The incarnation of all that coquettes are not, the heroine Mary Dupré tries to cultivate the flowers of her native Madeira in an English greenhouse. She receives a "curious book" (*WWR* 1:176) entitled *Experimental Botany* from her lover William Clavering. The tract is an embedded figure of the novel itself in that its horticultural hypothesis describes Norton's theory of English society:

> not only do plants flourish more or less in particular soils, but the colour of the flowers, nay, the very shape of the leaves, and its harmless or poisonous nature,
>
> Doth alter as it alteration finds.
>
> The blue scented blossom of a southern clime may be a small white unmeaning flower when transplanted to the north; and the fruit which is esteemed a delicacy in once country, be degraded to a showy berry, or sour poison in another.
>
> (*WR* 1:177)

Whatever Mary's horticultural successes, parallel social efforts are largely wasted in the hothouses—the clubs and ballrooms—of the fashionable world. Custom, as well as nature, limits the degree and kind of change achievable by human flora. The narrator of "The Creole Girl; or, the Physician's Story," for example, uses the same trope to explain the dismal fate of the protagonist, who was taken from the West Indies and deposited on English soil: "A flower transplanted to too cold a land,—/Which for a while gives out a hope of bloom/Then fades and pines, because it may not feel/The freedom and the warmth which give it room/The beauty of its nature to reveal" (*D* 83). Mary's hope of blossoming is not realized until she is grafted onto good English stock in the form of the ideal man, Clavering.

Mary's gardening seems a gesture of nostalgia and a sign of deracination; Clavering's gift appears to serve a romantic more than a botanical objective. Thus, while his reference to Sonnet 116 is appropriate to the state of his heart, the hypothesis of *Experimental Biology* constitutes an ominous warning about romantic sentiment:

> Love is not love
> Which alters when it alteration finds,
> Or bends with the remover to remove:
> O, no! it is an ever-fixed mark,
> That looks on tempests and is never shaken;
> It is the star to every wand'ring barque,
> Whose worth's unknown, although his height be taken.[32]

The law of love only appears to be opposed to natural law. Shakespeare's hypothesis of the permanence of true love is placed in doubt, first by Mary's tangled skein of promises to her father (to take care of her younger brother Lionel), to Clavering (to marry him), and to Lionel (to care for him rather than to marry) and second by Clavering's marriage to another following Mary's rejection of him. *Experimental Biology*, by contrast to the law of inalterable love, demonstrates that mutability is nature's rule. Although the death of his first wife enables Clavering to repeat the proposal of 15 years before, which Mary can now accept because her brother has died, romantic closure is disturbed by the sense that chance and contradiction play determining but undeterminable roles in human lives.

Unnameable species, like Altamont Percy, further document the difficulty of establishing laws of human behavior. At times a "small white unmeaning flower" and at other times a "blue scented blossom," he is a feckless man, who nonetheless possesses "a heart, and a kind one, though it beat under a velvet waistcoat" (*WWR* 2:250). When he finds "himself desperately and irremediably in love with the lovely wife of his best friend" (*WWR* 2:250–51), he is true to the moment and to the culture of velvet waistcoats, eloping with Clarice, to whom he remains loyal even after realizing his error. Sopsy's role in Norton's "experimental botany" is a minor one, but his example illustrates that social taxonomies possess comic but limited value. Readers are left to their own resources in interpreting a social jungle that is nothing if not Darwinian. The one principle on which they can rely is that the hothouse environment of the ton, like the garden in Hawthorne's "Rappacini's Daughter," is toxic to the very thing it engenders. Norton offers a limpid critique of the artificiality of Regency society, symbolized by the Fancy Quadrille of the Twelve Months at Almack's in which she and 11 other young women were paraded around a ballroom with baskets of fruits and flowers on their heads. Transplanted into the overheated atmosphere of "the world," women are likely to find themselves ill-suited for life outside its steamy environment.

NORTON AND THACKERAY I: VANITY FAIRS

In *The Four Georges: Sketches of Manners, Morals, Court, and Town Life*, Thackeray describes the court of George IV in precisely the terms employed in *Vanity Fair*:

> Shall we regard it as preachers and moralists, and cry Woe, against the open vice and selfishness and corruption; or look at it as we do at the king in the pantomime . . . ? It is grave, it is sad; . . . it is monstrous, grotesque, laughable, with its prodigious littlenesses, etiquettes, ceremonials, sham moralities; it is as serious as a sermon, and as absurd and outrageous as Punch's puppet-show.[33]

In writing his novel, Thackeray possessed the advantage of hindsight and the assistance of Norton herself. Their acquaintance began when she was already well known in literary circles and he was still a largely uncelebrated author of periodical reviews and satiric sketches. In 1845, she facilitated a meeting with Melbourne, and Thackeray later wrote to his mother that he had "been to dine with great people."[34] Several years later when she arranged a visit to the Duke of Devonshire, Thackeray unceremoniously broke a prior engagement, exhibiting the very sort of tuft-hunting that he mocked in *Vanity Fair*. A half-hearted apology to the jilted hostess, in which he recounts the wonders to be found at the table of her rival, demonstrates that, although he ridiculed the "(sm)all great," he also enjoyed their attention.

In taking the novelist under her wing, Norton acted with considerable generosity toward one who had harshly reviewed her publications. As early as May 1832, Thackeray noted in his diary: "came home & sat writing against Mrs Norton & poetesses till near one."[35] Even a caustic review of Norton's 1847 annual did not cause her to abandon her acerbic friend.[36] Whether or not Thackeray was "half-in-love" with Norton, as asserted by Micael Clarke, he undoubtedly garnered more than social capital from the friendship.[37] Several characters can be traced directly to Norton. Becky Sharp, for instance, encapsulates their shared aspiration to mingle with the ton. Clarke's comment on Becky's addiction to society—"she could no more exist without it than an opium-eater without his dram"—repeats the simile Norton employed to describe the temptations confronting wives left to their own resources by unvigilant or uncaring spouses.[38] While *Vanity Fair* is neither a roman à clef nor a historical novel recording actual events and people, it does offer a glimpse into a society that in many respects had not changed a great deal by the time Norton helped Thackeray to experience it firsthand.

While Becky is not Norton—their backgrounds, careers, and characters are quite different—there are significant parallels. In addition to beauty, wit, energy, and intellect, both possess the seductive charm of the slightly disreputable. In his biography of Melbourne, for example, Lord David Cecil describes Norton as "not quite a lady" and elaborates: "At twenty-two years old she had already seen a remarkable amount of the seamy side of human existence. The Sheridan family hovered on the fringes of society, showy and impoverished, and surrounded always by a faint aura of scandal."[39] Relationships with older lords (Steyne/Melbourne) provide distinction followed by disgrace. The tenuousness of each woman's position in society is demonstrated by the importance she places upon presentation to the monarch, an act each hoped would serve as a societal *nihil obstat*.

Thackeray satirizes the royal role in conferring respectability on those who curtsey before the monarch. If a woman of the world

> did not wish to lead a virtuous life, at least she desired to enjoy a character for virtue, and we know that no lady in the genteel world can possess this desideratum, until she has put on a train and feathers, and has been presented to her Sovereign at Court. From that august interview they come out stamped as honest women. . . . And as dubious goods or letters are passed through an oven at quarantine, sprinkled with aromatic vinegar, and then pronounced clean, many a lady whose reputation would be doubtful otherwise and liable to give infection, passes through the wholesome ordeal of the Royal presence, and issues from it free from all taint.
>
> (*VF* 553–54)

Becky's "aim in life" is indeed "to be thought, a respectable woman" (*VF* 556), and "presentation to the Sovereign" (*VF* 556) is the crowning moment of the governess's career. While some complained that "if dear good Queen Charlotte had been alive, *she* never would have admitted such an extremely ill-regulated personage into Her chaste drawing room," Becky "passed her examination, and, as it were, took her degree in reputation" from "the First Gentleman in Europe" (*VF* 554). Given that this "Gentleman" has just been shown entering and leaving Gaunt House with his mistress (*VF* 545), it is not surprising that Becky's diploma is a license for unseemly behavior. The ironic beatification of "George the Good, the Magnificent, the Great" (*VF* 555)—the very man who leered at Norton's Susan Glenalton—culminates in mocking silence and feigned blindness concerning his dealings with Becky: "What were the circumstances of the interview between Rebecca Crawley *nee* Sharp, and her Imperial Master, it does not become such a feeble and inexperienced pen as mine to attempt to relate. The dazzled eyes close before that Magnificent Idea" (*VF* 559–60).

The narrator is more forthcoming about other aspects of this event. Becky enters the scene as if "she were a princess and accustomed all her life to go to Court. . . . [S]he adopted a demeanour so grand, self-satisfied, deliberate, and imposing, that it made even Lady Jane laugh" (*VF* 555, 556). In imitation of the *Court Journal*, which reported in detail the gown worn by Norton when presented to Queen Victoria, Thackeray provides an extended account of Becky's "*costume de cour*" (*VF* 556). Her fine lace and brocade train are pilfered from Sir Pitt's house (Norton chose "Isle of Wight lace over white satin" and a poplin train), and her diamonds (Norton opted for pearls) are the clandestine gifts of married men, including her brother-in-law and Lord Steyne.[40] The gems are real, but the character presented by Becky is not. The entire scene is an elaborate charade anticipating the performances soon to be held at Gaunt House.

When Norton was finally presented to Queen Victoria in 1840, she, too, had acquired the reputation of being an "ill-regulated personage."[41] The scandal of 1836 had compelled the second phase of her real-life double plot. This courtship was not of her husband: their marriage was effectively, if not legally, ended by *Norton* v. *Melbourne*. Rather, she courted social exoneration, hoping for the "degree in reputation" that an introduction to Queen Victoria would provide. The odds were overwhelmingly unfavorable that a married woman separated from her husband and accused of having been the prime minister's lover would ever be presented to the youthful, unmarried, and rather prim Queen Victoria. Nevertheless, anxious for vindication beyond the verdict of the trial, Norton besieged Melbourne to secure a royal audience and sarcastically congratulated him on his "influence at the palace" when he did not do so. She angrily wrote, "We will see whether under the *mask* of justice, I shall be told by the Queen that I am not fit to associate with the ladies of her court" (*LCN* 148–49). When the royal introduction finally occurred, the event neither produced the hoped-for vindication nor silenced the scandal. Lady Holland, unofficial "queen of the Whig aristocracy and the hostess to the cream of the London *haut ton* for more than four decades," observed that Norton "is in greater beauty if possible than ever, but very cross & touchy they say. She expected her reception at Court would open all arms & doors to her. Not finding this or much beyond great civility for routs & balls, she is angry" (*LCN* 167).[42]

Norton's poem "Presentation at Court" (1849) treats this theme with the detached amusement not possible when she herself was competing for social preferment. Rather than adopt the view point of an older and wiser woman, she reprises the innocent perspective of Letitia Bellamont. This "little Nobody" sees the event, at which "two thousand Cinderella's" (*FDS 49*:29) will curtsey to the Queen, as a demeaning form of warfare:

> Such elbowing and pummeling, the strong against the weak, / I never could have dreamed among so fine a set to see,— / I thought the world of fashion must be full of courtesy; / But oh! the tumult and the strife,—the angry word and frown— / I assure you they did all, my dear, but knock each other down.
>
> (*FDS 49*:29)

Her lace in shreds as a result of the turmoil, Lady Crawl (whose name intimates her moral stature and recalls Thackeray's social crawlers, the Crawleys) abandons "the common crowd and herd" and, "with many curtseying dips, / Swims in the wake of Princes—as sharks swim after ships" (*FDS 49*:30). "Presentation at Court" describes the frenzied struggle for social preferment beneath the veneer of manners and breeding; it also reveals the scars from Norton's experience a decade earlier.

Court presentations are one form of public theater; less respectable are the charades for which Becky and Norton are infamous. After the former's Gaunt House performance, it is agreed "that had she been an actress none on the stage could have surpassed her" (*VF* 600). Becky begins the evening as Clytemnestra—which is appropriate given Haydon's casting of Norton as Cassandra. Steyne is "frantic with delight" at her performance. He jokes that she "was quite killing" (*VF* 596) in the part, although Steyne himself is the principal victim: "What a splendid actress and manager! . . . I am a greenhorn myself, and a fool in her hand—an old fool" (*VF* 599, 608–09). "The Royal Personage" (*VF* 600) is similarly afflicted, and Becky briefly entertains the notion that she "might play the part of a Maintenon or a Pompadour" (*VF* 560) in real life. Her hope is exceeded, if only figuratively and briefly, when she finds herself "another Cleopatra" (*VF* 600)—queen for an evening and outcast for the rest of her days.

Although symbolically linked to a series of tragic women, Becky is primarily a comic figure. The most appropriate title for her performance is unwittingly supplied by Lord Steyne. Looking at the jewels that he has saved her the embarrassment of returning to Mr. Polonius, he "quoted the hackneyed and beautiful lines . . . about Belinda's diamonds, 'which Jews might kiss and infidels adore' " (*VF* 559). Becky displays "the brilliants on her breast" (*VF* 620) when Rawdon finds her closeted with the man who gave them to her. Thus "Belinda" suits the times and the person more closely than either "Clytemnestra," "Philomèle" or "Cleopatra"—and clearly she is no Cassandra.

Conspicuous displays of jewelry are used by Norton to symbolize the vanity of the ton and are usually associated with foolish figures like Lady John Haslingden (*The Wife*), the Marchioness of Paramount ("Presentation at Court"), and the Marchioness of Updown (*Lost and Saved*). Diamonds also figure in Susan Glenalton's successful effort to woo the Prince Regent into her husband's social circle. On the evening of the party intended to ensnare her prey, Susan selects especially "splendid jewels," and her final gesture upon leaving for the party is to clasp "the last bracelet on her arm" (*WWR* 3:233). The narrator remarks, "Diamonds! What a strange passion; what a curious disease; what a topic for speculative curiosity, is the thirst which some women feel for these precious articles! . . . Of all the different madnesses and false tastes created by idleness and luxury, surely this is the most unaccountable!" (*WWR* 3:242–43). Unaccountable, perhaps, but effective: Lady Glenalton monopolizes the Duke's attention to the point that he "himself was less an object of attention that night, so wrapt was the little world of countesses and lords in observing this newly apparent flirtation in their orbit" (*WWR* 3:248). Applied to social relations, the laws of physics, no less than those of botany, are subject to alteration: beauty and wealth may—at least temporarily—eclipse the power of kings.

In many of the narratives that come after the silver fork phase, including that of Norton's own marriage, double plots are replaced by a single action that is bisected into radically distinct segments: an irretrievable past and an insufferable present. Marriage ends the wife's illusions, and her youthful energy and optimism devolve to the enervation and resignation of the prematurely aged. Becky Sharp momentarily experiences this sensation, for example, upon returning to Queen's Crawley and considering a life that might have been hers had she not married Rawdon:

She had been young there, or comparatively so, for she forgot the time when she ever *was* young—but she remembered her thoughts and feelings seven years back, and contrasted them with those which she had at present, now that she had seen the world and lived with great people, and raised herself far beyond her original humble station.

(*VF* 496)

Becky is cut off entirely from a past that she imagines might have been happy. Similar sentiments are often sounded in Norton's poetry. The speaker in "My Childhood's Home" (1829), a woman who once "stood in the courts of kings," now wishes for the simple pleasures of the past, such as "one of my nosegays of fresh wild flowers, / Instead of those jewels bright" (*SR* 180).[43]

In double-plotted narratives, by contrast, such feelings precede the resolution to revive moribund marriages and to recover a semblance of rural or youthful values within the confines of the London present. Hence for Susan Glenalton the

bright days spent . . . on the hills at Loch-Lyne, came back to her in that perfumed and crimson-curtained room. . . . [S]he would give all the brilliant worldly advantages she possessed, to be able to feel that she was beloved by her husband as in the days when that love seemed but importunity;—to be able to shake off the wearying trammels and fetters of society, and find peace and rest at home.

(*WWR* 258–62)

The silver fork fiction typically allows characters like Susan a second chance, something that, as the years of struggle with her husband dragged on, Norton increasingly recognized she herself would never have.

Satire and sentimentality are present throughout Norton's oeuvre, but they are increasingly complemented by an acute awareness of the mundane pain and daily anxieties of domestic life. As Barbara Leckie has observed: Norton "turns the genre of melodrama inside out: there is nothing natural about female suffering, and there is nothing fated about the cessation of such suffering. In real life, a hero does not always intervene to relieve the anguish of a woman's troubles."[44] This point is amply demonstrated in the final novels, *Lost and Saved* and *Old Sir Douglas*, in which satire and sentiment, romance and inverted melodrama are found in narratives of Victorian rather than Regency women.

CHAPTER 2

"STRANGE UNSTABLE WORLD": STRUCTURE AND SYNTHESIS IN THE FINAL NARRATIVES

The "sensation novel" of our time, however extravagant and unnatural, yet is a sign of the times—the evidence of a certain turn of thought and action, of an impatience of old restraints, and a craving for some fundamental change in the working of society.[1]

"Our Female Sensation Novelists"

Of all the personages who figure in history, in poetry, in art, Mary Magdalene is at once the most unreal and the most real:—the most unreal *if we attempt to fix her identity, which has been a subject of dispute for ages: the most* real, *if we consider her as having been, for ages, recognised and accepted in every Christian heart as the empersonation of the penitent sinner absolved through faith and love.*[2]

Anna Jameson, *Sacred and Legendary Art*

Norton's readers from the 1830s and 1840s would surely have recognized her hand in the novels of the 1860s. *Lost and Saved* adapts numerous aspects of her first long poem, *The Sorrows of Rosalie*, and *Old Sir Douglas* returns to the familiar Scottish setting and symbolic landscape of pastoral north vs. urban south that features prominently in both *The Wife* and *Stuart of Dunleath.* Recurring themes, tropes, and modes, however, cannot disguise significant changes and evolving styles. Most notably, Norton introduces sensational plots and villains that accentuate the moral vision of melodrama—a change attributable in part to public taste. A survey of new fiction in 1863 concluded that a "book without a murder, a divorce, a seduction, or a bigamy, is not apparently considered worth either writing or reading. . . . [A] tale must needs be full of horror, excitement, and crime."[3] Norton's shift in mode also reflects "an impatience of old restraints," personal as well as artistic, and a search for a form that will enable her to combine more effectively different voices—plaintive and passionate, satirical and sentimental—within a single work.

In the late fiction, the reductive moral equation of melodrama—the heinous male villain and pure female victim—is complicated by a careful examination of women at the crossroads. Reflecting her own protracted experience as a public figure living apart from her husband, Norton now portrays women's postlapsarian lives, precisely the material elided from the double-plotted narratives of the 1830s. An apt figure of this experience is Mary Magdalene, who embodies conflicted Victorian attitudes toward women and sexuality, sin and salvation. Even with more fully realized psychological portraits, however, Norton resorts to ethnic and racial stereotypes that remind readers of the simplistic formulae of melodrama. The net result is a complicated, if not confused, aesthetic mixture. The intersection of so many, sometimes contradictory, elements suggests that even Meredith's trope of the crossways is not quite adequate to bear the heavy traffic of competing voices that mark, and occasionally mar, the final works of Norton's long career.

1829/1863: *THE SORROWS OF ROSALIE* AND *LOST AND SAVED*

The Sorrows of Rosalie and *Lost and Saved*—nearly her earliest and her latest works—are parallel in structure, situation, and plot. The key difference is found in the treatment of the protagonist after her fall from respectability. In both works, a naive country woman elopes with an aristocrat from the fashionable world. Each is abandoned and gives birth to an illegitimate son who dies. Rosalie passes quietly into obscurity, longing for "peace in Heaven who not on earth may rest" (*SR* 54). With Beatrice Brooke, however, Norton envisions a fulfilling life for a woman after public disgrace and private sorrow—a possibility that challenges social and aesthetic convention. *Lost and Saved* offers a more nuanced ethical and artistic vision than Norton's silver fork literature and popular melodrama in general.

Both narratives open with stereotypically innocent protagonists whose naiveté is compounded by maternal absence. Their mothers dead, Rosalie and Beatrice maintain strong ties with their fathers in isolated natural surroundings. The former is described as a "laughing thing, half woman and half child," who gathers "many a diamond-spangled rose, / And many a simple bud that wildly blows" to place by her father's bedside each morning (*SR* 5). The latter's seaside home in Wales is the "most hidden of all in its surrounding hedges of honeysuckle, sweetbrier, and travelers' joy" (*LS* 11). As the novel opens, Beatrice has decorated her hair with seaweed for a family fête; the revelers drink tea out of conch shells, and the conversation wanders from mermaids and sirens to "a 'freakish fay'" (*LS* 17), all of which establish this as a world as alien to Almack's as any Mad Hatter's tea party could be.

Pastoral innocence for both is ended by the arrival of a fiend in the guise of an angel. As Rosalie tells it:

> In evil hour (for me unfortunate)
> Did the deceiver come; I will not say
> That he [Arthur] was all on earth most good and great,
> Or fairer than the other sons of clay;
> But he was all to *me*—a single day
> Spent without *him* was as a year of pain.
>
> (*SR* 7)

Beatrice's life is transformed in an equally dramatic fashion when Montague Traherne happens upon the seaside celebration: "the cloud and the breeze, which were to grow into murky tempest, came on, one fresh summer's day, and brought change, and darkness, and shipwreck, tears and sorrow, into the pleasant garden and the sunny chambers, and the hearts of the dwellers by the lone sea-shore" (*LS* 13). Having voluntarily left and irrevocably lost her home, each young woman idealizes her pastoral past. Rosalie is granted a "short year of bliss" (*SR* 20) during which she lives in a cottage rented for her by Arthur, but this life is "not like the happiness I knew / When in my first sweet home of peaceful rest" (*SR* 21). Beatrice briefly returns to "The Home" after her elopement with Montagu, but it, too, has changed from the days when "Charity and tenderness dwelt there; hope and help" (*LS* 13).

The fathers love but cannot protect their daughters. Each is rendered passive by grief over his wife's death, and the effects of self-pity are augmented by ignorance of the parental duties normally fulfilled by the mother. The only check to seduction comes from the daughters themselves, for the brief moment when they think of the pain their acts will cause their fathers.[4] After her child's death and Arthur's abandonment, Rosalie returns home because "a father *must* forgive! / The heart which judges truly cannot love" (*SR* 52). The ambiguity generated by the mesozeugmatic "truly" intimates her naiveté. Judgment may be incompatible with love, but the ominous sense that true judgment would end love haunts the scene. Rosalie's father is not put to the test since, unbeknownst to her, he has died. The absence of absolution leaves a bitter realization, "Thou art alone!" (*SR* 55). Beatrice, by contrast, intuitively measures her father's capacity to suppress judgment. He welcomes the prodigal home, but she carefully hides the fact that she has a son: "Come back to us once more. You were never forsaken; what are . . . fathers for, if they are to judge as strangers? Could you doubt your old father?" (*LS* 380). The question is intended to be, but is not interpreted as, rhetorical. Although not literally alone, Beatrice is lonely, since she can share her greatest joy with neither her father nor her child's father: "Her child was the child of shame, though not of sin. The sight of him would be a pang to her father" (*LS* 384). Concealment compounds shame, and she returns to the anonymity of London rather than continue to deceive her father. Norton implies that even benevolent paternal figures are incapable of fully understanding women or of forgiving their failings.

The male villains of these tales advance the plot but are of little interest in themselves. Lord Arthur and Montagu Treherne are aristocratic predators whose wealth and cosmopolitan manners facilitate the seduction of naive women with little knowledge of "the world."[5] The unmarried fathers continue to enjoy the pleasures of society while the abandoned mothers and sons suffer. When approached by their desperate mistresses, the young men plead their own suffering (*SR* 26, 43; *LS* 124). Neither finally rejects his lover in person, relying on a letter delivered by a surrogate. The discarded mistresses spurn offers of payment, leaving their seducers free to return seamlessly and guiltlessly to mainstream society and illustrating that "though the faults of women are visited as sins, the sins of men are not even visited as faults" (*LS* 432). When Rosalie travels with her son Albert to "the proud metropolis" (*SR* 37) to confront Arthur, she finds him amidst "the young, the gay, the free" and engaged to a "fair creature" (*SR* 41). Montagu also contracts a marriage that will enhance his wealth and status: "He was gone to be free—to forget her; while she remained thus chained down, by fetters more heavy than lead, to her fatherless child and her undeserved disgrace" (*LS* 314–15).

As these broad outlines suggest, the structure and formula of melodrama are consistent features of Norton's early and late work. Another common element is that men disingenuously rely on the rhetoric of romance to accomplish seduction and resist marriage, while women self-deludingly employ it to mitigate guilt and sustain the hope of marriage. The men temporize, hoping to quiet increasingly restive lovers with appeals to the sanctity of natural love. According to Arthur: "The links of love will best true love requite; / Cold are those worldly ties, and no delight / Can those unhappy find who love perforce, / Who drag the unwilling chain because tis *right*, / Struggling for duty, shrinking from remorse, / Sighing for earlier times when free their joyous course" (*SR* 22). In a similar vein, Montagu exasperatedly tells Beatrice: "There was LOVE in Eden before there were other ties, . . . and if you loved me, under all our difficulties, you would think of nothing *but* that love" (*LS* 163). Forced to reveal that their marriage ceremony was a sham, he makes a claim that only she believes: "they were as much married in the sight of Heaven, although the person who read the words was not in orders, as though a Bishop had consecrated the ceremony" (*LS* 219). The rhetoric of a rake is familiar; its invocation of free and natural love is credible only to those with a strong need to accept a lover's lies.

The women's version of the "tale of true love" is more ingenuous, less overtly manipulative; nevertheless, it disguises their moral failing and compromised social position. Both women are understandably but culpably ignorant of social law. Rosalie, for instance, seems almost to believe that the birth of her child weds her to Albert's father: a "beauteous boy was brought me, doubly dear, / For all the fears that promise caused to hover / Round him—'twas past—I claimed a husband in my lover" (*SR* 31). Arthur's promise of marriage may have been "only heard by Heaven above" (*SR* 34), but to Rosalie it is significant for that very reason. Beatrice similarly holds herself to be "married in the sight of Heaven." Even after Montagu marries another, she thinks: "While he lives, I never can become, I never ought to become, the wife of any other man" (*LS* 454). The loyal love of these abandoned mothers may be noble, but insofar as each believes herself to be married in God's eyes, she rationalizes her sin and espouses the very ideology that her lover enlists in order not to marry.

For the women, pregnancy sanctifies love and naturalizes the relationship, but for the men, it provides another means of temporizing. Arthur promises: "Soon as a son is born, to glad my life, / Oh, then shall Heaven and man behold thee Arthur's wife!" (*SR* 26). Montagu tells Beatrice "that as soon as he was legally of age, and master of his own destiny, a public marriage would not only justify her, but, as a matter of course, legitimate their son" (*LS* 219).[6] In reality, of course, the birth of the child makes his mother's banishment inevitable. Spurned by their lovers and shamed in the eyes of society, the mothers devote themselves exclusively to the infants: "By all unpitied, and to all unknown," Rosalie has only "my love—my grief—my child:—all else was gone" (*SR* 38). Albert is his mother's "Dear link of life, to whom I clung, whate'ver befell" (*SR* 45). Beatrice similarly invests herself in Frank, and Montagu is correct when he whines that Beatrice "was fonder of the child than of himself" (*LS* 249).

The difference between the Norton of 1829 and of 1863 is seen in the depiction of the women's lives after the deaths of their sons. Rosalie notes, "Years have gone by" (*SR* 53), but readers learn nothing of them. *Lost and Saved*, by contrast, carefully follows Beatrice's effort to rebuild her life. Lacking the knowledge of how to look for a job and the skill with which to procure one, she tries to sell her sketches. When that fails, she seeks employment as an artist's model, escaping the notoriety of modeling by accepting the only slightly more respectable work of lace-mending.[7] Throughout the process, she struggles to reconcile a comfortable middle-class sense of self with the indignity of physical labor. She tells the painter to whom she offers her services that she "should be more useful than a common model, because I should understand better what was wanted" (*LS* 330)—a statement that reveals her complete innocence of what might be expected of models, whether professionally or personally. Her condescension is further evident when her landlady, who recognizes Beatrice's irregular circumstances, confesses a youthful indiscretion of her own. Beatrice "felt dishonored and lost in the comparison made—and the equality which her forsaken condition seemed in her companion's eyes to establish between them!" (*LS* 317). Although she cannot entirely admit the realities of her situation, neither does she submit passively to them.

Beatrice resolutely labors to be independent even while chafing under the tedium and physical demands of work. *Lost and Saved* transcends the narrative of the fallen woman to consider the struggle of all women excluded from fulfilling labor and victimized by class bias:

> Beatrice had been used to more than daily bread: her hunger was of the soul. . . . She found no cause for pining or murmur, that with all her beauty, talents, and resources, she was reduced to become a lace-mender and clear starcher. . . . She missed no luxury, not even the luxury of leisure; but she

missed love—love, and cultivated companionship, and her vanished trust in human truth!

(*LS* 345–46, 348)

In documenting Beatrice's experience, Norton removes the quotation marks from "the world." The manners of the *haut ton* are noted, but the scope has expanded to include the daily lives and struggles with which she herself had become all too familiar.

Over the course of 20 years' wrangling with her husband, Norton came to understand not a little about the intricacies of British law, an experience enabling her to offer a counterpoint to the romantic rhetoric of higher love / law in the later narratives. It is not surprising, for example, that no mention is made of a breach of promise action in *The Sorrows of Rosalie*, even though Rosalie recalls her lover's false marriage promise no fewer than six times. When she laments that "human laws / Were fram'd against me," she refers only to the social code that condemns her to "shame and sorrow" (*SR* 59). Norton does not use the occasion to address legal inequities or the social values underwriting them. By contrast, when the narrator of *Lost and Saved* sardonically comments, "Some men swear easily" (*LS* 265), she need not add, "and know when to do so," because it is obvious from Montagu's self-interested manipulation of legalistic technicalities. Beatrice's reminder that he has promised not to see other women elicits laughter at her naiveté and an admission of the legalism by which he vitiates his word:

You swore by Frank's life that you were nothing to this woman; that she was nothing to you.

Yes, because you worded it so absurdly, my sweet Beatrice, I could hardly help smiling. Nothing between us that might not be between friends and acquaintances—I might easily swear that.

(*LS* 292)

He is able to keep his promise in a technical sense because in fashionable society friendship does not preclude sexual dalliances. He also knows his sham marriage is without legal force and that, were he subsequently to agree to a "sort of legal marriage" (*LS* 219), their son would not become his legal heir. Misunderstanding Beatrice's allegiance to a higher law, he assumes that educating her about human laws, now that it suits his purposes to do so, will mitigate the impact of his abandonment: "When she knows that our marriage, had it taken place, would have left little Frank in a most anomalous position, she may be more reconciled to her lot" (*LS* 308). After weaving any number of "legal fictions" to deceive Beatrice, Montagu exploits legal realities to escape their consequences.

While such legal fictions speak primarily to the character of their author, two additional observations can be made about them. First, the manipulative use of human law discredits the law itself and not merely those who take advantage of it. A system so easily employed to sustain the interests of aristocratic men at the expense of women and children signally fails either to offer equal justice or to fulfill its own mandate to protect the innocent and less powerful. Second, Norton's criticism of common law is not tantamount to an endorsement of narratives of natural law. As we have seen, Beatrice's insistence that she is somehow transcendentally united to Montagu blinds her to his character and to the harm caused by allegiance to sentimental ideology. Her romantic fictions are perversely complicitous with his legal ones, leading her to weave false hope after false hope. The failure to integrate principle and circumstance leads to tortured logic, for instance, when she reasons that she is an exception to her father's condemnation of hidden marriages and rationalizes Montagu's wish to conceal their union. Although readers' judgment is mitigated by her harsh circumstances and unfair treatment, Beatrice repeatedly relies on natural narratives to sustain illusions and, in effect, to delude herself.

Her experience dramatically reinforces Norton's insistence that women be educated concerning the laws that most directly affect them. The narrator challenges readers, who might think that Beatrice's legal ignorance is implausible, to consider

> what the ideas of law on these simple points may be, among very young ladies brought up in retirement, in this country where Gretna Green has only just ceased to be a Hymeneal temple,—in this country, the only one in Europe, I believe, where the innocent suffer for the guilty, and an after-marriage does *not* redeem the destiny of children.
>
> (*LS* 221)

No longer content simply to expose social cruelty or to indulge in pathos, Norton uses her fictional voice to dramatize the need for legal reform. That is not to say that Beatrice is represented merely as the victim of unfair laws. A "child of impulse and passion" (*LS* 160), she pays insufficient attention to social conventions, exhibiting the iconoclasm, if not the *sauvagerie*, of Gertrude Bouverie. Her dilemma is suggested by the author of "Our Female Sensation Novelists": "The heroine of this class of novel is charming because she is undisciplined, and the victim of impulse; because she has never known restraint or has cast it aside, because in all these respects she is below the thoroughly trained and tried woman."[8] The predicament is obvious: that which makes Beatrice charming also excludes her from polite society. Norton does not question that Beatrice is "lost" but asserts that "training and trying" may take place after events conventionally viewed as a social death sentence.

Reviewers took exception to the notion that Beatrice could be "saved" at all. Her seduction was not objectionable, but her refusal passively to accept further victimization elicited vehement protest:

> We must own to some surprise, how any cultivated mind, refined by poetry, and even genius, can possibly reduce a heroine to such extremities of degradation as are brought about in Beatrice's search for a living, after she is abandoned by Treherne. The belief in intrinsic purity ought to preserve any favorite conception of the imagination from such contacts, such base suspicions.[9]

Another reviewer warned of the "desperate and dangerous power of making 'the crooked *appear* straight.' Let us not be misunderstood: Mrs. Norton has laboured hard to make a moral tale out of an immoral subject; there can be but one opinion as to the purity of her intention, but the miracle was beyond her strength."[10] The implication is that an act of God, and not of a mere author, is required to save a woman like Beatrice. Were the title of the novel construed as "lost then saved"—with the caveat that there are limits to how lost the heroine can be—then it would conform to a simple and unobjectionable romantic formula. "Lost *and* saved," however, challenges Victorian proprieties. That Beatrice, an abandoned lover and mother of an illegitimate child, subsequently finds happiness in marriage and motherhood was too much for Mrs. Grundy to accept.

Norton defended the morality of her novel in a "Letter to the Editor" of the *Times* (May 22, 1863) but came under renewed attack from James Fitzjames Stephen, who assigned her a prominent place among perpetrators of what he called "the anti-respectability commonplace":

> In every generation . . . it occurs to some lively person who combines power of expression with more than average sensibility, that a certain proportion of those who are condemned, and even stigmatized, by the world at large—who fall, so to speak, under its official censure—are in reality better than others who are rewarded with its smiles and its favours.[11]

Norton's distinction between "the real bad woman" and "the nominal bad woman" (*LS* 267) tends to corroborate Stephen's observation. She does not, however, simply formulaically reverse the world's judgments. The dedication to Lord Essex refers to her intention to portray a flawed heroine: "I jested with you as to your notions of charm and perfection in woman, and told you I would s[o]me day create a heroine on that model, and bring her to grief in a novel" (*LS* iii). One can well imagine Essex's notions of female perfection: "the merry maid of sixteen, wild as a fawn and beautiful as a picture" (*LS* 12), that is, Beatrice before eloping. In a letter to her physician and friend, Sir Charles Locock, Norton elaborated upon her intention "to portray a *sensual* female nature—not in the common and grosser interpretations of that term,—but one in whom the animal nature is very strong."[12] Something of that physical nature is intimated by the footrace that opens the novel, and its fullest expression is found in Beatrice's assertiveness in the face of Montagu's deception. He is intimidated by "Beatrice, proud, passionate, strong and defying; rushing . . . to claim her 'rights' " (*LS* 198) and likens her to a "sort of Norma—a maddened Bianca" (*LS* 198). She is passionate and strong, but the comparisons speak more cogently of his insecurities than of her temper. Beatrice, unlike Norma, will not throw herself on the funeral pyre of her disloyal lover. She greets her abandonment with the resolution to "exert myself, for my dear boy's sake. I will not sink; nor will I be dependent on—on pity for past days" (*LS* 316). In that regard, a lack of social experience serves her well: she shuns the passive and self-destructive role expected of her both by society and according to aesthetic convention. Following Gaskell's *Ruth* and anticipating Hardy's *Tess of the d'Urbervilles*, Norton's *Lost and Saved* challenges society's image of "A Pure Woman" and predictably elicits the ire of reviewers, who are "but men."

Beatrice is not the "right worshipful heroine of Romance" (*DC* 2:171) that Meredith is loath to paint in *Diana of the Crossways*. In her refusal to maintain a posture of angelic passivity and in her flaws, she resembles her creator. For critics like Stephen, however, Beatrice possesses "nothing much to praise":

> No woman who had any proper feeling of self-respect and decency would have eloped with her lover in the middle of the night, at half an hour's warning, putting herself entirely in his power, in a foreign country, when she might have received the protection of one of her own sex, and when, at all events, by simply staying where she was, she might easily have obtained some proper guardianship.[13]

Stephen, of course, is right: neither Norton nor Beatrice defends these actions. Even allowing for the confusion attending her disembarkation with Montagu (in which she is far more culpable than Maggie Tulliver), Beatrice plainly acknowledges that her "father would never excuse or countenance" the decision to board "that strange coffin-like boat" (*LS* 95, 94).

Stephen, however, is also wrong. He fails to appreciate the resolve that follows Beatrice's error. When she learns that her marriage is invalid and that she is living as Montagu's mistress, not his wife, she issues an ultimatum that she does not have the resolve to keep: "*I will never come again, unless as a wife, to the house I imagined was my husband's home*" (*LS* 192–93). She is loyal to him even after repeated indications that their marriage will never take place and despite additional proofs that he is continuously unfaithful. Periods of anger—"Where was he—this mock-husband and no-father, who caressed other people's children and accompanied other people's wives?" (*LS* 259)—alternate with moments of rapturous hope that she will "see him again. I shall hear the voice, for the want of which I seem to have lived in a sort of gasping silence" (*LS* 401). The net result is a slow and painful process of disillusionment unrecognized by Stephen, whose preoccupation with the protagonist's faults prevents recognition of her virtues.

Stephen is guilty of simplistic binarisms, evidenced by his self-assured notion of how "girls of good feeling" will and will not behave. A distinguished jurist as well as literary critic, he nonetheless discounts extenuating circumstances, such as Montagu's deception and Beatrice's illness, on the one hand, and the factors militating against her obtaining "some proper guardianship" or confiding in her father, on the other hand. Norton seems to anticipate Stephen's criticism, as the narrator comments:

> No one expresses the least concern at a case like that which occurred a year or two since, when a father was sentenced to imprisonment for the costs of an action for the seduction of his daughter, which he lost only on the plea that the girl was old enough to give her own consent to sin.
>
> (*LS* 433)

Beatrice would have fared no better in court. Stephen's plea, in the legal sense, is the same as that of the defense in this case; Norton's demurrer, in the figurative sense, is the novel itself: a portrait of a woman lost *and* saved.

The novel concludes with a hurried turn of the plot. Beatrice meets, falls in love with, and is proposed to by her future husband, an Italian widower with a young daughter, in the space of about ten pages. Although seemingly a marriage ex machina, the rapid resolution is not entirely "an instance of that 'poetical justice,' more frequently found in novels than in real life" (*LS* 496), especially given Beatrice's torturous route to what must appear to readers as a kind of "anti-climax expedition." Her union with Ludovic Sforza, if not melancholic, is also not exuberant. Once married, she remains exiled in Italy, never fully able to escape her past. English travelers "have always the satisfaction of remembering that there was 'some sort of story against her—wasn't there?—before her marriage?' They cannot exactly say what it is, for nobody exactly knows; but there remains that shadowy SOMETHING" (*LS* 499). Her husband, who is fully aware of her past, proves that he, in contrast to Angel Clare, can act upon his principles: "What is the opinion to us, that is only founded on forms of thinking? Are you *in fact* degraded by that unhappy dream of the past?" (*LS* 453). He insists that only a woman wedded to shame cannot remarry: "That union is spiritual and sacramental—nothing can divorce her or set her at liberty to wed another. But with you, my beloved, it was not so. Live—live ever among the good and pure!" (*LS* 454). Although Ludovic's reference to and rejection of "forms of thinking" is consistent with the rhetoric of romance, in contrast to Montagu he holds that shame, not sexual experience, is indelible. When Montagu dies, marrying becomes easier for Beatrice; nonetheless, she must alter her thinking in order to do so without violating her principles. The couple's common desire but contradictory romantic narratives suggest that rhetoric in isolation has neither intrinsic value nor truth: lovers' discourse must always be read in relation to the objective it serves.

"OUR MODERN MARY MAGDALENE"

While Beatrice reminds Montagu of Norma, Norton was apt to have been thinking of Mary Magdalene, with whom she herself had been linked in *Norton* v. *Melbourne*.[14] Sir William Follett, counsel for the plaintiff, pointedly told the jury that the defendant had once sent Mrs. Norton "a curious book" allegedly proving "that Mary Magdalen was the most virtuous of her sex."[15] He implied that the man who would give and the woman who would accept such a tome were clearly profligate individuals. Norton was outraged by the insinuation, although she considered the case of Magdalene more positively in later narratives. In *Old Sir Douglas*, for instance, Mary Magdalene is associated with remorse rather than sexuality. The authorial spokesman, an ironic Scotsman named Lorimer Boyd, notes the "anti-Magdalenism in the Northern constitution. No Scottish Mary staunches her tears with her hair; though those lovely penitents are generally painted with golden locks, possibly to enhance and show the difficulty and value of their repentance" (*OSD* 2:213). Boyd's wry observation is directed equally at the self-righteousness of his countrywomen and the sensuality of European painters.

Norton may have been influenced by Anna Jameson's account in the monumental study *Sacred and Legendary Art*: "A noble creature, with strong sympathies and a strong will, with powerful faculties of every kind, working for good or evil—such a woman Mary Magdalene must have been, even in her humiliation."[16] Jameson contends that Magdalene's "combined character of Sinner and of Saint" has defeated painters, who err in emphasizing one dimension or the other: "Where the penitent prevails, the saint appears degraded; where the wasted, unclad form is seen attenuated by vigils and exposed in haggard unseemliness, it is a violation of that first great rule of Art which forbids the repulsive and the painful."[17] Norton encountered this dilemma when her depiction of "a *sensual* female nature" elicited the ire of critics like Stephen. Public unreadiness for a modern Magdalene not safely framed in religious art is further evident in the *Illustrated London News*, which objected that

> the story is too full of scenes which border so closely upon what it is considered improper to write about as plainly as the author does that one cannot but feel glad that she who has had the boldness to describe them in all their naked deformity is one so elevated, both by social position and literary reputation, as the Hon. Mrs. Norton.[18]

The muddled reference to the author's status is not clarified by the following remark: "Mrs. Norton is a woman, and, no doubt, understands her sex better than a man can pretend to do."[19] The critic does not so much conclude as dismiss the topic, and in the vein of Follett seems to imply that a woman who would read a book about Magdalene is certainly brazen enough to write one.

That Norton was linked with Magdalene in the public eye is evident from Henry Reeve's response to *Sacred and Legendary Art*. Jameson also commented on the anti-Magdalenism of the day:

> we have even done our best to dethrone Mary Magdalene; but we have martyrs . . . and *one* at least among these who has not died without lifting up a

voice of eloquent and solemn warning; who has borne her palm on earth, and whose starry crown may be seen on high, even now, amid the constellations of Genius.[20]

Her language echoes Bulwer's and Disraeli's, but Jameson never identified her modern martyr, prompting Reeve to speculate: "Who on earth or in heaven is our Modern Mary Magdalene? . . . Lady Blessington, Fanny Butler, Lady Flora Hastings, Mrs. Norton & I know not who besides have been suggested."[21] If his list is any indication, the number of potential Victorian Magdalenes is long enough to suggest that Jameson's report of her deposition was premature.

Had Reeve possessed the example of *Lost and Saved*, he might have narrowed the possibilities. Beatrice is shown at one point sitting with Frank in a pose suggestive of a maculate Madonna:

Motionless and pale as she sat there, supporting her child on languid, outstretched arms, as the famous, kneeling Magdalene supports the cross, she seemed to herself in a vision to rise up, and . . . pass under the Temple gateway into the garden down by the river, and plunging in with him, float and drift, and sink and drown, till both are borne onward to darkness and peace!

(*LS* 335)

The image is disconcerting: the expected association with the Madonna and Child is withheld; instead, Beatrice is likened to Magdalene at a moment of profound sorrow. Any subtext of hope implied by the crucifixion is erased by the image of mother and child sinking into the Thames and into damnation rather than salvation. The passage resonates with unsettled and unsettling significance. Norton suggests the co-presence of Madonna and Magdalene, virgin mother and motherless wanton. The antithesis is accentuated by Montagu's framing Beatrice as an erotic Madonna:

Sometimes, when he was struck by the extraordinary beauty of Beatrice as she held the poor little thing in her arms; by the expression of her face, the grace of her figure, more lovely than all the Madonnas he had ever seen in all the galleries of Europe, the fever of passionate admiration beat as quickly . . . as in the earliest days of his wooing.

(*LS* 250)

Casting Beatrice in the role of profane Madonna defines Montagu as a sensualist; constructing Beatrice as saint and sinner establishes Norton herself as a "Modern Mary Magdalene."

Little Frank plays an important role in this scene simply by falling from his mother's lap. In "a horrid waking dream," Beatrice

> turns a little faint: her arms relax their hold, and the sleeping child slips from them and falls to the ground, waking with a startled cry of fear and pain!
>
> Ah! how altered by that cry is the condition of Beatrice's mind! With what passionate tenderness she snatches up the helpless trouble of her heart, and searches with trembling hands and dilated eyes if so much as a scratch or a bruise have harmed the little one whose drowning death she imagined a few minutes since!
>
> (*LS* 336)

Beatrice is not the "pale angry Medea" (*LS* 311) for whom Montagu mistakes her. Her vision of a watery death finds an analogue in the parched and feverish death confronting the discarded concubine Hagar and her child (*LS* 336–37). In "The Departure of Hagar," Norton depicts the "banished slave . . . her young son in her hand," awaiting death in the desert. Just as Beatrice's "dilated eyes" look upon a watery waste land, Hagar's "hot, wild eyes" are "fixed with vacant glare, / On the dreary, level waste, that lies around her there" (*FDS 47*:11). The visage of these abandoned mothers expresses all of Norton's anger at social injustice and individual cruelty; indeed, she is one "who has not died without lifting up a voice of eloquent and solemn warning."

Were *Lost and Saved* to replicate the early satire "Marriage and Love," it might be titled *Maternity and Marriage*, since Beatrice's experience reverses the normative sequence of things. Frank's near drowning, however, marks a *peripeteia* and the point after which his mother is distanced from Magdalene. Shortly after Frank dies from natural causes, Beatrice meets a morose widower, Count Ludovic Sforza and his daughter Aurelia. In her loneliness, the girl "often prayed to the Madonna in church to be her friend. She liked all pictures of the Madonna, they looked so gentle" (*LS* 444). Her association of this religious icon with Beatrice, however, is fraught with contradictions and not only because she unwittingly echoes Montagu's comparison of his mistress to the great Madonnas of Western art. Their attraction for Aurelia originated in their resemblance to her mother, whose portrait hangs in her room. Since the Countess abandoned her daughter and ran off with "a gay French officer" (*LS* 441), motherhood for Aurelia is necessarily an overdetermined site of sacred and profane associations.

If Beatrice fits neither role exclusively, Magdalene or Madonna, her adopted and unmarried sister Mariana unequivocally embodies the saintly virgin. Mariana also plays Martha to her sister's Magdalene. Jameson notes that in Christian iconography Martha is depicted as "a chaste and prudent virgin. . . . As Mary Magdalene is the patroness of repentant frailty, so Martha is the especial patroness of female discretion and good housekeeping."[22] Gazing at her sister, Beatrice remarks, "Oh Mariana, what peace there is in your face! What can you be thinking of! You look like Ary Scheffer's picture of St. Augustine's mother, except for your youth" (*LS* 406). This painting shows St. Monica, sitting beside her son, apparently in contemplation of death and the afterlife. As it happens, Mariana is thinking of the Mater Dolorosa and "wondering whether any painter had ever made a picture of the last parting between the earthly mother and her divine Son—one conscious and the other unconscious of the coming fate" (*LS* 406). In her thoughts, Mariana reminds readers of the ultimate fate of all earthly mothers of human sons, but she also reinforces the connection between her sister and the archetype of maternal purity.

Old Sir Douglas provides a final glimpse of the Magdalene theme. The eponymous squire suspects, falsely, that his youthful wife harbors a secret love for his ne'er-do-well nephew. An involuntary groan escapes him during the gospel reading at Sunday services: "Then Joseph, her husband, being a just man, and not willing to make her a public example, was minded to put her away privily" (Matthew 1:19). Joseph is dissuaded from doing so by an angel, who appears in a dream and explains his wife's pregnancy. Norton reads the story as offering consolation to "women who have been falsely accused" since even the mother of God "had to endure *her* share of earthly shame!" (*OSD* 2:126). The narrator editorializes that even a "good man; merciful, affectionate, anxious to do that which was right in the sight of God" can extend mercy "only to 'putting her away privily' " (*OSD* 2:127). Douglas, too, is a just man, but he is just a man. Prey to jealousy and mistrust, he sorely misses the insight granted to Joseph: "the angelic vision [that] made clear that she who was condemned in the sight of man, was the chosen weak vessel for the mercy of God" (*OSD* 2:127). Incapable of confronting the situation directly, Douglas decides to "put himself away privily" as it were, abandoning his family for the battlefields of Crimea and leaving his wife to bear the false accusations of sexual misconduct. In a world in which even Madonnas may find themselves subject to suspicion and rumor, there would seem to be little hope for Magdalenes and Hagars.

The Uses of Race

Women of color appear in Norton's work at two distinct periods and in directly contrasting ways. Early in her career, she turned to the West Indies as the setting of stories depicting the fate of women of color who had the misfortune to become romantically involved with English sailors or colonists. These characters face the double prejudice of race and gender and invariably meet the fate of abandoned mistresses like Rosalie and Annie Morrison (*Woman's Reward*). Late in her career, Norton looked to India for characters whose depictions perpetuate the double bias that she had previously exposed and critiqued. In *Lost and Saved*, for example, cunning and amoral Asian women seduce Indian and British men alike, insinuate themselves into English society, and stop short of nothing, including murder, to maintain social status. Silver fork meets sensation; "the world" expands to include the Empire; and an insular nation, not simply the upper class, ruthlessly excludes the aspiring outsider.

While Thackeray mockingly proposed Miss Swartz as the heroine of his "novel without a hero," Norton's early fiction presented women of color as the sympathetic victims of British gender and racial bias.[23] "The Spirit of the Hurricane" (1832) focuses on the visit of Charles Louvel to his beloved "sister, or rather half-sister, since she was the daughter, not of his mother, but of a woman of colour whom his father (who was also a sailor) had fallen in love with when he came to Barbadoes many years ago" (*KB* 1:67–68). He arrives in the West Indies to find Pauline and her mother, a freed slave, in dire poverty. The mother, now an alcoholic, is near death, and Pauline is threatened with slavery. Charles steals from his ship to help his sister, is caught, and dies after being flogged. Pauline is left alone and wondering: "Oh God, . . . is this justice, or is it *murder*?" (*KB* 1:82).

The hurricane that follows Charles's death is described in biblical terms, suggesting divine wrath at the death of the gentle sailor:

> Suddenly the sound of a "rushing mighty wind" swept over the bosom of the earth, and ruffled the face of the waters. . . . Darkness was on the land and the sea—a horrid darkness that was not night; it seemed as if the last awful day had overtaken the sinful earth, and that its destruction had commenced.
>
> (*KB* 1:83–84)

When Pauline emerges after the storm, she is spied by several of Charles's shipmates:

> "Look! look! . . . a woman is standing there, unhurt and alone." "Hush!" said his companion, "it cannot be a woman; see how fearlessly she gazes round her over the ruined island: it is the Spirit of the Hurricane!" "Spirit of nonsense . . . it is a young and pretty creature, who has been saved by some strange mercy like ourselves. Come and speak to her, we may perhaps assist her."
>
> (*KB* 1:86)

The second speaker, under the influence of "native" superstitions, transmogrifies Pauline into an avenging phantom. He sees her not as a figure of ridicule, such as the "Belle Sauvage" (*VF* 244) mocked by George Osborne, but as an object of fear and blame. Standing in opposition to this mythologizing tendency is the first speaker, Henri Lafitte, a sickly orphan befriended by Charles when other sailors ridiculed him as " 'la petite blonde,' or 'Mam'selle Fanny' " (*KB* 1:65). Lafitte, a victim of gender and national stereotypes, is more humane than his companion. Rather than demonize Pauline, he sees a woman possibly in need of help and certainly linked to themselves and to all humanity in braving the unforeseen dangers of life.

Nature is an ineluctable and potentially destructive force visited upon humankind equally, regardless of gender or race. It is seen as a punishment only by the superstitious or by those fearful of the unknown. Human power, by contrast, is unfairly exercised and selectively cruel. Charles's punishment may be extreme—Pauline thinks it murderous—but he is guilty; she, on the contrary, is guilty of nothing except being a woman of color, yet she is threatened with slavery and decried as "the Spirit of the Hurricane." She survives the fury of nature but not the human storm. Upon learning that Charles is dead and having pledged to love only her brother, she dies and is buried next to him.

"The Creole Girl; or, the Physician's Story" (1840) reprises Pauline's tale with slight variation but with the same tragic resolution. The unnamed protagonist is "the child of Passion, and of Shame" (*D* 79). After her father, an Englishman "of noble birth," returns to England from the West Indies, the "unknown mother faded from the earth" (*D* 79). Their daughter is eventually sent to England, where her father hopes "to place her" in society (*D* 91). The Creole Girl remains a social outcast, however, and continues to suffer for the sins of her father. She is received by her father's friends with "cold compassion [that] made contempt seem light" (*D* 80). Hope for acceptance lies with a young suitor, who ultimately cannot free himself from the shackles of convention. The expected signification of "slave" is reversed as the young Englishman only

> *half* rebell'd against the chain
> Which fashion flung around him; though too proud
> To own that slavery's weariness and pain.
> Too proud; perhaps too weak; for Custom still
> Curbs with an iron bit the souls born free;
> They start and chafe, yet bend . . . to the will
> Of this most nameless ruler. . . .
>
> (*D* 84)

In the manner of Thackeray's "Hottentot Venus" (*VF* 256), the Creole Girl is feared as an exotic seductress, capable of hypnotizing potential victims with the "languid luster of her speaking eye, / The indolent smile of that bewitching mouth" (*D* 81). The hurricane in this case is sexual. A prophylactic and punitive narrative of race and sexuality, which is self-generated and socially sanctioned, preserves the son of England from a "spell" and "haunting" (*D* 87) entirely of his own construction.

This is "a physician's story" only in the sense that the doctor called in to care for the dying Creole Girl narrates her tale of desertion by her father and her lover. The doctor in detached tones indicts her indifferent father: " 'Why mournest thou?' / Because she was the unknown child of shame; / (Albeit her mother better kept the vow / Of faithful love, than some who keep their fame.) / Poor mother, and poor child,—unvalued lives" (*D* 93–94). While the physician pointedly marks the hypocrisy of the father toward both mother and daughter, he cannot mourn the young woman's death. She has left "man's injustice" for a realm where her "soul its chains of slavery [shall] burst" (*D* 95).

The late novels, by contrast, blatantly indulge in pejorative racial stereotypes. *Lost and Saved* offers two equally offensive examples of the "Hindoo character." Myra Grey, the daughter of a British magistrate and an Indian woman, poisons her husband, the Collector of Customs at Burrumpootra, but only after accepting bribes from "the native litigants under the pretense of influencing decisions" (*LS* 77). She then seduces the Governor of the Presidency, Pierrepont Treherne (Montagu's uncle), who barely manages to escape her marital grasp.

Settling for the Treherne family attorney, John Grey, she establishes a secure upper-middle-class life in London, where she is well served by "the Indian habit of intriguing for promotion" (*LS* 81).

Her niece Milly Nesdale outstrips Myra in social success and criminal excess. She manages to "captivate" and marry Lord Nesdale (*LS* 80). Myra possesses "cruel Hindoo eyes" to go along with a serpentine heart and tongue (*LS* 78, 372), but Milly is even more threateningly reptilian, capable of winding her very soul into a "corkscrew of spiral coils, preparatory to springing" (*LS* 231). With the wiles of an Indian seductress and the social skills of an Anglo-Saxon "woman of the world," Milly is a formidable foe "who, if she was 'coquette raffiné,' was so according to all rules and observances of fashionable life" (*LS* 254). Under the protection of her invisible husband, she conquers a series of men, including Montagu, who falsely assures Beatrice that he is indifferent to "the alluring coquetries of this woman of fashion" (*LS* 291). The narrator repeatedly associates Milly with offensive racial stereotypes, noting, for instance, that "[l]ike most persons of Eastern extraction, she had a positive pleasure in deceiving" (*LS* 229) and that she "got all she could from every one, not from necessity, but from habit, and because the predatory soul of the adventuress was in her, as in her aunt Myra, . . . no change of position would have extracted it out of either of them" (*LS* 229–30).

Old Sir Douglas turns from East to "West Injian[s]," describing them as little better than "wild savage[s]" (*OSD* 2: 226). Anita Frere, a Creole woman deserted by her Scottish husband, is not an avatar of her passive predecessors. She is more than a match even for her psychopathic spouse, pursuing him to England and confronting Alice Ross, with whom he has committed bigamy. When Alice derisively asks if Frere had married a slave, Anita says, "I am no slave but a planter's daughter! . . . and you had best keep your contempt for your own position. I am as educated as you are—and rich, rich, rich!" (*OSD* 2:229). While her appearance is that of "a Creole but a gentlewoman" (*OSD* 2:226), her behavior is vulgar, if not barbarous. She is impassive when splattered with the blood of a murdered man, and her husband calmly observes that "death need not be the horror to her that it was to the Englishwomen who witnessed it. Only in England is such a calm value set on human life" (*OSD* 2:258). Not a woman to "slay Jason's children to punish Jason" (*OSD* 2:258), Anita actively assists Frere to elude the police, proving the "soul of the adventuress" to be as much a West as an East Indian characteristic.

In "The Spirit of the Hurricane" and "The Creole Girl," racist attitudes are decried and employed metonymically to indict all forms of social injustice. Chauvinism of any kind—whether of gender, class, or nation—is identified as a reverse form of slavery. *Lost and Saved* and *Old Sir Douglas* are dominated by strong women who fall into two categories, those who nobly but passively resist victimization (the heroines, Beatrice and Gertrude) and those who actively but deceitfully refuse it (the villains, Myra, Milly, Anita, and Alice). Since women of color are found only in the latter category, Norton establishes a regrettable counter-narrative to her earlier work. The turn toward sensational plots involving murders, secret marriages, hidden identities, and narrow escapes caters to popular tastes—and prejudices.

STRUCTURE AND SYNTHESIS: *LOST AND SAVED* AND *OLD SIR DOUGLAS*

Except for the treatment of race, the novels of the 1860s constitute a synthesis of a lifetime's work. Many of the distinctive characteristics of her earlier narratives are present in minor keys. The silver fork preoccupation of the 1830s, for example, is found in minor figures such as the Marchioness of Updown in *Lost and Saved* and Lady Charlotte Skifton in *Old Sir Douglas*, characters whose social pretensions make them both the vehicle and the object of social satire. The political preoccupation of the 1840s is also de-emphasized but present: *Lost and Saved* critiques the exploitation of domestic labor, and *Old Sir Douglas* debates the wisdom of the British involvement in Crimea. New elements in these novels are the heightened rhetoric and action of 1860s sensation fiction, which was labeled, among other things, "Arsenical Literature" (documented by Myra and Milly) and "Bigamy Novels" (evidenced by James Frere).[24] The most significant change in the late fiction, however, is that the wives of invisible husbands have grown stronger and more resourceful than their predecessors. Instead of the death by broken heart visited upon the Creole Girl, Rosalie, and Eleanor Penrhyn (*SD*), the female protagonists resist, endure, and ultimately prosper. In the world of Beatrice Brooke and Gertrude Skifton, "[n]ot the most afflicted, but the most feeble, 'die of a broken heart' " (*LS* 358).

Each protagonist is pursued by a sensualist of Apollonian beauty and Dionysian character (Montagu Treherne, Kenneth Ross). Although these Byronic lovers prove to be entirely self-involved and ultimately self-destructive, their power to inflict emotional and social injuries upon the women they pretend to love is compounded by two forms of harm inflicted by women against women. The first is the class and social bias exemplified by the cutting behavior of Lady Updown and Lady Clochnaben. The second is the seemingly unlimited malevolence of characters like Milly Nesdale and Alice Ross (Douglas's half-sister), who perceive themselves to be excluded from a privileged seat at society's table and who derive vengeful pleasure from denying others the satisfactions withheld from them. Milly's aspirations are restricted by race, Alice's by character, on the one hand, and by legal and social practice, on the other. She is an unpleasant spinster entirely dependent upon her brother. She is tolerated by virtue of his status but wanted and welcomed by no one. These women represent a different order of villainy from class bullies of the Updown/Clochnaben variety. They raise evil from the level of snobbery and social cruelty to criminality ranging from theft to murder. Myra's penchant for poisoning her enemies misfires when she accidentally kills her lover, Montagu; Alice's feral stalking of her sister-in-law and bigamous husband are motivated by jealously and embittered vengeance.

The introduction of purely evil characters and violent plots does not, however, alter the fundamental structure of Norton's fictional world. One encounters, for example, both the geography and the ethnography of "Curious Customs in the County of Middlesex." Scotland and Wales offer greater individual autonomy and less oppressive civil rule than exist in England. Legal practices are more forgiving, and the social system is less bureaucratic. From the English perspective, Welsh codes offer a "confused sort of mercy without a poor law, which enacted that a man should stand free from punishment for theft of meat, if he could prove that he was a necessitous man and exiled" (*LS* 36). The confusion exists only in the eyes of the English; for the Welsh, a system of justice administered on the basis of need rather than property and inherited rights makes perfect sense. Conversely, Welsh innocence of British laws—marital in the case of Beatrice and commercial in the case of her father—produces consequences that seem punitively disproportionate to their cause: seduction and abandonment in her case, bankruptcy in his, and ruined reputations in both.

London, "the largest, the richest, the busiest—and the ugliest—capital in Europe" (*LS* 49), represents the antithesis of Scots and Welsh polity. Urban blight signifies this difference and plays an important role in Norton's fiction (although it had been chronicled in *The Child of the Islands*) for the first time:

Roaring, raging, rioting, rackety London; with its crowded streets full of busy bees and idle drones—swarming, crawling, moving ceaselessly to and fro; in gay fashionable dresses, in laboring mechanics' suits, in dapper holiday attire, in squalid filthy rags.... London, with its practiced beggars, halting on unnecessary crutches, peering from under blind eye-shades, compressing with mock bandages sinewy, healthy, and unmaimed limbs; whining for alms to spurious babes, hired for the day to stir the sluggish heart to pity! London, with its real misery, its real starvation, its back slums and fetid lodging-houses, its skeleton children playing by filthy sewers ...—its over-labored needlewomen, its gaunt and pallid men "out of work" ... its great bridges, spanning the fog-haunted river on whose disturbed and befouled waters tiny black steamers shoot hither and thither like insects of the beetle tribe; and where the cry of the drowning suicide is lost in the hum of gathered multitudes restlessly pursuing the pleasures of the business of life.

(*LS* 47–48; also see 245)

This survey of London life anticipates key themes in the novel. The "practiced beggars" provide a marked contrast to the necessitous thieves of Wales. The coachmen with their whips are a recurrent motif, reminding readers of the cutthroat, and in some ways lawless, world of the aristocracy. The imperious Marchioness of Updown, for instance, repeatedly demands that her driver cut in and out of the lines of cabs and coaches, even though "some of the draped and festooned aristocracy ... were in the very act of attempting to re-enter their carriages" (*LS* 349). The reference to the dirty waters of the Thames foreshadows Beatrice's contemplated suicide. All told, the panoramic glimpse of London's "apparently inextricable confusion of contradictory progress" (*LS* 47) suggests that Norton could no longer ignore the enveloping metropolitan poverty and filth nor rest content with unhappy protagonists isolated in gilded cages.

The mapping of city and country is paralleled by a symbolic European geography. The northern countries—"the digging and delving climes"—are imagined to be the locus of active energy, whereas southerners—the Italians in *Lost and Saved*, the Spanish in *Old Sir Douglas*—are viewed as a volatile mix of indolence and passion, sensuality and childishness. Northerners who lack self-discipline, like Kenneth Ross, are drawn to the land of the Lotos-Eaters. He is seduced by the "tranquil do-nothing-ness of the people" (*OSD* 1:111; also see 2:69). The Italian-Welsh heritage of the Brooke children is illustrated in the opening scene of the novel in which Beatrice and Owen spontaneously race along the beach, "their white teeth glittering with that smile peculiar to southern blood" (*LS* 15; also see 70–71, 75–76). She turns back in mid-course, returning to the starting place to claim victory. The referee, a cousin without "southern blood," rules that she is "a little unprincipled cheat" (*LS* 16).

That the siblings share the Mediterranean trait of "the rash eagerness of a child in all plans for their satisfaction" (*LS* 188) is confirmed by Beatrice's elopement and Owen's throwing a rock at the Queen's carriage in an attempt to deliver a letter to her: "His mother's blood ran in Owen's veins—that southern blood which, if it have not all the exaggeration of qualities attributed to 'the land of the cypress and myrtle,' has at least a quickness unknown to calmer souls" (*LS* 188).

Scotland, which served a purely symbolic function in *The Wife*, is fully rendered in *Old Sir Douglas*, from its wide natural vistas to its narrow social values. The Highlands are not simply a northern Eden, as Gertrude discovers when she tries to make a home for herself on her husband's estate. Unfamiliar with its customs, she painfully learns that good intentions may generate ill-will, and generous actions can be given negative interpretations. It is not that "THE WORLD . . . pronounced that [Gertrude] was a bad woman" (*OSD* 2:178); rather, actions such as distributing alms on the Sabbath are construed as signs of religious disrespect. She is blamed for Kenneth's infatuation with her, and rumors abound that she is "a creature more dangerous and subtle than any dancer, or Anonyma" (*OSD* 2:178). When Sir Douglas succumbs to the slander circulating about his wife, her fate is sealed: she is declared a "wily profligate woman [whose] husband had renounced her" (*OSD* 2:158). Gertrude's fatuous mother comically introduces the theme of the real vs. the nominal bad woman when she laments,

> I wouldn't mind if Gertrude was *really* bad; I mean I should think it quite fair; though of course I suppose I should be vexed, being my own child. But when I *know* her to be so good, and they are all so violent and unreasonable . . . I really do think the Queen ought to do something.
>
> (*OSD* 2:159)

Rural Scotland can be no less "a strange unstable world" (*OSD* 1:146) than London itself. *Old Sir Douglas* is Norton's last and darkest work. It suggests that irrespective of nationality, of setting, and even of upbringing, the most well-intended and loving couples are endangered by an array of social and personal threats.

The isolated Scottish setting shifts the emphasis from society to nature, but characters have no easier time interpreting and navigating their world. Nature may have its laws, but they are impenetrable:

> If there were not daily examples to familiarize us with the marvel, we might wonder at the strange way in which Nature asserts herself; or rather, at the effects of Nature and accident combined, in the characters of individuals. We see children, all brought up in one home, under the same tutelage, as different as night from day.
>
> (*OSD* 1:15: also see 1:98)

Reliable conclusions are impossible when a single cause produces contradictory results. If human nature is mixed, the narrator reflects, it is so according to no discernible formula:

> It may be true that human hearts are as a general rule "deceitful and desperately wicked," but some hearts are *more* deceitful and *more* desperately wicked than others. The leaven of sin may exist in all, but most assuredly it never was so perfectly mixed as to secure to each an equal distribution.
>
> (*OSD* 1:99)

Puzzlement at nature's indecipherable logic might lead to resignation in the face of divine mystery, but Norton prefers more secular and activist conclusions. If the unequal distribution and invisible working of "the leaven of sin" make it virtually impossible to read society, then humankind must labor dutifully—if with limited efficacy—to resist imposing irrational human structures on unreadable divine ones. To make this point, Lorimer Boyd echoes the view Norton expressed in *Letters to the Mob*: "God made gradation: it is no invention of man's. He made strength and weakness of body, clearness or dimness of intellect, capacity and incapacity of all sorts as he made men and angels" (*OSD* 1:212). He continues:

> I object only to the inordinate value set on *accidental* distinctions: distinctions inherited or acquired in some way totally independent of any merit in the possessor: perhaps possessed by persons of singular demerit. I hold the sort of blind adulation offered to mere rank, wealth, and what is called "position," to be as much intoxication of the understanding, as the state of a man who rises tipsy from table.
>
> (*OSD* 1:212)

In his view, a natural hierarchy of ability and character argues for a meritocracy, a system of government defended by Norton herself (see chapter 6). Even if happiness is out of direct human control, shedding blinders and "seeing things in their true light or relative proportion" (*OSD* 1:212) offer the only chance of even moderately efficacious action.

Boyd's—and Norton's—political philosophy accounts for the presence in *Lost and Saved* of a topic that would otherwise not be expected in a novel of sensation: the plight of the working poor. In having her middle-class heroine descend to the rank of seamstress, Norton challenges class assumptions and defends the values of work and self-reliance, especially for women. Beatrice's earliest consciousness of labor occurs on a visit to the home of the Wollinghams, where she is astonished by the number of servants: "I sometimes wonder what work they can possibly find to divide among them" (*LS* 66). The good-natured Helen Wollingham explains the various functions of hall porters, grooms of the chambers, butlers, under-butlers, steward-room boys, coachmen, and what appear to be "a hundred more slaves of the lamp in this Aladdin's palace" (*LS* 67). The conspicuous consumption of human labor is carried to its ridiculous extreme by Helen's mother, who employs three maids merely to "wait . . . upon the empty dress" that she will wear to a ball (*LS* 175).

One of these servants, Miss Parkes, is cruelly bullied by the Marchioness. On the evening of the ball, Parkes visits Beatrice, who has fallen ill under the combined strain of mending lace for the Updowns and caring for Frank. Parkes herself is "very tired in her ankles, having stood all day superintending the sowing [sic] on of the jeweled barnacles on the white and gold-embroidered hull" (*LS* 175), that is, on the Marchioness's gown. Duty prevents her from reaching Beatrice until "two in the morning, looking very yellow and tired" (*LS* 350), and she must be back by four to "put the diamonds and emeralds into their cases, and see to her pearls; it's rather a fagging night, dear, and though it's true she mightn't be home till five or six, she'll be so very angry if we're not all in waiting" (*LS* 351). When her absence is detected by the Marchioness, the Good Samaritan Parkes is summarily dismissed and refused the reference that would enable her to secure other employment. Norton's depiction of aristocratic callousness and cruelty combines the silver fork subject matter of the earliest work and the political and social preoccupation of poems like *The Child of the Islands.*

The social villainy of the Marchioness of Updown has a parallel in the religious hypocrisy of the Countess of Clochnaben,

> whose understandings really seem to be turned upside down. . . . She is always wrong, and always thinks she is right. It is a pity we can't pack a few moderate

sensible thoughts on the top of her mind, and then ticket her, "This side uppermost." But she will never be converted.

(*OSD* 2:265)

She and Alice Ross "belonged to that wide-spread and influential sect, the Pharisees. They were continually thanking God that they were better than their neighbours; and lost in contemplation of the mote in their brother's eye" (*OSD* 1:195). Self-justifying narratives enable them to simplify the confused face of humanity and neatly to distinguish saints from sinners. Clochnaben, the social villain, and Alice, the sensational one, are Sabbatarians who condemn all who do not share their practice. Norton writes that "stricter Sabbath rules, and the vehement battle of sects as to how to keep God's day holy, do not make Scotland a more moral country" (*OSD* 2:263–64). The point is underscored by the fact that extended Sunday observance tends to be inversely correlated with true piety (*OSD* 1: 218, 288).

A final element of Norton's fictional synthesis is a brief return to the political interests that occupied a central place in her life from the time of the First Reform Bill until the passage of the Divorce Act of 1857. With the death of her friend Sidney Herbert in 1861, Norton's thoughts returned to a man whose dedication to public service—he served as secretary of war during the British involvement in Crimea—was widely held to have contributed to his early death. Her decision to place Douglas Ross "in the centre of those scenes of military suffering and proud English endurance" (*OSD* 2:168) recalls the final section of Tennyson's *Maud*, in which the speaker escapes tortured thoughts and emotions by enlisting in the national cause. Unlike Tennyson, however, Norton directly confronts the controversies surrounding the wisdom and waste of the war.[25] Douglas yearns "for death on the battlefield" but finds only "the slow, ignoble, sickly wasting away of life" (*OSD* 2:293). Gertrude herself worries about the "mismanagement of supplies" and "the horrid red-tape-ism" that has reached the level of "criminal folly" (*OSD* 2:171; also see 2:291–92). Norton's view falls between the jingoism of Tennyson's speaker and Gertrude's emotional criticism of Britain's conduct of the war. The narrator notes the suffering that governmental blunders have caused but is troubled that efforts to remedy those mistakes have led to further criticism and dissention: "My heart is made very sore by the abuse of men in power here; who are, as I believe, doing their very utmost to retrieve mistakes and alleviate suffering. You will say that such mistakes ought never to have been made; but that is over" (*OSD* 2:176).

The narrator eulogizes the English soldiers who died in places with obscure names like Bulganac, Bouliok, Alma, Balaklava, Sebastopol, Varna, and Scutari (*OSD* 2:287–89). She honors those who returned to loved ones "but who were so worn and shaken by the past tempest of that wintry war, that, like nipped trees, they stood for a little while, and then succumbed and fell" (*OSD* 2:289). Gertrude herself not only defends the cause in which her husband is engaged but also associates loyalty to him with loyalty to the nation. Her strength of character provides Norton the opportunity to extend her arguments for the place of women in politics to the role of women in times of war. In a letter to Lorimer Boyd, Gertrude proclaims:

> I have heard women say that they did not comprehend the feeling of patriotism; I think I do, not so much for my country as for my *countrymen*. I believe in the full measure of good which might be done; I believe in the full value of individual exertion. It has been my dream from the first, and will be my dream to the last, to watch the lives that leave their tracks of light behind, like ships on the waters. Though the wave close over the light, the tracks once explored will be crossed again even to another hemisphere, and the influence of one man's mind may outlive not only his existence, but the very memory of his name.
>
> (*OSD* 2:176)

Gertrude's belief in individual action—in a woman's action—and her faith that human effort will produce lasting and beneficial ends are surely Caroline Norton's as well, and in this statement Norton provides her own eulogy.

Part II

Law

Chapter 3

"The Brethren of the Long Robe": Legal Satire and Courtroom Humor

When all is done that cunning man can do,
The suitor ruined, and the opposer too;
When baffled, wearied, saddened, soured, and vexed;
By failure or success alike perplexed, . . .
One thing alone seems clear, without a flaw,—
LAW is not JUSTICE; JUSTICE is not LAW![1]

Caroline Norton, "Cromwell and the Lawyers"

All preconceived ideas on any subject I can scout,
And demonstrate beyond all possibility of doubt,
That whether you're an honest man or whether you're a thief
Depends on whose Solicitor has given me my brief.[2]

W. S. Gilbert, *Utopia Limited*

Apart from marrying one and then having him fling his copy of Blackstone at her, Norton could not have expected to have a great deal to do with attorneys or their law books. Her husband's accusation of adultery in 1836, however, began what would prove to be a lengthy and generally unhappy exposure to legal processes and players, an exposure not terminated even by her husband's death in 1875. While not expecting the terms of his will to be favorable, she was shocked to learn that their sole surviving son had been disinherited.

Their legal wrangles thus continued from the grave, further justifying her comment that "the accursed tribe of Lawyers have had their fangs in me . . . and I can't get away."[3]

Norton selected as the epigraph to *English Laws for Women* Mrs. Bagnet's comment concerning the arrest of George Rouncewell: "It won't do to have truth and justice on his side; he must have law and lawyers" (*BH* 656). She, too, posits a negative correlation between justice and its earthly agents. The disjunction is exacerbated by two features of "legal optics": first, the obligation of attorneys to see either side of a case (with the corollary that once they are hired, the opposing position becomes untenable), and second, the radical separation of "the legal world" from other realms of experience (with the corollary that anything falling outside its purview is invisible to the law). The " 'hired Masters of the Tongue-fence'—as Milton calls lawyers" (*ELW* 93)—are imagined to be skilled prestidigitators whose audience nonetheless feels an "inward consciousness that some juggler's trick, the 'hey presto!' of some earthly magician, might so change the whole face of things, that all this power might be brought to bear *on the contrary side of the argument*" (*PL* 116). This unsettling feeling is illustrated by an attorney's story concerning

> one of his brethren of the long robe, who, mistaking the tenor of his brief, argued with great skill and apparent warmth the cause of his client's adversary; but on being made aware of his error, said, with admirable composure—"*This*, my lord, and gentlemen of the jury, is what might be urged, and I have no doubt *will* be urged by the counsel on the other side;"—and proceeded to answer his own objections, to destroy point by point the whole framework of his own oration, and to build a directly contrary argument on the ruins of his own train of reasoning.
>
> (*PL* 116)

For all that lawyers might resemble Janus in their ability to look in two directions, these "Cyclops of the law" (*LQ* 144) are strangely monocular when it comes to considerations other than those of law. They "can only see with one eye, narrowly peeping at, and puzzling over one single aspect of their many difficulties," carefully discounting "the special circumstances that mark the individual human lot" (*LQ* 144). Their powers of discernment may be legendary within the hermetic world of legal statutes, but they are willfully blind to the faults of a system in which eloquence is more powerful than truth.

Legal diplopia and myopia have become standard features of legal comedy, but Norton is unusual in that she both wrote and inspired such satires. *Norton* v. *Melbourne* generated several parodic redactions, but more surprising is the frequent interruption of the proceeding itself by general hilarity. The attorney general, Sir John Campbell, was especially effective in exploiting stereotypical images of women and servants to elicit laughter in the service of a verdict for Melbourne, all the while adding insult to the injury already inflicted upon the plaintiff's wife.

COMMON LAW COMEDY IN *NORTON* V. *MELBOURNE*

This trial was eagerly anticipated by a public that had been reading of the affair for over a year in gossip columns and scandal sheets. Typical of these efforts is this "LAMB-POON"—a pun on Melbourne's given name, William Lamb—appearing in *The Satirist* on June 21, 1835: "Though if for ever my renown may blot, / I'll still stand up, dear CAROLINE for thee, / For, Oh! How oft (the marriage vows forgot!), / Hast thou consented to lie down for me."[4] The broad humor to which the allegation of adultery gave rise did not stop when the trial began, despite the efforts of George Norton's attorney, Sir William Follett, to maintain the seriousness of the proceedings. Recognizing the delicacy of the material to be introduced in court, as well as its susceptibility to coarse comedy, he instructed jurors to "dismiss as far as you possibly can from your minds the idle rumour and the talk to which this case has given rise."[5] Eschewing any hint of the comedy surrounding the figure of the cuckold, he earnestly appealed to the jury to defend the sanctity of fatherhood.

Follett moved quickly to call attention to "the deepest injury . . . which one man can inflict upon another" because it "poisoned in its sources the dearest of all earthly affections: the love of a father to his child."[6] He made sure that his fellow men on the jury understood that only the grievousness of the wound could lead a father to bring such a painful matter to public attention: "a husband sustaining an injury of this sort, has no mode whatever of obtaining redress, or guarding against a spurious offspring being palmed upon him, but by first bringing his case before a jury and seeking for damages for the injury he has sustained."[7] He appealed to the jury as "men of the world, with a knowledge of the feelings of your brother men," first, to ask themselves "what must be the meaning of the visits of Lord Melbourne to this young and beautiful woman?"; second, "as fathers—and . . . as men—to consider what his [the plaintiff's] sufferings must be"; and third, to remember "the defendant's rank and station" in considering "the amount of damages you shall award."[8]

Although aspiring to the gravitas of domestic tragedy, Follett could not prevent the proceedings from occasionally descending to the level of bedroom farce. An audience primed for sexual disclosure seized upon tidbits, such as his offering the fact that Lord Melbourne often used the rear entrance to the Norton home as evidence of the clandestine and illicit nature of his visits. Follett was visibly embarrassed when the statement that Melbourne "invariably went in . . . by the passage behind" was greeted with explosive laughter.[9] Although failing to anticipate the courtroom's reaction in this instance, he must surely have recognized that a reference to "a curious book . . . prov[ing] that Mary Magdalen was the most virtuous of her sex" would elicit sniggers, which he hoped would redound to its readers and not upon himself. Christine L. Krueger is correct in suggesting that "Norton becomes a character in Follet's [sic] titillating melodrama which, like pornographic representations of women, forms a conspiratorial and voyeuristic relationship between author and audience that Norton herself could not challenge"; however, this tack can be attributed a fortiori to Sir John Campbell.[10] Melbourne's attorney consistently and deliberately relied on salacious insinuation to ingratiate himself (and his client) with jurors, not as aggrieved husbands but as knowing men of the world. And while Follett and Campbell opposed one another, neither was on Magdalene's side.

The attorney general could do little to dispel the aura of sexual license surrounding his client, whose wife had been the public lover of Lord Byron and who himself had been the defendant in a previous criminal conversation action. Perhaps he made a virtue of necessity; nonetheless, it is surprising that Campbell would engage so freely in sexual humor and banter. His strategy suggests a homeopathic remedy: if sexual misconduct is the charge, then sexual humor is the means of addressing it. By establishing a comfortable rapport with the jury on the subjects of male sexual mores and foibles, Campbell countered Follett's appeal to them as responsible fathers and upholders of public decency. Unlike his adversary, he was more than willing to capitalize on the potential for humor and openly played to the audience in the packed courtroom.

In his cross-examination of the servants, whose testimony concerned Melbourne's visits to their mistress, Campbell demonstrated that virtually all were unreliable, having themselves been fired for sexual indiscretions. Several had been invited to the Norton family estate prior to the trial, where they had been entertained and coached. In summation, Campbell ticked off the list of disreputable witnesses, only to be interrupted by Follett at the name of Trinette Elliot.

Whether Follett's exasperation happened to boil over at this moment or whether he actually believed Elliot to be more credible than the others, his interpolation elicited sarcastic ridicule. Elliot, Campbell righteously proclaimed, was

> a discarded servant, and a witness of bad character. His learned friend said no; why, she admitted that she, being a single women, had become with child, and that she had been turned away by her mistress. But his learned friend seemed proud of her; she was his trump card; he gloried in her. Compared with other of his witnesses she was chaste as drifted snow. However, by some accident or another, she had been got with child. (A laugh.) He . . . might be in the habit of drawing false inferences, but he could not help suspecting that if an unmarried woman became with child she must have had illicit intercourse with some man (a laugh), and if she had, she must have committed a breach of chastity. (A laugh.) He suspected that if she had had a child she was not a pure virgin.
>
> (Laughter.)[11]

Campbell's pretense of self-deprecation and his mocking ratiocination were directed to an audience of knowing men all too familiar with the morality of servants. Elliot ceased to be an individual; she was merely one of innumerable "discarded servants—a race the most dangerous in all cases, but particularly in cases of this sort."[12]

In the one instance in which neither moral turpitude nor subornation could be proven, Campbell condescendingly questioned the witness (Eliza Gibson, who served as housemaid and lady's maid) in a manner that established an implicit understanding between himself and the jury concerning innocent young servants and lascivious lords:

> *JC*: Did he [Melbourne] ever kiss you, Eliza?
> *EG*: No, Sir, never.
> *JC*: He never took any improper liberties with you? (A laugh)
> *EG*: No.
> *JC*: On no occasion?
> *ED*: No.
> *JC*: I am very glad of that.
>
> (Laughter.)[13]

Clearly, naive domestics might expect to be innocently teased by avuncular aristocrats both in court and out. The attorney general's affable condescension is entirely for the benefit of the male jury, who are joined with him in patronizing the witness and misdoubting the seriousness of the charge against Lord Melbourne.

Another servant, a coachman named Fluke, provided the most sensational moment in the proceedings, testifying that he had walked in on his mistress closeted with Melbourne in a state of dishabille. She was "lying down on her right side with her feet towards the door, and her head upon the hearthrug. . . . Mrs. Norton's clothes were up, and I saw the thick part of her thigh."[14] This sensational exposure gave way to general hilarity when the attention of the colorful coachman was diverted to the circumstances of his dismissal. The cockney comedy of a real-life drunken coachman, compounded by Fluke's Wellerian manner, transformed the proceedings into a Dickensian farce:

> *JC*: How was it that you left Mr. Norton's?
>
> *JF*: To tell the truth, I got a drop too much. (Laughter.) It was a Court-day, and we generally have a drop at such a time. Mr. and Mrs. Norton fell out in the carriage, and of course they put the spite on me, and so I was discharged.
>
> (Laughter.)[15]

"Laughter" and "Great laughter" culminate in "Roars of laughter" during Fluke's increasingly lively narrative of events. With the coachman incapacitated by drink, George

> mounted the box in his opera hat . . . and I being a goodish sort of a coachman did not wish to see my master make a fool of himself in a crowd; so I said "If you will drive you must drive by yourself." . . . I preferred walking; a pretty good proof that I was not very drunk. (Laughter.)[16]

The comic cross-examination successfully besmirched the witness and diverted the courtroom.

While Campbell might have been expected to let the glimpse of Norton's thigh remain cloaked by the curtain of comedy, he returned to the potentially damning testimony in his concluding oration, recognizing an opportunity to deliver the coup de grâce. Fluke had testified that

> Mrs. Norton, the moment I got into the middle of the room, when I was going to deliver my message, shifted herself with her hand, and rose up a little. Lord Melbourne looked at her, and she looked again at his Lordship: she then turned round and never said any thing, but gave me a bow, as much as to say "That is enough," after [I] had delivered my message. . . . I left the room.[17]

In Campbell's summation this testimony is rewritten in novelistic fashion. It is "a winter's day in November" when the coachman enters and spies

Mrs. Norton, not on the sofa, but lying on the rug, with a roaring fire, like a Spartan virgin, exposing her thigh to the view of the witness, without making any effort to rise or to adjust her dress. . . . [T]hey looked at each other, and he delivered his message, and she nodded to him, and he went away.[18]

The scene is contradictory (a roaring fire and cool Spartan virgin), the action enigmatic, and the communication oversubtle. How is the scene to be interpreted? The answer, Campbell reveals, lies in its improbability:

Was this testimony credible; was it to be supposed that the act of adultery had taken place, and that when Flooke [sic] came in she should continue in that posture and make him a bow, or that she should lie like a statue without any effort to recompose her dress, for the mere purpose of allowing Mr. Flooke [sic] to gratify his curiosity? The most profligate woman could not have behaved in such a manner.[19]

In this retelling, the exposed thigh reveals only the prurience of a bibulous coachman. The tale had to be the product of either the overheated imagination of a spiteful former employee or the overzealous coaching of the plaintiff's friends. Fluke is lectured that he "was under the greatest delusion if he supposed that 12 intelligent men," who apparently know very well how profligate women behave and sexual affairs are conducted, "would believe his evidence."[20] Follett's melodrama of seduction is rendered by Campbell as camp pornography in order that it might ultimately be reduced to banal realism.

In his instructions to the jury, Lord Chief Justice Tindal identified Fluke's credibility as the crucial issue in the trial:

None of the other witnesses spoke to any act approaching to an act of adultery. . . . The witness had described the way in which Mrs. Norton was lying on the rug. That was a situation of high indelicacy at least; whether it was before or after the supposed act of adultery was left entirely to conjecture.[21]

After informing the jury that it was up to them "to determine whether they believed the witness or not," Tindal summarized the testimony in a manner that made his own assessment unmistakably clear: Fluke "had given an account of himself not favourable to his dealings as an honest man."[22] Having narrowed the relevant testimony to that of a single witness and questioned that witness's honesty, Tindal left little room for deliberation. It is not surprising, therefore, that the jury returned a verdict for the defendant without leaving the courtroom. Their decision was greeted with "loud bursts of applause, an expression of feeling which was promptly re-echoed by shouts from the mob without the doors."[23]

Clearly, Campbell's sexual comedy proved more popular than Follett's domestic tragedy. That the fate of the prime minister hinged on the testimony of a man named Fluke suggests the kind of aptronym more readily found in literature than life. Indeed, *Norton* v. *Melbourne* owed a good deal to literary conventions: the spirit of farce ignited by Fluke and stoked by Campbell, the risqué humor attending "a situation of high indelicacy," and the conventional accounts of servants' and women's behavior. These elements united the male jurors and courtroom audience in a comfortable appreciation of the human comedy. Campbell's homeopathic defense deflected the charge of sexual misconduct, a strategy so effective that he decided not to present a single witness for the defense. His tack guaranteed that there would be no counterpoint to the comedy of the day and enabled the famous defendant—heretofore the cynosure of public attention and the object of numerous satiric barbs—to escape virtually unnoticed.[24] Homeopathic rhetoric shifted attention from his case to encompassing social narratives about sexuality, gender, and class. Melbourne was acquitted, not because he had been proven innocent but because those testifying against him were proven guilty. By establishing "a conspiratorial and voyeuristic relationship" between jurist and jury, Campbell reinforced comfortable masculine narratives concerning the race of discarded servants and the behavior of profligate women. The result was not simply a verdict of innocence, but an amplification of social narratives that would predispose future juries to similar verdicts and future attorneys to similar tactics.

The curtain thus descended upon a scene of uproarious good humor—and of order restored. The disruptive servants had been dismissed anew; the wrongly accused leader's political standing was reaffirmed; and the audience departed, relieved by laughter and primed for celebration. And so the story would have ended, except for one of the principal players, notable for her absence. While Melbourne was "safe from all risk, & sitting in triumph" (*LCN* 96), Norton felt that she had been "made to appear a painted prostitute in a Public Court before a jury of Englishmen" (*LCN* 98). In addition to the public shame, her private life was now in shambles. Alienated from her husband, separated from an influential friend, and barred from living in her home and seeing her children, she found the situation anything but a cause for festivity.

One of the most galling results of the proceeding was Norton's learning that, although the woman's reputation was invariably on trial in such cases, she could not be a party to the action. She wrote to Shelley immediately after the verdict:

> Well, a woman is made a helpless wretch by these laws of men, or she would be allowed a *defence*, a counsel, in such an hour. . . . I could send notes to disprove the evidence of each witness, and they were of no use unless they bore upon the *defendant's* case. To go *for nothing*, in a trial which decides one's fate for life, is hard.[25]

A second lesson was the realization that attorneys on neither side were concerned with her fate. Their obligations were to clients, not truth: "Between these two interests of plaintiff and defendant therefore the woman's character is left to take its chance; the one interest being directly opposed to hers, the other completely independent of it" (*LQ* 81). Norton was especially frustrated by Campbell's decision not to present a case for the defendant, which "depriv[d] the lady of the benefit of the cross examination of respectable witnesses who had known her and been in the service a considerable time."[26] Beyond wishing her husband's story to be discredited, she wanted her own to be told. The verdict in *Norton* v. *Melbourne* had not provided vindication; rather, it unceremoniously deposited her at a crossway. She was not guilty but also not innocent, and the law left no alternative to its own indifference to her fate.

CRIMINAL CORRESPONDENCE: "*GRANDIS ET VERBOSA EPISTOLA*"

When a young court reporter recalled Follett's use of Melbourne's letters and inserted the scene into his serial fiction, one of the funnier moments in the trial became one of the most famous moments in *The Pickwick Papers*.[27] Follett possessed only three brief notes to Norton from Melbourne, all in this vein: "How are you? I shall not be able to call to-day, but probably shall to-morrow."[28] Had he possessed Norton's correspondence to the defendant, the hilarity would very likely have been much greater and the verdict might well have been different. Her letters include jokes about kissing, wordplay on his name ("my pet Lamb"), and suggestive banter on his "favorite subject," flagellation (*LCN* 42, 54, 56, 157).

Without references to kissing and spanking, however, Follett was forced to make do with innocuous notes about visiting, and his arguments indeed seem risible:

> These three notes, which have since been found, relate only to his hours of calling on Mrs. Norton, nothing more; but there is something in the style even of these trivial notes to lead at least to something like suspicion. . . . They seem to import much more than the mere words convey. They are written cautiously I admit—there is no profession of love in them, they are not love-letters, but they are not written in the ordinary style of correspondence usually adopted in this country between intimate friends or mutual acquaintances.[29]

The argument must have seemed far-fetched at best, and Follett's explanation of why more letters were not produced could not have strengthened it. He suggested that Norton's brother had stolen and probably destroyed the correspondence. Since there was no evidence for this supposition, Campbell was able to counter that "his Learned Friend had been led into statements which he could not afterwards support" and to insinuate that the rest of the plaintiff's case was equally insupportable.[30] Campbell, however, indulged in a fiction of his own when in closing remarks he claimed that the extant letters were numerous and the notes read by Follett were "selected no doubt from a variety as the worst that could be found."[31] He grandiloquently proclaimed that if "this is the *grandis et verbosa epistola*. 'I will call about half-past 4 or 5. Yours, Melbourn [sic],' the jury were called upon to presume from this letter that there had been an adulterous intercourse. . . . There was nothing in the evidence that could induce the jury to believe that she had broken her marriage-vows and dishonoured her distinguished family."[32] Knowing that he had the last word, Campbell took full advantage of the license of the bar to construct an alternative to Follett's fiction that he had no responsibility to prove and that the opposing side had no chance to rebut. Each fiction features a large body of letters that, in Follett's narrative, is so damning to the illicit lovers that it was brazenly stolen, and, in Campbell's, so innocuous that—to borrow the words of one of Norton's characters—there was not "a line or a syllable which might not be read at Charing Cross" (*WWR* 1:258).

These fictions illustrate the "hey presto!" of legal magicians and explain Norton's private ire and public satire. It likely mattered little that the letters were invisible, existing only in the lawyers' stories. Were they to be found, it is certain that their content would be interpreted in opposite ways. This point is corroborated by Norton's letters to her husband, to which Follett obviously did have access. To hear him tell it, this correspondence was evidence of nothing so much as the skill of a consummate actress. His reasoning once again reversed the obvious: if Melbourne's notes, which contained "no profession of love," concealed an illicit passion, then it should not be a surprise that openly affectionate letters to George disguised disdain in order to dupe the recipient. They are "written by a person pretending to be an affectionate wife" and are "calculated to disarm suspicion, and . . . to leave not the least doubt of her fidelity."[33] Predictably, Campbell insisted upon the plain meaning: "written as they were in that playful, touching, affectionate style," the letters are evidence that her devoted love continued "to the year 1836, until Mr. Norton had been induced in an evil hour to part with an affectionate wife."[34]

To buttress the point, Campbell again appealed to the "Jury as men of the world, and as men of experience," who would surely recognize that not even an unrepentant Magdalene could have acted as brazenly as it was alleged that Norton had done:

> Was it possible that if the mind of Mrs. Norton had been alienated—if her affection had ceased to belong to her husband—if she had become an adulteress, and had continued in a long course of the utmost depravity—was it in human nature that she should have continued to have lived affectionately and harmoniously with her husband?[35]

If Follett's logic seemed at best counterintuitive and at worse farcical, Campbell's argument about women's behavior answers to no logic at all. Furthermore, his presumptive narrative is a blatant fabrication, one that he knew to be false but did not fear would be strongly contradicted (and not just because he was the last to speak). Were Follett too successful in painting a bleak portrait of the Nortons' domestic life, he potentially lessened the damages awarded the plaintiff for the loss of a wife not worth keeping.

THE EQUIVOCAL VALUE OF VISIBILITY II: IN THE COURTROOM

In drawing upon *Norton* v. *Melbourne*, Dickens and Gilbert changed the substance of the case from criminal conversation to breach of the promise to marry. This less sensational topic had the advantage of retaining the potential for laughter at the same time that it enabled the authors to avoid the unseemly issue of adultery. The safer subject of broken promises—as opposed to violated marriage vows—yielded an even more important advantage: it enabled authors to bring women into the courtroom. Unlike Norton, who was not on trial and could not defend herself, plaintiffs in breach of promise trials typically did appear in court, and their presence contributed to the stereotype of the action as an opportunity for beautiful women, who had successfully seduced hapless defendants, to exercise their sexual power upon equally vulnerable juries.

Diana of the Crossways is one of the few literary treatments of the Norton case to retain the charge of adultery, yet Meredith acknowledges the chauvinism of breach of promise narratives by introducing a picture of the beautiful protagonist into the courtroom: "it is reported for positive that a miniature of the incriminated lady was cleverly smuggled over to the jury, and juries sitting upon these cases, ever since their bedazzlement by Phryne, as you know. . . ." (*DC* 1:9, Meredith's ellipsis). This "dot language, crudely masculine" (*DC* 2:245) references a story so familiar that it need not be elaborated, a tale having to do with beautiful women and male jurists and jurors—whether they serve in the imaginary tribunals of the Beautycultural Society or in the courtrooms of the county of Middlesex. Meredith merely confirms what the laughter elicited by Campbell had already intimated: Victorian juries were as susceptible to Phrynian avatars as their Athenian forebears were to the original. Publishers were no less aware of this power than attorneys; hence the irony of the fact that, although Norton was nowhere near the courtroom, only her image (Fig. 5) appears in *Extraordinary Trial! Norton* v. *Viscount Melbourne, for Criminal Consort. Damages laid at $10,000*!!!, the book hastily prepared for an audience hungry for the details of the trial as well as a glimpse of the notorious lady.

When Diana, on the eve of the trial, leaves the furor of the city for the relative quiet of the country as Norton had done, she also distances herself emotionally by satirizing the British judicial system. She imagines a conversation with a chivalrous juryman, who explains what female plaintiffs might expect in court:

> anything short of downright bullet facts went to favour the woman. For thus we right the balance of legal injustice toward the sex: we conveniently wink, ma'am. A rough, old-fashioned way for us! Is it a Breach of Promise?—She may reckon on her damages: we have daughters of our own. Is it a suit for Divorce?—Well, we have wives of our own, and we can lash, or we can spare; that's as it may be; but we'll keep the couple tied, let "em hate as they like, if they can't furnish porkbutchers" reasons for sundering.
>
> (*DC* 1:176–77)

Figure 5 "The Hon. Mrs. Norton," *Extraordinary Trial!* (1836?)
Source: Courtesy of the Cornell University Law Library.

Bullets and cleavers would seem to be the only means male litigants have of influencing jurors. While the "old-fashioned way" appears to be of immediate benefit to Diana, she suggests that rough justice is perhaps not the ideal system:

> My goodness! what a funny people, sir!—It's our way of holding the balance, ma'am.—But would it not be better to rectify the law and the social system, dear sir?—Why, ma'am, we find it comfortabler to take cases as they come, in the style of our fathers.—But don't you see, my good man, that you are offering scapegoats for the comfort of the majority?—Well, ma'am, there always were scapegoats, and always will be; we find it comes round pretty square in the end.
>
> (*DC* 1:177)

Law "in the style of our fathers" might benefit an occasional female litigant, but it bodes ill for women and the cause of social justice in general. The foreman voices a familiar social narrative, one that legitimizes chivalrous protection, allegedly for women's benefit, but at the cost of equal justice.

Meredith's satire on haphazard but "comfortabler" justice is supported by the fact that *Norton* v. *Melbourne* "kept the couple tied" and unhappily so for almost 40 years. Reactions to the verdict exhibited the paternalism of Diana's fictional juror. The *Times*, for example, chided the thoughtlessness of the careless wife and appeared content to make her the scapegoat:

> To the fair portion of the reading public the trial may suggest a very useful caution: it shows that a young and beautiful woman cannot receive with impunity the constant visits of a gentleman, even though that visitor may be more than twice as old as herself, and though his sole object may be to waste her time and his own with the most contemptible and unmeaning frivolities.[36]

It is as if Norton had taken on the role of Eliza Gibson. The journalist further noted that she had been left fatherless at an early age and that it was Melbourne's particular responsibility as a friend of her father's to be her protector. If not an adulterer, he was nonetheless a blameworthy surrogate parent, who led his daughter "to neglect the duties of a wife and mother for such conversation as an elderly idle statesman could afford, and to direct her course of reading to dissertations upon the chastity of the Magdalen."[37] Such conversation might not have been criminal in the accepted legal use of the phrase, but the trial occasioned sermons on paternal duty and uxorial decorum from the organs of public virtue—civic homilies that ironically corroborated Norton's satires on the subject of invisible husbands.

Although "bedazzlement by Phryne" did not occur in *Norton* v. *Melbourne*, the plaintiff later accused his wife of seducing his legal representatives. When John Bayley, who assisted Follett during the trial and subsequently acted as George's representative during custody negotiations, admitted the justice of the mother's request to see the children, George insisted that he had "become completely infatuated by a beautiful and talented woman"—an allegation reminding us that Hyperides was Phryne's lover as well as her attorney.[38] Another victory at the Caudine Forks must have seemed Pyrrhic, but Norton herself encouraged such associations, for example by joking privately with her brother: "I have seduced N's referee—he seems most kind honourable & gentlemanlike—he was here for two hours last night."[39] Her public statements sound a quite different tone: "My husband is fond of paying me the melancholy compliment, that to my personal charms, and not to the justice of my cause, I owe, that *all* concerned in these wretched affairs take my part against him, so soon as they have any explanation with me!" (*ELW* 129, also see 137). In *Thrupp* v. *Norton*, an 1853 trial for unpaid debt, Phryne did testify. According to George, "the judge, and every one engaged for or against her in the cause, seemed overpowered by Mrs Norton's demeanour; and those who had a turn for the drama (of whom, unfortunately, my own solicitor was one), were suspended in breathless, helpless inaction" (*ELW* 98). Her personal charm may have been undeniable, but in the paradoxical circumstance of feminine visibility and legal invisibility, the latter proved to be the more significant factor. Throughout the protracted negotiations over the terms of separation and in several trials for debts that followed his failed lawsuit, George successfully manipulated the law to his own benefit, confirming Diana's sense that it was time to "rectify the law and the social system."

Norton's understanding of the gendered narratives in which she was entangled is evident from her employing one for purposes of debunking it. In commenting on Bayley's alleged seduction, she begins with a maternal tale of the kind employed by Serjeant Buzfuz in behalf of Mrs. Bardell, casting herself as the Mater Dolorosa:

> Now, it would certainly have been strictly probable that any man . . . would,—on finding instead of the painted wanton he expected to find, prepared to struggle for her "rights" and her "interests,"—a miserable, sobbing, worn-out young woman, appealing to him for nothing but the mercy of getting back her children . . . being but man and not the angel of justice, he might have leaned most unfairly, unduly, and compassionately, to the person whose bitter grief, and single, simple stipulation, came upon him by surprise.
>
> (*ELW* 129)

In this account, the seduction of Bayley is accomplished by a mother, not a siren. This story, however, turns out to be a teasing turn of the screw. Norton's "strictly probable" account is proposed so that it can be disposed: "I thank heaven it was not so" (*ELW* 129). Neither the wanton nor the mother unduly influences Bayley's recommendation, which follows solely from "the justice of my cause."

Norton provides one final turn of this narrative screw. After debunking her maternal narrative, she revives it in another guise: As a mere reporter and not a self-interested fictionist, she has learned that the progress in her case is due to "no weak leaning of any man, but to the sympathy of a true and gentle *woman*, . . . Sir John Bayley's *wife*":

> She did not know me; I was, to her, nothing but a slandered stranger: but she came to see me and comfort me. Pure-hearted, high-minded, and herself a mother,—she strove to stand between me and my bitter disappointment. *She* . . . wrote to Mr Norton,—*she* pleaded for those children,—who did not live with him, who were no pleasure to him, who were merely his imprisoned hostages for power; *she* dug for pity in that sterile heart.
>
> (*ELW* 129–30)

As if further proof of his villainy were needed, George remained impervious to Mrs. Bayley's heartfelt pleas, and her effort amounted to "water poured upon sand" (*L* 3:15).

Norton's elaborate scheme of proposed-rejected-reported narratives ultimately reinscribes the maternal prerogative and invites comparison with the drama of outraged motherhood staged by Dodson and Fogg during the proceedings against Mr. Pickwick. In opting for a plaintiff more strikingly a mother than a siren, Dickens echoes the sexual anxieties concerning beautiful women in the courtroom but also complements this narrative with one of maternal power. Although Mrs. Bardell is "a comely woman of . . . agreeable appearance" (*PP* 229), her litigative advantage inheres not in her face but in the person of young Master Bardell, whom she kisses "in a frantic manner" (*PP* 556) upon entering the court. Once the trial begins, the fatherless child is placed in "a commanding position in which he could not fail to awaken the full commiserations and sympathy of both judge and jury" (*PP* 554). Mrs. Bardell, by contrast, is seated on "the low seat just beneath the desks of the King's Counsel . . . *invisible* to the great body of spectators" (*PP* 553, my emphasis). While *Bardell* v. *Pickwick* is justifiably famous for its mimicry of Follett's use of Melbourne's notes, Dickens's indebtedness to the narrative tactics of Melbourne's attorney have not been noted.

One of Campbell's strategies in *Norton* v. *Melbourne* was to bring the invisible wife into the courtroom as a dutiful mother. He cross-examined the servants carefully on the subject of Mrs. Norton's devoted mothering, ignoring the apparent inconsistency in finding them trustworthy on this subject but not on that of sexual misconduct. Several were asked, for example, if Mrs. Norton were not "remarkably fond of her children," and each responded to the effect that she was "devotedly attached" to them.[40] Appealing to what he held to be the "natural laws" of female behavior, Campbell reasoned that since "a woman who forgot the duties of a wife, forgot those of a mother," Mrs. Norton could not have been an adulteress: "In the history of such cases the parties had generally lived happily until the paramour had been introduced, and . . . she forgot all her domestic duties, which ended in a discovery of her infidelity and separation. Was there any single circumstance in the present case like that picture!"[41] Speaking in his own voice—and on his own authority—the attorney general asserted that

> Mrs. Norton continued to the last as fond of her husband and children as when their intercourse with these witnesses first began. He (the Attorney-General) declared to his God, he made the declaration in the most solemn manner, that this circumstance alone bore to his mind the most convincing proof of her innocence.[42]

Campbell contended that the crisis in the Nortons' marriage had been precipitated, not by her infidelity, but by his forcibly removing the children from the home and not allowing their mother to see them. In this regard, Dickens could do no better than to imitate this pathetic tale of a desperate mother:

> Mrs. Norton was thrown into the deepest consternation, and almost into a state of distraction, at finding that her children were to be thus separated from her. She pursued them all over the town, until she found them in Berkeley-street, where her tears and her entreaties to see them were unavailing.[43]

Campbell stopped short of smuggling pictures to the jury, but he did his utmost to maintain Norton's maternal presence in their minds. He was more than willing to exploit her when it suited his purposes, arguing, in effect: she is a good mother, therefore, my client cannot be guilty. His tactic merely corroborates Norton's recognition that once a woman's story is introduced in court, her "character is left to take its chance."

BREACH OF PROMISE: SUITORS ON TRIAL

One year prior to her bitter lesson in marriage law and two years before her legal history was immortalized in *Bardell* v. *Pickwick*, Norton included a breach of promise trial in *Woman's Reward*. *Bigley* v. *Dupré* is a set piece largely unrelated to the plot, and its irony is inconsistent with the generally melodramatic tone of the novel.

The questions raised by what appears to be a gratuitous episode are accentuated by an improbable plot turn near the end of the book. Readers are casually informed that the plaintiff in the trial "is to be married to the gentleman who was employed to defend Mr. Dupré's case, and who is very much in love with her" (*WWR* 1:296). This unlikely marital alliance between legal antagonists invites comparison with another case indebted to the Nortons' history, Gilbert and Sullivan's *Trial by Jury* (1875). The breach of promise case, *Angelina* v. *Edwin*, ends with the Judge's proposal to the beautiful plaintiff. Norton's literary trial is less well known than Gilbert's, yet both speak to latent fears about suitors—in the romantic sense—in the courtroom.

Norton satirizes the law by opposing an authorial narrative, that of childlike lovers dabbling in romance, to the lurid melodramas composed by their attorneys once the issue finds its way into the courtroom. Neither Lionel Dupré nor Rosabel Bigley suffers deeply or long as a result of their failed romance, and nothing in their adolescent comedy of errors suggests a lawsuit. Once a legal action is initiated, however, the forms of law discount individual circumstances and discourage attorneys from taking them into consideration. Norton thus anticipates *Bardell* v. *Pickwick* in questioning the law's ability to regulate promises of marriage.

From a commonsense perspective, neither Lionel nor Mr. Pickwick is guilty of the breach of which he is accused. Yet in both instances there is sufficient legal proof of the engagement and its breach. The evidence may be ambiguous in Pickwick's case, but it is unequivocal in Lionel's. From both Eton and Oxford, he has written letters referring to Rosabel as, among other things, "my little wife" (*WWR* 1:257). The poem with which he expresses his feeling (and in the eyes of the law becomes engaged) speaks more effectively of his immaturity than his passion: "Oh! save me from the broken charm, / Give me thy heart while fresh and warm, / Its innocence is living" (*WWR* 1:227). When he later claims not to have written "a line or a syllable which might not be read at Charing Cross" (*WWR* 1:258), he is obviously exaggerating—and obviously unaware of the fairly lax standards of proof applied in breach of promise cases. The narrator reports that "it was surprising to see how little what had been written, without a thought of its being read by more than the person addressed, would bear public inspection" (*WWR* 1:262). With epistolary proof of the kind that Follett could only have dreamed of, the plaintiff's attorney expects an easy time of it. He is forced to withdraw the case, however, upon learning that the documentary evidence "had been garbled, and added to, in the most material parts" (*WWR* 1:268).

It might be said that justice wins out in the end, but the more basic question is whether justice—or at least judges—should have been involved in the first place. Norton's skepticism is suggested by the fact that Lionel escapes punishment as a result of individual conscience, not due process. The plaintiff stops the proceedings exactly when she stands to gain the most, financially speaking. Rosabel is initially an enthusiastic party to suit: "with feelings almost as fiery" as her father's, she is resolved "to avenge the insult they had mutually sustained" (*WWR* 1:261). When she discovers that her father, an attorney, has altered the evidence, "her supposed wrongs vanished from her mind; she only thought of the baseness of the forgery" (*WWR* 1:267). Her change of heart reveals the dramatic irony of Lionel's poetic proposal. He has pleaded, "Oh! Save me from the broken charm," which is precisely what Rosabel does, although not in the sense he intends. She rescues him from a seemingly inescapable guilty verdict. Because Lionel's exoneration owes everything to the character of his accuser and nothing to the enlightened working of the system, Norton implies that in affairs of the heart, character and common sense are more important than common law.

Over and above Norton's general suspicion about the role of law in matters of love, the fact that Mr. Bigley's fraud is entirely unnecessary focuses particular criticism upon breach of promise laws. Had the system been left to run its course, Lionel would surely have been convicted of a breach that arguably did not occur. Rosabel may have temporarily succumbed to her father's pressure, but she is no Phryne. In fact, she appears in court only to utter "a few hurried sentences" (*WWR* 1:267) that explain her father's malfeasance. In Norton's depiction, men, their laws, and their lawyers are defeated by the integrity of a young woman shocked at the "way the law could so twist and turn *facts* as to 'Make the worse appear the better reason' " (*WWR* 1:267). Virtue wins out, but a damaging indictment of breach of promise laws is made: not all plaintiffs can be expected to exhibit Rosabel's integrity and not all defendants can count on the ineptness of attorneys like Samuel Bigley.

The critique of the legal system is amplified by the parody of its representatives. The plaintiff's attorney—admittedly duped by his clients—constructs a compelling story, featuring a young and innocent girl misled by a treacherous and worldly young man. It is a formulaic, but also a completely false, tale. Melodrama inheres only in the interested narratives of lawyers, not in the ordinary lives of their clients:

> he expatiated so movingly on the extreme youth, beauty, and innocence of the fair plaintiff—dwelt so much upon the treachery of the young man who had made so base a return for her father's hospitality, and appealed to the jury in so impassioned and indignant a style, as to the amount of damages, that the imaginary worth of Miss Rosabel's wounded and misplaced affections, rose in the judgment of those who listened, to an inestimable value.
>
> (*WWR* 1:263)

When the plaintiff's counsel finishes, it seems "impossible . . . that excessive and enormous damages should not be awarded" (*WWR* 1:263)—"excessive and enormous" making clear what Norton thinks of the proceedings.

Mr. Jennings, counsel for the defendant, "heard, unmoved, the pathetic address of his opponent, and sate [sic] *feuilletant* his own brief, in which an equally affecting case was made out for the wronged Lionel" (*WWR* 1:264). In his version (the telling of which is preempted by Rosabel's revelation), the roles are reversed: "The arch-traitor was here represented as a young and innocent orphan, who, left without friends to guard him, found only a grasping mercenary in the person appointed to watch his fortune [Mr. Bigley], and had thus been made the victim of a deep-laid plot" (*WWR* 1:264). The rebuttal is neither less melodramatic nor more accurate than his adversary's tale. Jennings knows he cannot deny the breach, but he will contend that circumstances demand "the damages, if laid at all, should be laid at one farthing" (*WWR* 1:264). Since the verdict appears to be a foregone conclusion, none of Lionel's attorneys musters even a semblance of interest in the perfunctory proceedings. The junior counsel occupy themselves with "scribbling notes to each other, reading the newspaper, eating hard biscuit, yawning in the jury's face, and drawing caricatures on scraps of paper" (*WWR* 1:265). Jennings is preoccupied with his next case, which promises to be more challenging—and remunerative. He passes the time, not attending to the claims of the plaintiff's attorney—after all, he need hardly do so, since they are entirely predictable—but "feeding his imagination with his own questions" (*WWR* 1:266). These questions pertain not to the matter at hand but to an upcoming case "in which the fair plaintiff had been more deeply injured than Rosabel, and which excited considerable interest and expectation" (*WWR* 1:265).

In the prospective trial he plans to assuage the paternalistic concerns of the jury by treating the "fair plaintiff" in a kindly fashion:

> I will call her '*My dear*,' thought Mr. Jennings, with a professional luxuriousness of sentiment; . . . but I wont do so insolently, neither, poor little soul. No, I'll be gentle; I'll make no jokes; women on a cross-examination always burst into tears when one attempts a jest. I will be grave and compassionate.
>
> (*WWR* 1: 265–66).

His solicitude is meretricious, and his idle thoughts reveal both a low estimate of women's ability to withstand irony and a general condescension toward female plaintiffs. Jennings's reverie is brought to a sudden end by the commotion surrounding Rosabel's entrance into the courtroom and the abrupt withdrawal of her suit. His recognition of her person is indicated by nothing more than "dark flexible eyebrows [that] rose to the very margin of his white well-fitting barrister's wig" (*WWR* 1:266).

An unintended consequence of the trial is announced much later: the seemingly indifferent Jennings—of whom we hear nothing after learning of those raised eyebrows—is reported to have become engaged to Rosabel. This development is unexpected not only because Jennings exhibits no interest whatsoever in the plaintiff but also because Norton exhibits no interest in either of them. Jennings makes no other appearance in the novel, and his engagement is announced in an off-handed comment by a minor character. What might be inferred from this seemingly gratuitous romantic development? If Rosabel represents a kind of integrity seen nowhere else in the courtroom, it is difficult to explain either her attraction to one shown to profit from this system or his attraction to her. Are we to imagine that his "white well-fitting barrister's wig" provides such a contrast to the shabby appearance and behavior of her father, "a yellow-wigged Norfolk attorney" (*WWR* 1:259), that she cannot resist his offer of marriage? Or perhaps there is more than meets the eye in a raised eyebrow: has the newly visible Rosabel elicited love at first sight? Alternatively, it may be that Jennings's professional sangfroid has melted as a result of Rosabel's unprecedented example of integrity and courage. Any number of explanations might be hazarded, but none seems more probable than another, and Norton provides no basis for deciding among them. Readers can draw one—literally only one—conclusion: the courtship had to have begun in the courtroom.

The comic resolution of a minor subplot in *Woman's Reward* is spectacularly exceeded in the topsy-turvy world of W. S. Gilbert.

Angelina v. *Edwin* comes 40 years after *Bigby* v. *Dupré*, during which time breach of promise trials had become both more frequent and more dubiously viewed.[44] Gilbert, a solicitor who abandoned law for literature, freely exploits the stereotype of women's seductive power. The opening lines of the operetta set the tone as the Usher, who, despite urging that "From bias free of every kind, / This trial must be tried!" (*TJ* 25–26), counsels the jury: "listen to the plaintiff's case: / Observe the features of her face— / The broken-hearted bride" (*TJ* 21–23). Physiognomy is proven more compelling than facts, since the jurors clamor for "substantial damages" (*TJ* 231) well before the trial has concluded and immediately following the Judge's pronouncement on Angelina's appearance: "Oh, never, never, never, never, since I joined the human race, / Saw I so exquisitely fair a face" (*TJ* 219–20). At the conclusion of the farcical proceeding, the Judge resolves the case by offering to marry the plaintiff himself (*TJ* 410–11). His actions indicate that justice is anything but blind and further suggest that breach of promise trials (in which the plaintiff is always unmarried and usually female) are likely to provoke particular interest from bachelors in the courtroom.

Gilbert's satire is built upon two distinct narrative modes, the personal (natural, truthful) and the legal (artificial, false).[45] When merely relating their feelings, the litigants speak with considerable candor. Indeed, they make simple appeals to nature and natural urges to explain their behavior. Edwin, for example, tells a tale of falling in and out of love with Angelina (*TJ* 57–73) that is definitely not calculated to correspond with legal forms and that will certainly not produce a verdict favorable to himself. He calmly admits that he has become bored with Angelina and is now "[a]nother's love-sick boy" (*TJ* 69). His only defense is an invocation of Nature.[46] He has acted, he explains, in harmony with the cosmos, whose first principle is change:

> The moon in her phases is found,
> The time and the wind and the weather,
> The months in succession come round,
> And you don't find two Mondays together.
> Ah! Consider the moral, I pray,
> Nor bring a young fellow to sorrow,
> Who loves this young lady to-day,
> And loves that young lady to-morrow.
> (*TJ* 298–305)

This distinctly unsentimental formulation might appeal to devotees of Pan, but it is not likely to impress the legal representatives of John

Bull. Indeed, it is precisely because Edwin's comments do not fit the requirements of a formal plea that they should be read as a personal rather than a legal statement.

From this perspective, it is not quite so surprising that the plaintiff—speaking in the character of lover rather than litigant—confesses that, in truth, "I am no unhappy maid!" (*TJ* 214). Like Rosabel, Angelina is a healthy daughter of Nature, who seems little troubled by her lover's desertion. Such "personal" moments, like Rosabel's unscripted entry into court, stand out against the background of legal and, by implication, untruthful speaking. Angelina also believes that the cycles of love echo those of nature, and she maintains that the seasons of love alternate with and depend upon one another:

> O'er the season vernal,
> Time may cast a shade;
> Sunshine, if eternal,
> Makes the roses fade!
> Time may do his duty;
> Let the thief alone—
> Winter hath a beauty,
> That is all his own.
> Fairest days are sun and shade. . . .
> (*TJ* 205–13)

Comic exuberance and vitality clearly take precedence over serious representation of legal processes. Edwin argues for the changefulness of passion and against licensing or regulating the variable emotions of the heart; Angelina insists upon the mixed quality of all experience. *Trial by Jury* thus expresses a hearty appreciation for the lustiness of youth and a concomitant disregard for any attempt to regulate love through social or legal proscriptions.

In the course of the trial, however, the former lovers are compelled into formulaic narratives of exactly the kind emanating from the barristers in *Bigley* v. *Dupré*. Angelina changes her tune, insisting: "I worship and madly adore; / My blind adoration is always increasing, / My loss I shall ever deplore" (*TJ* 341–44). She asks the jury to keep this fact in mind when "assessing / The damages Edwin must pay!" (*TJ* 347–48). In response, Edwin professes to smoke and drink, and assures the jury, "I should thrash her, perhaps I should kick her, / I'm such a bad lot" (*TJ* 351). His surprising "defense" can be explained by the dilemma facing defendants in such cases: on the one hand, the jury must be convinced that Angelina loses little in losing so unworthy a lout as Edwin, therein diminishing the basis for "substantial damages"; on the other hand, should Edwin go too far in convincing the jury of his bad character, he will corroborate Angelina's claims by showing that he is exactly the sort to abandon an innocent and loving woman. Predictably, the warning that he is a potential wife-beater is seized upon by Angelina's attorney, who feigns surprise: "I never had a notion / That a man could be so base, / Or deceive a girl confiding, / Vows, *etcetera*, deriding" (*TJ* 237–42). "Etcetera" brilliantly confirms the formulaic nature of this discourse and conveys the backdrop of legal noise against which the "natural" voices of the lovers stand out and are applauded.

Edwin's appeals to free love and to the weakness of men's moral character are not entirely ill-advised in light of the fact that the all-male jury confesses to having been scamps, rovers, and cads themselves (*TJ* 75–76). Any hope for the defendant, however, is dashed when, upon seeing the plaintiff, the gentlemen of the jury forget their claim to have foresworn philandering: "We love you fondly and would make you ours" (*TJ* 225). In professing to Angelina, "Just like a father / I wish to be" (*TJ* 280–81), the Foreman exposes the close link between paternalistic rationalization and sexual motivation. In the name of the father, he wishes to save / seduce the daughter, who, at this rate, appears destined to a career resembling Becky Sharp's rather than that of an idealized "Angel(ina) in the House." As a knowing appeal to fellow men and "rovers," Edwin's strategy must fail precisely to the degree that its rationale is correct. Nothing makes this paradox more clear than the instructions of the Usher to attend to the plaintiff's face. When the "ruffianly defendant speaks— / Upon the other side; / What *he* may say you needn't mind" (*TJ* 29–31). Ushered in here is the gender bias—satirized by Meredith—favoring attractive plaintiffs and guaranteeing Angelina's legal victory, as well as her continued sexual subordination.

Faced with the prospect of paying damages to his jilted lover, Edwin offers to wed "this lady to-day, / And I'll marry the other to-morrow!" (*TJ* 316–17). When this seemingly preposterous suggestion is endorsed by the Judge, counsel for the plaintiff quickly counters that "[t]o marry two at once is Burglaree!" (*TJ* 324). One expects "bigamee" rather than "burglaree" here, especially since neither rhyme nor meter precludes the more obvious and accurate term. Why, then, the substitution, and what—if burglary is the correct term—is stolen from whom? One possible gloss is that Edwin proposes helping himself to more than his share of the marital market. If this is the intended meaning, then Angelina's attorney has in common with Mr. Jennings a rather low estimate of women as property owned by and stolen from men. Another explanation is that the theft is of damages rightfully owed the plaintiff and, of course, her attorney (although a sharp-eyed lawyer might see the "burglaree" as the source of more litigation and fees).

A third meaning becomes evident when considering the Judge's role. He has committed the most serious larceny, having become engaged to a "rich attorney's / Elderly, ugly daughter" (*TJ* 149–50) in order to be taken into his prospective father-in-law's practice. After accumulating considerable financial and experiential capital, he spurns his fiancée, now described as an "incubus" (*TJ* 148), breaking both the promise to the daughter and the "gentlemen's agreement," if such it is, with her father. He laughingly boasts that the "rich attorney my character high / Tried vainly to disparage" (*TJ* 151–52). "Tried" must be taken to mean both "attempted" and "sued." If *Angelina* v. *Edwin* is read in light of the precedent established by the Judge, then "burglaree" is the correct term because jilting is a calculated means to an acquisitive end.

Having risen in the profession—in his own words, "my being made a nob / Was effected by a job" (*TJ* 169–70)— the Judge now hears cases of exactly the kind in which he was once a defendant. Hence the double irony of his description of his judicial accomplishments: "And many a burglar I've restored / To his friends and his relations" (*TJ* 144–45). The Judge apparently dedicates himself to returning the favor initially granted to him. Not only has he escaped punishment for inconstancy and exonerated fellow thieves, that is, jilts, but he has also positioned himself to use the courtroom to attempt additional "burglarees." A short-lived interest in the First Bridesmaid is abruptly terminated at the sight of the plaintiff's "exquisitely fair . . . face" (*TJ* 220). He retracts the love note given to the former and passes the very same billet-doux to the latter. Although this missive places the Judge, who outdoes even the defendant in the rapidity of his heart swings, in some danger of being "tried" again, the abrupt and chaotic conclusion of the trial preempts any reference to the First Bridesmaid's becoming a suitor. His "character high" is finally brought "low," but only comically so, when he leaps from the bench to propose marriage to Angelina. In one fell swoop, he defeats the Foreman's amorous designs upon the plaintiff, resolves Edwin's dilemma, renders the accusation of robbery irrelevant, and convicts the defendant of a new charge: Edwin is a "snob" for rejecting Angelina, the "fob" now accepted by the Judge (*TJ* 413–15, 418).

The chaotic and comic conclusion of the trial has a single quiet counterpoint. Edwin thinks of the newly engaged couple and wonders: "Whether they'll live together / In marriage tether / In manner true?" (*TJ* 397–99). This "natural" question lingers, but only faintly, at the end of the play. At the close of the trial, the Judge sends the attorneys home, telling them: "Put your briefs upon the shelf, / I will marry her myself! (*TJ* 384–85). His wording recalls one of the numerous phrases for spinsters, who are said to be "on the shelf." Angelina is apparently taken down from the shelf, and the now unneeded briefs are put in her place. Gilbert ironically implies that the law itself is the old maid: it has no place in the land of love. But what of the converse: is there a place for love in the land of law? Gilbert's cynical conclusion appears to be that lawyers can do more for their clients by marrying them than by representing them. Plaintiffs in breach of promise cases are, by definition, candidates for an unmarried life, and they are already virtually spinsters, at least according to popular stereotype and in their attorneys' courtroom narratives. The term for their legal status, feme sole, is another synonym for an unmarried woman. Since wives are prevented from either initiating or being named in a lawsuit (according to the doctrine of coverture), it might be argued that by effectively screening ineligible (read "married") women from participation, the legal system functions not so much to protect unmarried women from burglars as to expose them to legal thieves, who remove them by marriage from both the romantic and the juridical economies.

Norton's and Gilbert's breach of promise actions entail a symbolic romantic substitution in which lovers who have become litigants are replaced by litigators who become lovers. The exchange of amorous attorneys for unloving defendants might appear to humanize impersonal agents of the law, but only in the sense of showing them to be as prone to opportunism and self-interest as the next person. The symbolic substitution produces a satisfying romantic closure (a "verdict" of marriage) but only by rendering the law either ridiculous or entirely irrelevant. In actuality, of course, the legal system could not sentence unsuccessful defendants to marriage, but it could impose "substantial damages." In Norton's and Gilbert's formulations, by contrast, the legal system's solution to broken promises is neither monetary compensation nor punishment but replacement of the reluctant bridegroom with one of its own.

The replacement of lovers-turned-litigants by lawyers-turned-lovers necessarily initiates a second promissory cycle (involving the plaintiffs and their new lovers), which in light of the first broken cycle offers a mildly dissonant counterpoint to comic closure. The courtroom becomes the site not to enforce promises but to generate more of them. The proliferation of proposals by lawyers and judges suggests that legal institutions promote the profligate promising that they are charged with regulating. This promissory supplementarity is an inevitable consequence of symbolic substitution but also an inherent counterpoint to it. The "verdict of marriage" is always subject to appeal; that is, it is always threatened by the possibility that occasioned the legal action in the first place, broken promises. The curious romantic / juridical economy of substitution and supplementarity generates an unresolved tension between closure and continuation, between poetic and legal justice. In transforming the courtroom into a courting room, Norton and Gilbert satirize men and their laws, but overwrite this critique with a masculine fantasy of rescue by marriage that reinforces precisely the ideology responsible for the laws they appear to mock. This romantic resolution is questioned, however, because the sequence of love and litigation cannot be terminated as neatly as the judge's gavel ends a trial. There may be an attractive romantic logic (and sense of poetic justice) in this idea, but promises of love gone wrong outside of courtrooms cannot be resolved by promises of love made inside them. Norton's gratuitous and Gilbert's comic engagements expose a cynical perspective on the law as impotent and ultimately irrelevant to fundamental human concerns.

CRIMINAL CONVERSATION: *NEWCOME* V. *HIGHGATE* AND *WARWICK* V. *DANNISBURGH*

Norton v. *Melbourne* may have inspired comedy, but it was no laughing matter to Norton or to Thackeray and Meredith, whose work directly confronts the unpleasant reality and tragic consequences of trials for the woman not present at them. *The Newcomes* and *Diana of the Crossways* document the unhappiness caused to all parties by the cumbersome and humiliating process of seeking a divorce. The humor of *Newcome* v. *Highgate* and *Warwick* v. *Dannisburgh* is bitter rather than gentle; the focus is not on the comedy of the law but on the difficulty of living with its consequences.

Newcome v. *Highgate* reflects many of the popular prejudices evinced in *Bardell* v. *Pickwick*, including the widespread belief that plaintiffs and attorneys alike are more interested in damages than justice. Serjeant Rowland, counsel for Sir Barnes Newcome, is a master of what Pickwick's ineffectual attorney calls the art of effect. He "wept freely" (*N* 593) while presenting the evils resulting from Clara's elopement, which he describes in the hyperbolic diction of popular melodrama:

> how grandly Serjeant Rowland stood up for the rights of British husbands! with what pathos he depicted the conjugal paradise, the innocent children prattling round their happy parents, the serpent, the destroyer, entering into that Belgravian Eden; the wretched and deserted husband alone by his desecrated hearth, and calling for redress on his country! . . . At not a shilling under twenty thousand pounds would he estimate the cost of his client's injuries.
>
> (*N* 593)

In researching *Norton* v. *Melbourne*, Thackeray had learned that Follett repeatedly called jurors' attention to "the elements of your consideration of the amount of damages you shall award," requesting them "as men to consider what the plaintiff's sufferings must be, and to mark by your verdict, in the only way that the law allows, your sense of the conduct of the defendant and the irreparable evil he has inflicted."[47] Because Clara openly left her home in the company of her lover, Barnes knows that Lord Highgate must pay "full measure . . . for his delinquencies" (*N* 594) and for possession of a wife whom her current husband is happy to be rid of. Even Highgate's attorney admits as "[a] man, a husband, and a father, [he] could not attempt to defend the conduct of his unfortunate client" (*N* 593). The narrator's dismissive summary makes his disdain for the proceeding obvious:

> quick, let us hire an advocate to roar out to a British jury the wrongs of her injured husband, to paint the agonies of his bleedingheart, (if Mr. Advocate gets plaintiff's brief in time, and before defendant's attorney has retained him,) and to show Society injured through him. Let us console the martyr, I say with thumping damages; and as for the woman—the guilty wretch!—let us lead her out and stone her (*N* 563).

The irony of a process whose objective is "damages" is not lost upon the narrator, whose abridgement of Campbell's lengthy cross-examination omits testimony and summarizes the casualties:

> Many witnesses were mauled and slain. Out of that combat scarce anybody came well, except the two principal champions, Rowland, Serjeant, and Oliver, Q. C. The whole county looked on and heard the wretched story, not only

of Barnes's fault and Highgate's fault, but of the private peccadilloes of their suborned footmen and conspiring housemaids.

(*N* 594)

In addition to the race of discarded servants, Thackeray introduces the loyal domestics that Norton complained were left waiting in the witness room when Campbell decided to truncate his defense. When challenged on the tale of "connubial happiness which he had depicted so pathetically" (*N* 593), Rowland can produce no one to verify his fiction of domestic bliss. Oliver, in turn, asserts that 20 witnesses could document "neglect so outrageous, cruelty so systematic, that he wondered the plaintiff had not been better advised than to bring this trial, with all its degrading particulars to a public issue" (*N* 593). In cross-examination when "Barnes's counsel . . . tried to impugn their testimony, they dared him and hurt the plaintiff's case very much" (*N* 591). The judge undoes the damage, however, disabusing the jury of any idea that Highgate might be exonerated: "Mr Justice C. Sawyer charged the jury at great length—those men were respectable and fathers of families themselves—of course they dealt full measure to Lord Highgate for his delinquencies!" (*N* 594). Cutting through any possible extenuating circumstance, Sawyer leaves only one narrative intact, that of the incontrovertible rights of husbands and fathers.

While *Warwick* v. *Dannisburgh* is a more accurate reflection of the Nortons' factual circumstances than Thackeray's divorce trial, Meredith is less concerned with the conduct than the consequences of the proceeding. Diana's brief foray into "Lawyerland" (*DC* 2:197) and exposure to "lawyers' lingo" (*DC* 1:164) are not encouraging. Her attorney "could sit listening to her for hours" and believes "that she was as innocent as day; a wonderful combination of a good woman and a clever woman and a real beauty" (*DC* 1:219), but his assessment is personal rather than professional. After the initial consultation, she spurns further legal advice, becoming to "the legal profession generally . . . nothing other than 'the woman Warwick' " (*DC* 1:154). Even "her decorous and crudely-minded defenders" make painfully obvious "the estimate of discarded wives entertained by men of business and plain men of the world" (*DC* 1:154).

Of the trial itself, Meredith makes only an occasional reference to random details of the 1836 proceeding, such as Augustus's taking his wife's papers and the servants' testifying concerning their employers' behavior (*DC* 1:137, 146). His larger purpose is to expose the punitive nature of English marriage law. With the failure of his action, Augustus has no basis for obtaining a divorce, and two hopelessly alienated people are left chained together. Diana is trapped in "miserable suspension, neither maid nor wife, neither woman nor stockfish" (*DC* 2:42). She "was exonerated. But she was not free" (*DC* 1:182). Although she lives alone and supports herself, she is subject to her husband's veiled threat to force her return by suing for restitution of conjugal rights. There would seem to be no possibility of eluding "the meshes of the terrific net of the marital law brutally whirled to capture her by the man her husband" (*DC* 1:183) and resuming anything resembling her premarital existence.

She quickly learns that actions taken independently of her husband, even though they are separated, are likely to produce legal crossways: "It is the married woman's perpetual dread when she ventures a step. Your Law originally presumed her a China-footed animal" (*DC* 2:104). Finding the familiar comparison to the Orient inadequate, Diana strains to describe the effect of law upon women. She thinks of a "poor vulture hovering for the horse in the desert to die" (*DC* 2:111) but rejects the simile as overstrained and invokes a Gothic analogy: "Nothing in nature, only gruesome German stories will fetch comparisons for the yoke of this Law of yours. It seems the nightmare dream following an ogre's supper" (*DC* 2:112). Her thought builds in a crescendo of rhetorical figures until the law becomes an insatiable monster: "the world of the Laws overloading her is pitiless to women, deaf past ear-trumpets, past intercession; detesting and reviling them for a feeble human cry, and for one apparent step of revolt piling the pelted stones on them. It will not discriminate shades of hue, it massacres all of them (*DC* 2:112–13). While Thackeray sardonically suggests stoning the adulteress, Meredith hyperbolically implies that the legal system treats all woman as if they were adulteresses.

When Diana's name is subsequently linked with Percy Dacier's, she is warned of "the things that lawyers could say on the subject" (*DC* 2:22). Her husband's letter "of supplication, interpenetrated with the hint" (*DC* 2:69) of another criminal conversation trial impels her to accept Dacier's proposal that they elope to the Continent:

> We can start this evening. Once away, we leave it to them to settle the matter, and then you are free, and mine to the death. . . . [I]f we delay, I'm in danger of losing you altogether. . . . There's a process of the law. But stop it. Just this one step, and it ends. Whether intended or not, it hangs over you, and you will be perpetually tormented. Why waste your whole youth?—and mine as well!
>
> (the second ellipsis is Meredith's ; *DC* 2:35)

Dreading "that 'process of the Law' a second time" (*DC* 2:41), Diana temporarily agrees to a plan that would place her in the situation of Clara Newcome. Although she ultimately does not elope, Meredith exonerates her neither in this relationship nor in that with her husband: "her own mistake and the world's clumsy machinery of civilization: these were the capital offenders" (*DC* 1:184). Such errors, however, do not merit "piling the pelted stones on [her]." The far greater liability lies with legal machinery that creates the "wife and no wife" (*DC* 1:217) and then indifferently banishes her to a social desert.

Chapter 4

"Ink Stands and Law Books": Domestic and Legal Violence

The miller's daughter of fourteen could not believe that high gentry behaved badly to their wives, but her mother instructed her—"Oh, child, men's men: gentle or simple they're much of a muchness."[1]

George Eliot, *Daniel Deronda*

To _____.
Here lies a Beauty,
Whom to love was a duty,
She married a Fool,
Not to make him a tool,
But only to vex
Both herself and his Sex.[2]

Benjamin Robert Haydon, *Diary*

The honeymoon ended quickly (literally and figuratively) for the Nortons, who were married on June 30, 1827. The couple returned to London after a brief wedding trip and spent a few days in George's chambers at the Temple before moving into their own apartment. While there, George, reportedly under the influence of drink, hurled an "ink stand, and most of the law-books, which might have served a better purpose, at the head of his bride" (*ELW* 15). He could scarcely have chosen more appropriately symbolic objects, for the pen—hers, not his–became a primary point of conflict between them and the law became the principal means by which he attempted to accomplish what physical violence could not: suppression of his wife's independent spirit and spirited language. When the tailor in *Daniel Deronda* remarks that a "quarrel may end wi' the whip, but it begins wi' the tongue, and it's the women have got the most o' that" (*DD* 401), he succinctly diagnoses the origin of the Nortons' troubles. Sarcasm at her husband's expense—in this instance, to the effect that he might make better use of the instruments of his profession—was the weapon that Norton most often employed against the man whose violence did not end with these errant missiles. Unequal to the "javelins hurled by an Amazon," George on another occasion doused her writing materials with brandy and set them afire, warning her "not to brave him" in the future (*ELW* 32).

When Daniel Maclise drew Norton demurely superintending the ceremony of tea, he could have no idea that her husband would "deliberately [take] the tea-kettle, and set it down upon my hand; I started up from the pain, and was both burnt and scalded" (*ELW* 32). A violent quarrel in the summer of 1835 prompted her to leave home. She agreed to return—a fateful act in the eyes of the law, for in so doing she "condoned" his violence and would be unable to secure a divorce on grounds of cruelty. The abuse resumed almost immediately, and she suffered a miscarriage in August.[3] In March of the following year, George removed the children from the family home and left his wife to fend for herself. Despite attempts to reconcile after the Melbourne trial, they would never again live together. Separate establishments brought an end to the physical violence—except on the occasions when Caroline tried forcibly to remove the children from their father's custody—but the legal assault, symbolized by the objects George first threw at his wife, persisted for many years.

It is likely that this experience accounts for a three-word paragraph in *Woman's Reward*: "He struck her" (*WRR* 2:308).[4] Lionel Dupré's attack upon his wife is an isolated occurrence, as is Stephen Penrhyn's angry assault on his wife in *Stuart of Dunleath*, but neither assault is a surprise. Each man is a thorough egoist, indifferent to his spouse, except when she disrupts his convenience. Lady Clarice is eventually driven to leave Lionel not so much because of a single violent episode but because of his "cruel neglect, the utter forgetfulness of [her] suffering" (*WRR* 3:3). Unhappy couples occupy a significant place throughout Norton's fiction. In two of them, however, spousal neglect is punctuated by violence, and broken bones and bruises become the stigmata of the invisible injuries resulting from indifference and infidelity.

THE GREENACRE LETTERS

Physical abuse was not the only form of violence that typified the Nortons' long and unhappy marriage. The conclusion of the Melbourne trial left them legally bound but emotionally alienated. In the following years, George repeatedly promised and withheld visitation rights and financial settlements. The correspondence immediately after the trial reveals tangled negotiations involving the children, money, and the terms upon which the couple might resume communal living. This "double courtship" occurred primarily at arm's length and was conducted either in writing or through third parties like Bayley. Neither trusted the other nor seemed committed to the second wooing. Since George's letters made repeated references to debts and actions for unpaid bills, there is reason to agree with her suspicion that for him "*money* is the avowed object of our attempted 'reconciliation'" (*LCN* 140). And because her letters persistently demanded that she be reunited with the children, there is also reason to admit his suspicion that her "wishes are limited to the enjoyment of [her] children's society" (*L* 2:30). After almost a year of negotiation, he wrote that they had reached an impasse and that no further discussion would take place. "[F]eeling completely hopeless as to obtaining just terms from Mr Norton," his wife ironically observed that she possessed "no legal remedy against him, except an action for 'Restitution of Conjugal Rights'" (*L* 1:24). The bitter joke (a married woman could not sue her husband) concerning how far she would go to see her children revealed her impotence and her humiliation—points reaffirmed by a macabre epistolary turn in the summer of 1837.

George inexplicably reversed positions and wrote to propose a meeting at the vacant residence of his now deceased friend, Miss Vaughan. Fearing the isolated setting—and having always perceived Vaughan as a pernicious influence upon her husband—Norton instead proposed coming to his house, which at least offered the protection of witnesses. The meeting yielded

> a long and very distressing interview. . . . He proposed to me to *return to him, and to forget the past*; he assured me he had been hurried on, when sore and angry, by the persuasion and advice of others, to that dreadful trial. . . . He was very kind in manner, and I agreed to all he proposed, being quite worn out.
>
> (*L* 1:26–27)

In planning to remove the reunited family to a new home, George inquired if his wife had any furniture to contribute to the joint establishment. She made "a sort of bitter answer, asking whether he had sent for me as Greenacre sent for Mrs Brown, to ascertain her property" (*LCN* 140). The reference to a sensational murder of the previous year captured George's imagination. Greenacre had been executed for killing his fiancée, Hannah Brown, whom he had lured to a vacant house to discuss the distribution of property prior to marriage. After murdering and robbing her, he enlisted the help of his common-law wife to dispose of the dismembered corpse. Oblivious to this bitter barb at his material preoccupation, George embraced the part with enthusiasm: "come on Friday night, bring all you have got, and we'll be married on Christmas Day. . . . Your affectionate intended, Greenacre" (*L* 2:38–39). It is difficult to understand how he thought that addressing his wife in the voice of a murderer would further the objective of reconciliation, especially given the ominous overtones of the suggestion that they be married on the day that Greenacre and Brown were to have wed. His history of abuse makes the allusion both an unfunny joke and an unsubtle threat.

George may simply have been criminally obtuse, but Caroline believed he had gone insane. His first letter under the *nom de plume* Greenacre supports her conclusion. It begins in a tone of accusation and mistrust. He feels that she has not done enough to dissuade her creditors from seeking payment from him. It goes on to treat, without apparent distinction, the children, the objects of Miss Vaughan's that he is buying at auction, and the yearly allowance that his wife might expect from him. He adds, ominously, given Greenacre's attempted bigamy, that his money "is in dangerous hands,—those of a man trying to furnish two houses at once" (*L* 2:38). The letter seems almost to taunt her for the hardship that his withdrawal of support and retention of her possessions have imposed: "Pray *Mrs Brown*, how many chairs have you got—also tables? Have you e'er a dining one?" (*L* 2:38). This question, too, seems a veiled threat, since Greenacre claimed that Mrs. Brown's death was the unintended consequence of his kicking a chair out from under her during their quarrel over money.

A second Greenacre letter sustains the focus on furnishing Miss Vaughan's house for the newly reunited family. George requests that she "not pawn or otherwise dispose" (*L* 2:43) of any possessions that might be used at Kettle-Thorpe. In this letter, too, he jumps rapidly from one topic to the next. For example, he asks, "what allowance will do for you until, as I trust, we shall be *happily, safely*, and *comfortably re-united*" (*L* 2:42), and then abruptly raises the issue of a deed of separation, apparently unaware of the contradiction. The letter is signed, "Your intended victim, Greenacre" (*L* 2:43). It is hard to know in what sense George views himself as his wife's victim, unless he jokingly refers to his retying the knot—an event destined, like the marriage of Greenacre and Brown, never to take place.

Property, whether stolen or merely disputed, proved fatal to both couples. Faced with legal action by his wife's creditors, George issued an ultimatum that was answered with impassioned eloquence:

If things, as you say, "resume their old way again," . . . it will for ever bar all possibility of my hoping anything or expecting anything from personal communication with you. *You sent for me, offered to take me back, offered to send for the boys, allowed my innocence*; and now you write on money matters, as if the children's coming were to be *bought* by me!

For God's sake, George, think well of what you are doing; they advised you ill *once* to an action of law; they may advise you worse now!

(*L* 2:47–48)

It is unlikely that his next step was taken with the counsel of others, since George himself must have known that it would be difficult to elude responsibility for his wife's debts. Nevertheless, he placed a notice in several newspapers on March 30, 1838, accusing her of deserting the family and of living extravagantly at his expense. The public insult effectively ended any chance of reconciliation. From this point on, the Nortons seemed determined to air their grievances in as public and embarrassing a manner as possible. Perhaps the most flattering thing that can be said of their history is that at least there were no murders.

The possibility of homicidal husbands was clearly on Norton's mind even before the Greenacre episode. In "The Unexpected Rencontre," published in *The Keepsake* (1836), Rosalie Benoit flees her husband and settles in England, where she becomes the lover of Arthur Glanville. Adolphe Benoit tracks her down and compels her return to Paris. Chancing to see Arthur four years later, she explains:

I spare you the details of the scene—the violence of his temper—the threats of vengeance. . . . I knew him capable of all—how then to avoid the horrors of my situation? I was his wife, and no law could justify my desertion of him—I felt at his mercy entirely.

(*K* 87)

Arthur laments that Rosalie did not confide in him because the "laws of England afford protection to a wife against a husband's ill-treatment" (*K* 87). In the context of the story, Arthur's faith in English law seems justified, since French law does not prevent Rosalie's eventual murder by Adolphe. In the context of the Nortons' history, however, the lines seem bitterly ironic: English law protected neither Mrs. Brown nor Mrs. Norton.

Although the impact of spousal abuse was felt throughout her lifetime, once separated, Norton had more to fear from legal than physical violence. She was still writing about the Greenacre case, however, almost 35 years after the fact and only a few years before her death—of natural causes. The appendix to an otherwise unrelated pamphlet, *Taxation. By an Irresponsible Taxpayer*, revisits the Greenacre case and recounts Brown's murder and dismemberment in meticulous detail. Mary Poovey is surely right to suggest that the return to the scene of the crime was an indictment of "George Norton, the ex-magistrate, [who] is aided by the laws of his country in the brutal (if metaphoric) 'assassination' of his wife."[5] Norton was far more outraged by the violence of British marriage laws than by the unfairness of metropolitan tax rates:

> the very reason this burden of increased taxation falls so heavily that I am tempted to resist it, is, that in my case I am pronounced to be *non-existent* in law.... Non-existent for protection, but not, it appears, "non-existent" for oppression. Non-existent as to compelling payment due *to* me, but not non-existent as to extortion of payment due *from* me. Liable as a "female occupier" to pay taxes, but not able as a "female occupier" to hold my house except through trustees, or to compel, by *any* process of law, the payment of an agreed income.
>
> (*T* 17)

Initially a veiled and private threat of personal violence, the Greenacre letters have assumed the status of "*grandis et verbosa epistola*" in Norton's mind. They signify the systemic violence of British law against married women.

DOMESTIC AND LEGAL VIOLENCE IN *STUART OF DUNLEATH*

This work owes much to Norton's experience but varies considerably from it. While the marriage of Lionel and Clarice is a secondary plot in *Woman's Reward*, that of Eleanor Raymond and Sir Stephen Penrhyn is the focal point of *Stuart of Dunleath*. The result is a much fuller treatment of spousal cruelty. Norton ultimately subordinates domestic strife to an extended consideration of philosophical and religious issues pertaining to marriage, such as the opposed imperatives of "strict justice" and "charity" (*SD* 1:154–55) and the relationship of God's law, common law, and uncommon need. The characters' circumstances at the outset are fairly close to the Nortons'. Sir Stephen Penrhyn marries with very little knowledge of the woman to whom he has twice proposed by letter (as George had done). Eleanor Raymond accepts the offer without a strong attachment because, among other things, she faces poverty and no other desirable alternative. Mistakenly thinking marriage to be a haven, she encounters two forms of spousal violence, a literal blow of the hand and the figurative assault of the law.

The nadir of the Penrhyns' eight-year marriage occurs when, in a fit of anger and jealousy, Sir Stephen breaks Eleanor's arm. Norton's depiction of the moment carries the figurative impact of the blow itself. The discovery that his wife has misled him about David Stuart (the former guardian whom she still loves) and the fear that she may be guilty of infidelity ignite Sir Stephen's volatile temper. Not a word precedes his attack:

> He rushed towards her, as she made a breathless startled pause at the door; he seized her arm with his right hand, he grasped her shoulder with his left, and he shook her as passionate nurses shake a rebellious child. . . . [A] wild short sharp cry escaped her; and when he relaxed his grasp at the sound, she staggered to the nearest chair, and dropped into it; her eyes fixed on his face with speechless amazement and horror.
>
> (*SD* 3:180–81)

No words are uttered during the scene until Sir Stephen reminds his wife that her life is in danger:

> "I wonder you are not ashamed to look at me," said he fiercely, panting with anger and excitement; "I wonder you are not afraid for your life, after your conduct towards me."
>
> "Oh!" said Eleanor, with a bitterness and desperation which did not seem to belong to her nature, and in a tone as vehement, though not so loud as his own—"I am afraid of nothing—you can only kill me!"
>
> (*SD* 3:181)

The impact of her words is not immediately felt. Stephen initially trivializes his action, dismissing it with a casual apology and appeal to "kiss me, and let us be friends" (*SD* 3:181). The aftershocks of her utterance build during the night until he is "sickened" by what he has done and haunted by her indifference to life:

> You can only kill me! Was it Eleanor who had spoken these desperate words? Was it Eleanor, whose voice echoed in his ear alternately in tones of command and of anguished defiance: Or was it all a strange dream? . . .
>
> Sir Stephen could not recover from the impression made by the tone in which Eleanor had spoken. . . . It was as if some great crash had broken a sweet instrument, and jarred it into strange discord. The phrases . . . repeated themselves in his brain over and over again, in spite of his struggle to drive them out.
>
> (*SD* 3:188–90)

A tormented evening of fitful sleep follows: "Disturbed dreams coursed one another through his mind—he started and muttered in his sleep. His hand clenched and struck out" (*SD* 3:192). It is not clear at whom or what the unconscious gesture is directed: at his wife? at himself? He seems to want to obliterate his action and its effect upon his self-esteem. The very gesture, however, mirrors his attack against Eleanor and reconfirms the violent nature that he wishes to ignore.

Sir Stephen avoids the implications of his act by treating it as a physical ailment. He "wishes to be blooded in the arm," and with the flow of blood from the offending limb "the fever is drained away; and the vague thirst of vengeance is quenched; and the taunting dreams are banished; and the sense of coolness returns; and let who will lie awake again to-night, Sir Stephen slumbers sound, and wakes refreshed, as he had done hitherto all his life" (*SD* 3:196). Although Eleanor's arm heals, her marriage is irremediably broken, which leads to the second form of unexpected violence—that of English law toward married women.

Stuart of Dunleath is the first of Norton's works to engage questions of law directly and to use the novel to make readers aware of women's legal status. Eleanor is entirely innocent of her legal and financial circumstances until she seeks to use what she thought was her own money. She discovers that she has, in effect, been twice robbed of her personal fortune by those empowered to protect it, her guardian and her husband. Each theft is immoral, but neither is illegal. In the first instance, David Stuart, seeking his own financial gain, risks and loses the funds he was commissioned to manage for her. He eventually repays the money, to the delight of her husband, who had accepted her without a dowry and interprets this windfall as a reward for his generosity. Eleanor does not realize that the restored wealth enriches her husband a great deal but herself not at all, hence the second loss of her fortune. The cherished hope of purchasing Dunleath for David is dashed when Sir Stephen explains marriage law:

> "D—n it, how stupid women are, in all matters of business. Your fortune's mine: do you understand that?"
>
> "The fortune my father left me!"
>
> "The fortune your father left you. No married woman has a fortune of her own, as you call it, that isn't specially settled upon her. There's no such settlement in your case, the money has fallen in, and been replaced, that's all. I'm your husband, and it's mine."
>
> (*SD* 3:72–73)

Eleanor's ignorance is understandable, given that the law does not accord with basic notions of fairness. Norton exposes this inequity and impugns the society that sanctions it. In posing the leading question, "But will you not suffer me to employ my money in that way, even if the formal law gives it to you?" (*SD* 3:73), Eleanor succinctly isolates the problem. The sentimental ideology of marriage suggests that husbands, of course, will be fair-minded about the wealth possessed by their betrothed. When such is not the case, however, positive law always favors the husband, regardless of any intuitive notion of justice.

Sir Stephen's claim to the money restored to Eleanor by David Stuart is justified by the principle of coverture, the legal fiction that marriage transforms two individuals into a single legal entity represented solely by the husband.[6] *Stuart of Dunleath* addresses the plight of nonexistent wives, anticipating Maeve Doggett's analysis of coverture "as an acceptance of the husband's right to physical control of his wife which lay at the heart of the legal construction of the marital relationship. Far from being a *consequence* of coverture, the husband's right of control was its very *essence*."[7] It serves, therefore, less as a foundational principle than an ex post facto rationalization of physical control. Sir Stephen's violence is continuous with his legal authority over his wife; he has as much right to dispose of her person as he does her property.

This point is made insultingly clear to Eleanor after she leaves her husband. She will not divorce him, choosing instead to move into the loveless but respectable home of her brother. She may remain there, however, only if Sir Stephen chooses not to exercise his right to the restitution of conjugal rights. Norton, of course, lived under this threat, and she offered her own calculation of the mathematics of marriage: "to reside apart from her husband for ten, fifteen, twenty years,—with every human circumstance, except death, that can put division between them,—does not affect the legal fiction which assumes that a married couple are *one*" (*ELW* 156). Sir Stephen is as well informed on conjugal rights as on spousal property, and through his lawyer he makes sure that Eleanor understands that fact (*SD* 3:304–06). Only her premature death releases Eleanor from his grasp—as well as from the cold comfort provided by her brother, Godfrey Marsden, who "contrived to make generosity a burden, advice an insult, and abiding with him a daily penance" (*SD* 3:306).

Godfrey, although a judgmental and unempathic man, at least recognizes that his sister cannot possibly be expected to return to the "husband who had maltreated her" (*SD* 3:304). Human laws may seem counterintuitive, if not perverse, but Godfrey's appeal to natural law is easily brushed aside by his brother-in-law's attorney:

> [T]here was no doubt that the court would order Eleanor to return; that the peccadilloes of which her husband had been guilty—though they were such as frequently created dissension in families, and were greatly to be condemned and regretted, would not form a sufficient ground of resistance to the order of the Court . . . especially as Eleanor had clearly "condoned" all she complained of, by continuing to reside under her husband's roof long after she became aware of the facts.
>
> (*SD* 3:305)

The "peccadilloes" here referred to include maintaining an illegitimate family in addition to breaking his wife's arm. "Masculine errors" (*SD* 3:305) may be discounted, but masculine rights would seem to be inalienable.

DIVORCE: "A MOST INDECENT FICTION OF THE LAW"

Norton's comment that *Stuart of Dunleath* "contains at least my real opinions on the subject of so many angry pamphlets and discussions" is not entirely helpful since so many different opinions are aired during conversations concerning abstract notions of justice and concrete questions of law.[8] These dialogues might easily be excerpted and published in pamphlet form; however, by placing the concept of divorce in various dramatic contexts, Norton both lightens the polemic and moderates the anger. Dialogic complexity enriches the issue, encourages recognition of the value of contradictory positions, and ultimately complicates the heroine's decision neither to divorce nor to live with her husband. Eleanor eventually accepts the fact of marriage as an inviolable principle, but by refusing to live with Sir Stephen she redefines its meaning. Actions must be principled, but principles would seem to be qualified, if not redefined, by actions.

Permutations of circumstance and character document the difficulty of applying general rules to particular situations. For instance, when a sympathetic but flawed character like David Stuart argues for Eleanor's divorce, readers, desirous of a happy resolution for the lovers, must remind themselves that his position is compromised by self-interest: he feels guilt for having recommended the marriage in the first place, and he wishes to marry Eleanor himself. Conversely, when a "perfect panoply of self-satisfaction" (*SD* 1:76) like Godfrey Marsden condemns divorce, readers may be inclined to resist the argument simply because of its advocate. When Eleanor considers but rejects divorce as "a question of principle" (*SD* 3:259), her decision is complicated by the circumstances it generates. Her refusal to live with her husband may seem reasonable; however, since her only other option is Godfrey's frigid hospitality, this choice is tantamount to a slow suicide. This untenable middle path is only one of the factors exposing the brutality of what Meredith called the "clumsy machinery of civilization."

Eleanor's situation fits none of the legal formulae for leaving a brutal and adulterous husband, and the law makes no provision for the welfare of the "nonexistent" wife. For example, David Stuart's advice—that a Scottish divorce is preferable because easier to obtain than an English one—is legally sound, but the mere fact of his giving it tends to discredit the recommendation. Eleanor wonders whether marriage can be one thing in England and quite another in Scotland. Legalities are not irrelevant, but neither are they the primary factor in her reasoning. Her process of thought entails a two-step sequence. Only after considering her motivation for seeking a divorce does she raise the issue of its morality, which reverses the expected sequence of applying principle to circumstance. The second step in this paradoxical process depends upon completing a preliminary stage that is subsequently determined to be irrelevant. That is, only after studying her own heart is Eleanor able to consider divorce in ethical and philosophical terms, and only then is she able to reach the conclusion that the state of one's heart is beside the point: divorce is immoral regardless of motivation. Experience and ethics, therefore, are dramatically at odds, and Eleanor learns what Norton has long since known: that the rights (legal as well as moral) and wrongs of a situation can be hopelessly complex. Encountering a crossway, Eleanor knowingly chooses a path leading to a dead end.

The incisive questions of Eleanor's London attorney quickly expose the hidden motivation for leaving Sir Stephen. Although she knew of his mistress Bridget Owen "for five or six years," she did nothing until David Stuart discovered it and contacted the attorney on her behalf: "She could not forget the look of astonishment in his clever countenance, as she gave those hesitating answers; nor the pause he made, as if reflecting; nor the keen intelligence of his eyes, when lifting them once more to her face" (*SD* 3:250–51). Discerning the truth, he "did not look at her, but turned over the papers on the table; and then questioned her in quite a different tone, and on another branch of the subject, as though he were satisfied, and had given her time to recover herself" (*SD* 3:251). Eye-to-eye contact implies mutual understanding; eyes cast down to documents signal avoiding the human dimension and refocusing on legal requisites. A rift opens between personal opinion and professional counsel: the attorney detects her motivation, recognizes its relevance to the objective at hand (divorce), and determines that a new legal strategy must be devised. Since foreknowledge constitutes condonation, adultery is not a legitimate plea. A Scottish divorce on the grounds of cruelty, however, is likely to succeed. The portrayal of this "brother of the long robe" is far from satirical. His consideration for Eleanor shares nothing with Jennings's condescension toward female litigants. Furthermore, his legal pragmatism seems directed to his client's rather than his own benefit, and it can be advantageously contrasted to Godfrey's moral absolutism.

Eleanor, however, pursues the human inquiry foreclosed by the attorney's chiefly legalistic considerations. She confronts an unflattering possibility: "Wronged as she had been, was what she was doing, in reality an appeal to justice, or a desperate yielding to temptation?" (*SD* 3:250). The answer is ineluctable: "it was not her husband's sin that had brought about this separation; it was the visionary sin of her own love; the desire to swear at the altar of God to be true to David Stuart till death,—that prompted her to plan the breaking of her first vow" (*SD* 3:251). Although she follows her attorney's instructions and reviews Ferguson's *Law of Divorce* after leaving his office, she finds the study "distasteful" and the legal tome a "useless book" (*SD* 3:256, 255). Thus, in the second stage of her thought process, she asks a leading question of the sort not admitted by a lawyer: "What was the marriage-vow but a mockery, if the oath God witnessed, could be absolved by men? if the dread sentence, 'What God hath joined, let no man put asunder,' were to be nothing but a form of words, and part of an unmeaning ceremony?" (*SD* 3:252). With God's law established, there is no chance of human law countermanding it: "The whole question was, whether that sin could be lessened by being legalized.... Eleanor could not bring herself to believe that it did" (*SD* 3:268). On the one hand, she resolutely rejects the romantic rhetoric of sensualists like Montagu Treherne; on the other hand, she no less firmly refuses the consolation of legal sanctions such as hoped for by Beatrice Brooke. Eleanor systematically rehearses and discounts all extenuating circumstances that might justify marrying David: her husband's breaking his marriage vow (to say nothing of her arm), her youthfulness at the time of marriage, and the coercive factors, such as David's advice and her poverty, that contribute to her "unloving vow" (*SD* 3:369). In the process of relentlessly excising the very things that others would consider significant, Eleanor reaches a position entirely consistent with her brother's view that divorce is "a most indecent fiction of the law" (*SD* 3:281) and with a legal positivist's insistence that a principle is a principle.

The anomalous situation that results—her becoming "a wife and no wife"—exemplifies Norton's tack of repeatedly constructing fictional situations that resist, or at least complicate, moral and legal absolutism. Throughout the text, characters and their conclusions seem to be at odds. For instance, Godfrey and the attorney would both appear to represent masculine logic and the rule of law, yet their adherence to law leads to opposite conclusions about Eleanor's situation. Godfrey and Eleanor, by contrast, have virtually nothing in common apart from their mother, yet their views on divorce are identical. Similarly, when Godfrey and Margaret Fordyce debate moral principle, she answers his simplistic position, "Right is right and wrong is wrong" (SD 1:241), with the plea: "How can we talk of dealing strict justice? Charity is what is expected of us.... We are all as different as possible; we are all faulty, and we owe each other a continually running debt of indulgence" (*SD* 1:154–55, 158). Yet here again, Norton presents a paradox, for it is Margaret who insists: "the marriage vow... is irrevocable; nothing but death should part you" (*SD* 3:259).

Norton's statements on the subject of divorce outside of *Stuart of Dunleath* are of a similarly complicated nature. Following the publication of the novel, she added her voice to the parliamentary debate of marriage law, supporting Lord Campbell's view that an important alteration has been made in the law of the country. Up to a recent period it had been a question agitated by lawyers, whether marriage was not a religious contract, requiring the sanction of the church. That question has been settled by the Legislature, and marriage is now a Civil Contract.

(*LQ* 26)

This position would appear unequivocally to establish the possibility of absolving the contract. Nevertheless, Norton also aligned herself with characters like Eleanor and Margaret in a letter to Gladstone dated March 29, 1854:

To me the ceremony of marriage in our church seems utterly indissoluble and though in earlier life I might at one time have *wished* my marriage dissolved according to the laws of men,—it would have been with a secret conviction that no law could really annul it, and make me the wife of any other man,—& with a perpetual remorse.[9]

Both *Stuart of Dunleath* and her own experience, however, demonstrate that "perpetual remorse" may also attend not annulling a marriage, suggesting that regret might be the only constant factor in matters of divorce.

Having enclosed a copy of *English Laws* with her letter to Gladstone, Norton is at some pains to account for the discrepancies among the views expressed in her letter, her novel, and her essay:

I have not expressed this opinion [that just quoted] in my pamphlet: partly because, though I think the *factor of my case* should weigh with those who read, I cannot expect my *opinions* should do so.... But I did express it in a form where opinions are less challenged, in the description of fictitious characters in a novel I published two years ago [*Stuart of Dunleath*]. I am quite willing to accept marriage as it is accepted in the Roman Catholic Church—as a sacrament.[10]

Her "case" argues for divorce as a matter of public policy; her "opinions" reflect matters of private belief. In effect, she argues for the availability of a legal course that she herself would not choose to follow. Opinions are irrelevant to the public debate, which she enters in the spirit of Eleanor's pragmatic attorney. Liberalizing divorce law would remove obstacles to women's exercise of free choice and minimize the adverse consequences of these choices. Thus she urges Gladstone, in contradiction to her private feelings, to support changes in divorce law that would delimit husbands' power over wives, that would give women "a right to sue for divorce in extreme cases, & in cases of desertion," and that would "free both parties . . . to marry again."[11]

Stuart of Dunleath avoids the argumentative tone of "so many angry pamphlets and discussions," including Norton's own, not because "opinions are less challenged" in the novel but because they are inseparable from the complicated situations from which they emerge and to which they are applied. In that regard, her accomplishment resembles Eliot's in *The Mill on the Floss.* Eleanor's conclusion about the marriage vow anticipates Maggie's argument that "if the past is not to bind us, where can duty lie? We should have no law but the inclination of the moment" (*MF* 601–02). The parallels in the books are striking: Tom Tulliver plays Godfrey's role as the disapproving brother; Dr. Kenn reprises Rev. Fordyce's role as the wise clergyman and counselor; and Stephen Guest articulates the "natural arguments" of David Stuart, for example, telling Maggie that "natural law surmounts every other,—we can't help what it clashes with . . . . What is mere outward faithfulness?" (*MF* 601–02). He also vents the romantic rhetoric of Norton's importunate and coercive lovers: "Good God! . . . what a miserable thing a woman's love is to a man's. I could commit crimes for you—and you can balance and choose in that way" (*MF* 603–04). In resisting such arguments, Eleanor and Maggie make principled decisions that are at once honorable and regrettable. David Stuart and Stephen Guest are good, albeit flawed, men, whose offers of love promise a moiety of happiness on earth. Rejecting them ultimately entails a Jamesian resignation that is at once ennobling and unrelated to questions of law. In Eliot's words:

> The great problem of the shifting relation between passion and duty is clear to no man who is capable of apprehending it: the question, whether the moment has come in which a man has fallen below the possibility of a renunciation that will carry any efficacy, and must accept the sway of a passion against which he had struggled as a trespass, is one for which we have no master key that will fit all cases.
>
> (*MF* 627–28)

Godfrey's simplistic philosophy of right and wrong is inadequate to guide or to guard those negotiating the crossways of human existence.

Stuart of Dunleath places the issue of divorce in the larger context of moral choice. Godfrey, a naval officer who takes military law as the model of all justice systems, symbolizes one alternative. With some justice, he maintains that the "conduct of a man without strong principle becomes a mere series of accidents" (*SD* 3:283). David represents the opposite approach, arguing that "a certain latitude and discretion" (*SD* 1:242) must be allowed. From the former's perspective, David's is an "indian-rubber conscience" (*SD* 1:243); from the latter's, Godfrey's beliefs are draconian and inhuman. However unappealing Godfrey's character might be, he seems to be right about David, who himself recognizes that his life has largely been shaped by "the hazard of the die" (*SD* 3:220), not by his own initiative or ability. He has paid insufficient attention to Reverend Fordyce's sermon on the text, " '*unstable as water, thou shalt not excel*' " (*SD* 1:61, also see 1:87–88).

The chief instance of David's "failure to excel" comes when, after having advised Eleanor to marry without love, he asks her to divorce for love. Learning that she refuses to do so, he responds as Stephen Guest does: "If you loved as I do, these scruples would be threads that would snap asunder, not chains to bind you down to a miserable form of virtue, in which the spirit is wanting" (*SD* 3:295). He eventually finds consolation in marriage to Margaret, a worthy woman who is nonetheless a stand-in for Eleanor. In the resulting ghostly ménage à trois, only his wife is happy for only she possesses the illusion of love: "Margaret believes herself to be the crowning joy of David Stuart's life . . . but is not! . . . Eleanor . . . whom he loved and injured; haunts that home of his youth, for the regaining which he risked her fortune, and ruined her future" (*SD* 3:342–43). Margaret will surely provide the anchor that David lacks, but without the safe harbor of a conventional romantic resolution, readers may feel themselves adrift at sea.

This subdued resolution reinforces Norton's theme of responding to human limitation with tolerance. Given the relativity of perceptions and the opposition of values, righteousness or zealotry is likely to compound rather than to mitigate suffering. Margaret recognizes that egocentric vision contributes to misunderstanding when she asks Godfrey: "Who made your mode of thinking and feeling the standard and example by which your fellow-creatures are to be tried?" (*SD* 1:154, 157–58). David's similar challenge is every bit as impassioned as Virginia Woolf's protest against the twin goddesses, Proportion and Conversion: "Your own convictions, late or early, do not transform you suddenly into a sort of John the Baptist, a wandering preacher, calling on others to repent. Every one must abide by their own heart; you are not their self-appointed judge" (*SD* 1:242). The Duke of Lanark, Margaret's brother, wisely observes that "we are all of us very hard upon faults we do not understand" (*SD* 3:17). He classifies kinds of tolerance, demonstrating that "a continually running debt of indulgence" is neither weak nor undesirable. He distinguishes among "the tolerance of tenderness,... the tolerance of carelessness, which I should be sorry to see in any one I love; and the tolerance of justice, which I agree with Margaret in thinking the nearest approach we can make to the angelic nature" (*SD* 2:170). While the first is closest to sympathy or charity, it risks devolving to mere sentimentalism unless tempered by the third. While the second is preferable to Godfrey's intolerance, it is little other than callous indifference, insensitivity, and complacent self-interest. The third unites justice and fellow-feeling, judgment and compassion; it represents the ideal to which all may aspire, but which none in this novel ultimately achieves.

Norton's "tolerance of justice" is close to Dr. Kenn's view that "moral judgments must remain false and hollow, unless they are checked and enlightened by a perpetual reference to the special circumstances that mark the individual human lot" (*MF* 628). A final example will illustrate this principle and demonstrate Norton's allegiance to and evolution beyond the silver fork tradition. The Duchess of Lanark is introduced as one of "the class of conquest-makers" (*SD* 1:204), a coquette familiar to readers of the early fiction. The geography of vanity partially extenuates her guilt, at least insofar as in London "[h]er frivolity seemed less, where all were more or less frivolously occupied; her kindliness greater, where so few were kindly, so many much the reverse" (*SD* 2:135, also see 3:148–49). The duchess may be damned with faint praise, but flirtatiousness does not mean that she is uncaring or callous. Her strong and happy marriage owes much to the character of her husband, who provides the anchor that she is missing:

> For the thousandth time, she felt—incorrigible as she was—the superiority of this man without beauty; without what is called charm; with only his frank high soul and singleness of heart as grappling-irons in the shifting anchorage of her love,—over all those to whom she had from time to time accorded a momentary and wavering performance. For the thousandth time she acknowledged with a secret sigh, the worth of his regard, the value of his approbation, and shame at not being more deserving of both.
>
> (*SD* 3:152)

In a coda in which Norton summarizes her characters' future, the duchess is assigned the role in the double plot of coquetry previously filled by Susan Glenalton. The duke claims always to have known that the duchess "would steady, and get rid of her one fault," and "she owns that she has been more touched and governed by his trust, than she could have been by lectures or control of any sort" (*SD* 3:341–42). This comic subplot does not counterbalance the somber fates of David Stuart, Margaret Fordyce, and Eleanor Penrhyn, but it does suggest that, while the "tolerance of justice" may be too lofty a goal for those of less than "angelic nature," the "tolerance of tenderness" is accessible to all, and is all the more important for that reason.

NORTON AND THACKERAY II: THE NORTONS AND *THE NEWCOMES*

In a study of domestic violence in literature, Kate Lawson and Lynn Shakinovsky speculate that in the 1850s "the reform of marriage laws and the introduction of the Divorce Court in England made the miseries of marriage an object of widespread interest."[12] The marital unhappiness of the Nortons re-emerged in the public eye in 1853, when an unpaid bill for carriage repairs led to a legal action (*Thrupp* v. *Norton*) and the renewal of the allegations and resentments generated by *Norton* v. *Melbourne*. The dispute subsequently spilled into the pages of the *Times* in an exchange of letters to the editor. The recrudescence of public unpleasantness perhaps reminded Thackeray to research "the trial of *Norton* v. *Melbourne* having a crim. con. affair coming on in the Newcomes."[13]

Although he drew upon the Nortons' troubled marriage, Thackeray invented freely; for example, Clara Newcome bears little resemblance to Norton, possessing neither wit, intelligence, flirtatious temperament, nor imposing physical presence. Under the physical and emotional abuse of her husband, Norton was fiery and rebellious; Clara is merely cowed and despondent. After she "came into Barnes's hands, a dreadful weight fell upon her. . . . She blundered, her eyes filled with tears; the little wit she had left her in her husband's presence" (*N* 561). Despite such differences, Thackeray borrowed many elements from the Nortons' history, including a turbulent private life behind a facade of social tranquility. The Newcomes' days are filled with "quarrels and recriminations, misery and heart-burning, cruel words and shameful struggles," yet they "appeared before the world with smiling faces, resuming their battle when the feast was concluded and the company gone" (*N* 527). The "story of the bruised cheek" (*N* 563) contradicts appearances, and Clara's elopement explodes the domestic fiction, as did the Nortons' separation and sensational divorce case. A key difference, however, is that after published reports of "The Elopement in High Life" (*N* 597), Clara disappears from the limelight. Even the narrator loses interest after her remarriage: "she no more belongs to our story: with the new name she has taken, the poor lady passes out of the history of the Newcomes" (*N* 595).

Clara's example provides a cautionary tale, the moral of which is pronounced by Pendennis: she is a "virgin offered up to the devouring monster, Mammon (with many most respectable female dragons looking on)" (*N* 595, also see 276, 584). Her experience encourages Ethel Newcome to break her engagement to Lord Farintosh: "I have thought of what has happened here,—of the wretched consequences of interested marriages; the long union growing each day so miserable, that at last it becomes intolerable, and is burst asunder, as in poor Clara's case" (*N* 610). Ethel warns her fiancé to avoid Barnes's error and admits their complicity in it: "Oh, what perjuries poor Clara was made to speak—and see what has befallen her! We stood by and heard her without being shocked. We applauded even. And to what shame and misery we brought her! Why did her parents and mine consign her to such ruin!" (*N* 612). Thackeray follows the pattern of several of Norton's tales: Clara's punishment exceeds her crime, and the more culpable party is not punished at all. Barnes carries on without the burden of guilt or social opprobrium: "Why should Sir Barnes Newcome's conscience be more squeamish than his country's, which has put money in his pocket for having trampled on the poor weak young thing, and scorned her, and driven her to ruin?" (*N* 595).

Thackeray, however, does attempt to balance accounts. Barnes may be insulated from hardship by wealth and from criticism by callousness and an impermeable sense of self-approval, but his harsh treatment of Clara alienates virtually all of his acquaintances and family, even those who find her actions abhorrent. His hypocritical forays into public sentimentality, including lectures on "The Poetry of Childhood" and "The Poetry of Womanhood, and the Affections" (*N* 652), expose him to reviewers' satire. Mr. Pott maliciously employs double entendre to remind readers that the effusive speaker was an abusive spouse:

> The performance . . . was so pathetic as to bring tears into the eyes of several of our fair friends. We have heard, but never believed until now, that Sir Barnes Newcome possessed such a genius *for making women cry*. . . . Bets were freely offered in the room last night Sir Barnes would *beat any woman*—bets which were not taken, as we scarcely need say, so well do our citizens appreciate the character of our excellent, our admirable representative.
>
> (*N* 668)

Pott's verdict is reaffirmed by the electorate, who pelt the incumbent MP with vegetables and greet him with jeers: "Who beat his wife? Who drove his children to the workhouse" (*N* 681). The gibe about the workhouse refers to Barnes's illegitimate family, something—in addition to wife-beating—that he has in common with Sir Stephen Penrhyn. Clara may disappear, but Barnes is driven, from the novel: "What about Sir Barnes Newcome ultimately? My impression is that he is married again, and it is my fervent hope that his present wife bullies him" (*N* 773).

The Newcomes reflects many aspects of Norton's work. Clara experiences all the hazards of which women who leave their families are warned (*N* 594) and of which Norton wrote in "Marriage and Love," "The Forsaken Child," and *The Dream*. A significant difference between Thackeray and Norton in this regard is his lack of interest in children and their mothers. The death of her two children is traumatic for Eleanor Penrhyn and severs the only remaining tie to her husband. Clara, however, is indifferent to her children with Barnes (*N* 500) and, submerged in Tennysonian depression, evinces no greater interest in her Belsize offspring: "More and more sad does the Lady Clara become from day to day; liking more to sit lonely over the fire; careless about the sarcasms of her husband; the prattle of her children. She cries sometimes over the cradle of the young heir. She is aweary, aweary" (*N* 532, also see 594–95).[14]

CODA: CRIMINAL LAW

Norton's writing on divorce demonstrates that neither the narrative of civil law, according to which two become one, nor that of divine law, according to which one may not return to two, offers protection for abused wives. When she turns from marriage law to the Old Bailey, the story is modified but only in the sense that gendered injustice is refigured in broader social terms. Legal violence is inflicted by the administration of criminal codes and not simply by inequitable marriage laws. In an occasionally bitter mood, Norton depicts the law feasting on hapless defendants irrespective of gender.

The Child of the Islands (1846), her long poem on the condition of England, offers a typifying example of the exercise of legal might. By remaining firmly entrenched in the world of legal statute and jargon, lawyers effectively silence voices that might counter their own. In this example, a "criminal . . . in the felon's dock" is bludgeoned into insensitivity by the process that ultimately authorizes taking his life:

At first he grasps the rail with nervous hand,
Hearing the case which learnedly they state,
With what attention ignorance can command:
Then, weary of such arguing his fate,
Torpid and dull he sinks, throughout the long debate.

Vapid, incomprehensible to him
The skilful pleaders' cross-examining wit;
His sullen ear receives, confused and dim,
The shouts of laughter at some brilliant hit,
When a shrewd witness leaves the Biter bit.
He shrinks not while the facts that must prevail
Against his life, unconscious friends admit;
Though Death is trembling in the adverse scale,
He recks no more than if he heard the autumn gale.
(*CI* 71)

In this case, the shrewd author bites the profession that under the cloak of coverture authorized her legal execution. She appealed the verdict vociferously, if fruitlessly, but this "scaffold-sentenced" victim stands mute "like a dog, new-sentenced to be shot!" (*CI* 72). The accused is reduced to a state of abjection by words wielded as weapons, and through him Norton voices a protest against the brute imposition of legal force.

A similar point is made in "Palace of Justice, Bruges," which contrasts the edifices of human law to the "glorious Temple" of divine justice (*FDS 47*:59). The character of earthly law is established by its contrast to God's tribunal:

There, shall no ignorant wretch
Essay to cast each word,
In eloquence unknown,
So that he *might* be heard;
Or, casting all his woe,
On one more fit to plead,
Stand trembling by, to watch
What help it gives his need.
(*FDS 47*:60)

In this poem, the "savage thirst to kill" (*FDS 47*:59) is exhibited by the representatives of law, not by the unfortunate accused brought before their courts. Although the stark contrast might seem to be an instance of the "anti-respectability commonplace," the conclusion underscores that the very concept of a "there," where "all is true and plain," heightens the torment of the accused in human courts: "How oft must sufferers yearn, / With wild impatient thought, / For the realms where RIGHT is all, / AND MIGHT, at length, is nought" (*FDS 47*:60). On the few occasions that Norton enters the Old Bailey, lawyers are the criminals, and criminals can only wish that, like married women, they were "non-existent in law."

Part III

Politics

Chapter 5

"Half a Life": Narratives of Women and Politics

Does it not provoke you sometimes to think how in vain the gift of genius is for a woman; how, so far from binding her more closely to the admiration and love of her fellow-creatures, it does in effect create that "gulf across which no one passes," and all to be forgotten! Witness its being impossible to find out when or how Aspasia died, who I believe to have been Pericles's superior in all things except the power to steer the ship of which you speak.[1]

Caroline Norton, Letter to Mary Shelley

A woman's life is only half a life, as she cannot have a seat in Parliament.[2]

Anthony Trollope, *Phineas Finn*

Following the death of Lord Palmerston in 1865, Norton wrote a letter of condolence to his widow, Lord Melbourne's sister. Lady Palmerston, the "doyenne of Cambridge House, herself successor to Lady Holland of Holland House and the Whig tradition of political entertaining," was, according to K. D. Reynolds, the "woman against whose success all others were constantly measured."[3] Norton implied that her own accomplishment as a petticoat politician was comparatively modest and eloquently described the limits as well as the significance of women's contributions to public life:

> It was my dream when I thought to marry and live among the men who influenced their time, to be what I think you were, in this, the only reasonable ambition of woman, and though it may seem a light thing to speak of, in face of the solemnities of Death, it is *not* as light a thing as it *seems*, to have added so far to the happiness and security of a career of public usefulness and public elevation—beyond and besides the inner life of home, which *all* women have power over.[4]

Her words recall Gertrude Ross's dream of being able "to watch the lives that leave their tracks of light behind, like ships on the waters." In reality, Norton felt less like Lady Palmerston or even Gertrude, whose goal of observing is even more modest, than Mrs. Transome, of whom Eliot writes concerning her son's political aspirations: "In this way poor women, whose power lies solely in their influence, make themselves like music out of tune, and only move men to run away."[5]

Lionel Dupré's misogynistic tirade in *Woman's Reward* illustrates George Eliot's point and dramatizes women's thankless, secondary role in politics:

> A woman wishes her husband to be prime minister, or her lover to be lord chancellor, or her son to be an ambassador; . . . women love men—they have no abstract love for their country; they don't understand it, they take different sides and abuse the opposite party with a most fierce and contradictory spirit; for that comes by nature, but they have no patriotism, and about as much idea of *public* ambition as my Neapolitan greyhound.
>
> (*WWR* 2:99)

Lionel does not admit the justice of his sister's riposte: "Whose fault is it that women have no spirit but that of party—no idea of ambition, but that of arriving at power? You allow we are only your echoes, that you influence us, that you lead our enthusiasm" (*WWR* 2:99). He disparages women for the doglike submission that he demands from them. Although he treats Mary like a Neapolitan greyhound, he takes full advantage of her tireless efforts on his behalf during two political campaigns (the first successful, the second not) while simultaneously deriding the loyalty and energy of which she is the exemplar. His subsequent marriage questions Norton's observation that women have power over the inner life of the home, since his wife is little more than a domestic lap dog to be displayed, ignored, or kicked as her husband sees fit.

Norton's undistinguished marriage to a man whose political history exactly parallels Lionel's impeded her dream of "living among the men who influenced their time." Becky Sharp's marriage provided a similar obstacle to social success, and she turned her considerable social talent to nursing the fledgling career of Sir Pitt Crawley, promising to intervene with Lord Steyne and telling her brother-in-law, "Poor little penniless I have got a little interest—and who knows, perhaps the mouse may be able to aide the lion" (*VF* 528–9). For Norton, whose political interest and knowledge in contrast to Becky's were considerable, the most likely avenue of influence was the literary salon. The career of Lady Blessington suggests the option realistically open to her. Indeed, their names were often linked, in part because of a common Irish heritage, reputation for beauty, and appetite for public attention.[6] In the absence of wealth and patronage, literary success provided the cachet required of the political hostess. Both Blessington and Norton were prolific and popular authors, identified in *Reynolds's Miscellany* as "amongst the most eminent female writers of the age."[7] Lady Wilde held Norton to be the better writer, noting that Blessington "had neither Lady Morgan's wit nor Mrs. Norton's agonizing pathos; and if compared with the lady authoresses her contemporaries, must in all things be named lowest in the list."[8] Both Blessington and Norton served as editor of *The Keepsake* as well as other annuals, which was lucrative literary labor for independent women of limited means attempting to maintain salons and visibility.

Reynolds observes that "one characteristic that the successful Victorian political hostesses seem to have shared was unorthodox social position."[9] Blessington more than made up for any perceived lack of pathos by leading a daringly scandalous life. Her open affair with Count D'Orsay added a particular cast (decidedly bohemian) and character (almost exclusively male) to her salon, which was sedulously avoided by proper ladies. Prominent politicians and artistic figures, however, were frequent visitors, including many of those known to or intimate with Norton. Even as he was professing his passion for Norton, for instance, Haydon observed: "Everybody goes to Lady Blessington's. . . . She is the center of more talent & gaiety than any other woman of fashion in London."[10] Norton's more conventional background (the Melbourne affair was as yet the subject of rumor, not legal action) may have excluded her from the center of literary bohemianism, but she was a prominent figure on its periphery. Samuel Rogers, Sydney Smith, Disraeli, and Bulwer Lytton all found their way to her door, as well as to Lady Blessington's.

Blessington's first novel, *The Repealers* (1833), offers a fleeting portrait of her literary and social rival in the person of the "celebrated Mrs. Grantly."[11] Even though, as Michael Sadleir contends, not all of the praise in this *roman á clef* is ingenuous, the fictional attention enhanced Norton's standing in silver fork society.[12] Mrs. Grantly, readers are told, is

> no less remarkable for her beauty, than for her genius and talents. Does she not look the very personification of a muse? What a classical style of beauty, and how much expression is joined to that oval face, and those exquisitely chiseled features! How delightful to witness such a rare union of beauty and genius![13]

Blessington's encomium anticipates Bulwer Lytton's mythologizing and documents one of the reasons for the popularity of Norton's gatherings.

The Equivocal Value of Visibility III: In the Salon

That the voice of "the Byron of modern poetesses" emanated from a woman in the "classical style of beauty" was certainly a boon to someone not associated with a prominent political family either by birth or by marriage. Although never a rival to Lady Palmerston, Norton hosted salons at two distinct periods: the first in the early thirties with a circle boasting Lord Melbourne at its center and the second in the early forties with a cadre of politicians linked to a rising Tory star, Sidney Herbert. Both forays into political society were abruptly ended by scandal: the allegation of adultery in the first instance and the suspicion of disclosing confidential government information in the second.

The role of political hostess was a natural one for Norton not only because of her political passion but also because of her delight in fashionable society and her striking social manner. If the showy behavior remarked upon by both Lord and Lady Holland put some off, it was an incentive to others, such as "off-hand premiers," like Melbourne, and aspiring ones, like Disraeli. Greville noted in his journal: "Great talk about . . . Melbourne's affair with Mrs. Norton, which . . . , if it is not quashed, will be inconvenient. John Bull fancies himself vastly moral, and the Court is mighty prudish, and between them our off-hand Premier will find himself in a ticklish position."[14] Such "great talk," however, was not necessarily a disincentive to young politicians seeking preferment and visibility. Nor was it necessarily a liability to the hostess herself; as Reynolds notes, "With uniformly eccentric social and/or moral backgrounds the career of political hostess gave these women the opportunity to establish themselves and their families in the highest ranks of society, from which they might otherwise have been excluded."[15]

That an item of underclothing, the petticoat, came to designate a political woman is not inconsistent with the aura attending salons like Blessington's and Norton's.[16] If the "optics of authorship" defines one aspect of the gendered paradox of being simultaneously seen and invisible, then the "optics of politics" constitutes another. Recalling Maginn's observation that the woman writer should be treated gently by reviewers, "except she writes politics, which is an enormity equal to wearing breeches," we are reminded of the contradictory constructions that greeted Norton as a writer. A parallel authorial paradox obtains in politics: on the one hand, the woman inclined to independent thought and activism is associated with masculine wear: breeches, bloomers, or cerulean socks; on the other hand, she is linguistically garbed in more feminine and slightly salacious attire—new clothes that metonymically emphasize exactly what they are purported to quarantine: sexuality in politics.

The political hostess may be a center of attention, but her influence need not translate into power outside the salon. As Barbara Leah Harman writes, opponents of the bluestockings "defined public life as a prohibited realm for women, associated with indecorous self-display, illicit sexuality and infidelity, and the destruction of the family."[17] "Celebrated Mrs. Grantlys" in real life might find themselves excluded from home and hearth. If the siren's power could not be diminished, it could be restricted to primarily masculine salons. Thus, while men passed willingly through the Caudine Forks, women closed ranks. Norton's personal attractions were begrudgingly acknowledged, but her unconventional behavior was invariably disparaged. Mrs. Frederick Sullivan, for example, observed, "I never saw anything so tormentingly beautiful. One is attracted by her consummate beauty, one is repelled by her odious manner!"[18] Men, too, felt compelled to condemn the woman to whose beauty they were susceptible. Greville's comment about Blessington might also be applied to Norton:

> There is no end to the men of consequence and distinction in the world who go there occasionally... but all this does not make society in the real sense of the term.... The reason of this is that the woman herself, who must give the tone to her own society, and influence its character, is ignorant, vulgar, and commonplace.[19]

Once again, the visible woman found herself both the envied cynosure and a censored object of the male gaze.

THE FIRST TERM: POLITICAL INFLUENCE FROM 1830 TO 1836

When George Norton's position with the Bankruptcy Commission was terminated by the new Whig administration in 1830, his wife wrote to Lord Melbourne to beg a political favor for her unemployed husband. In writing to a man whom she had never met, Norton was presuming upon some old ties: the home secretary had been a fervent admirer of her grandfather and had, in fact, begun his biography, which was turned over to their mutual friend, Thomas Moore, to be finished.[20] Furthermore, Melbourne and her father, Thomas Sheridan (d. 1816), had been good friends, "not far apart in age, and . . . closely knit by sympathy in taste and turn of thought."[21] Perhaps out of loyalty to these old friends, Melbourne responded favorably to the request, beginning a friendship that continued until his death in 1848.

The friendship fueled Norton's unlikely hope that she might attain "the kind of behind-the-scenes influence exercised by the great Whig ladies of the previous century, such as the duchess of Devonshire . . . and Viscountess Melbourne, Byron's confidante and the home secretary's mother."[22] Her dream was linked directly but narrowly to Melbourne, whose presence transformed the Nortons' drawing room into a "tiny salon frequently crowded with guests wishing to curry favour with the new Home Secretary."[23] In this salon, for example, Disraeli—not even a member of Parliament at the time—approached Melbourne, who

> offered to help him: "Well now, tell me, what do you want to be?"—"I want to be Prime Minister." Melbourne shrugged his shoulders and sighed. " . . . No, go into politics, you will be right; you have ability and enterprise, and with patience I dare say you will do very well. But you must put all these foolish ideas out of your head."[24]

Although banter rather than business was the norm, Norton briefly served as Melbourne's representative in secret negotiations to form a new government following the resignation of Sir Robert Peel in 1835. Disraeli noted:

> my old friend Mrs. N[orton] opened a communic[ati]on with me, in order to form a co-alition between the constitutional Whigs and Sir R[obert]

P[eel].... I had several conferences with her prompted by L[yndhurst] and paid her visits sometimes of two hours (tho' our acquaintance o[the]rwise had quite ceased).[25]

The plan never materialized, but few women of her time could boast such direct political experience. The episode was neither typical of the roles filled by political hostesses nor was it ever repeated.

Disraeli's credentials as a fashionable novelist rather than as an aspiring politician provided the more likely entrée to Norton's gatherings. Agitation for reform might have been swirling outside, but the climate inside was decidedly lighter. André Maurois reports that the "conversation was an enchantment to Disraeli.... [Mrs. Norton] delighted to leave an intolerable husband, liked to have Disraeli as her escort for the theatre or a ball. He found it agreeable to show himself in her company."[26] Enchanted by the wife but bored by the husband, Disraeli was more devoted to the eldest of the Three Graces. He accurately predicted to Helen Sheridan Blackwood that political loyalties would separate him from her more ardent sister:

I do not send you my pamphlet, because the politics will not please you, altho' I am not a Tory, and never intended to be one. I saw "Starry Night" [Caroline] yesterday, and am going to write something for her Mag[azine], I wo[u]ld do it for none else but your sister. It is the last testimony of my affection, as I have a melancholy presentiment that horrible politics will ultimately, if not very soon, dissolve that agreeable acquaintance which has been the consolation of my life.[27]

Helen's indifference to politics appealed to Disraeli but frustrated her sister. On one occasion Helen refused to hear the content of a letter from the Duke of Wellington, saying, "don't look so eager Caroline, and above all things don't read it to me if there *are any politics in it*, for I know I shall be bored & tried to death" (*LCN* 170). *Stuart of Dunleath* reprises this situation in Lady Margaret Fordyce's finding "political life... a stirring and glorious career" (*SD* 2:159). She instructs Eleanor on the need to entertain politicians: "Ministers are but men; and men from their hard occupied intellectual lives [are] very glad to unbend. They are as merry as schoolboys, at a fish dinner at Greenwich" (*SD* 2:159). Her protégé's attitude, by contrast, resembles Helen's as she finds politics "a surgical profession; painful, tedious, often revolting, the operations necessary to amend the diseased condition of society" (*SD* 2:136). Margaret envisions "the pattern of gorgeous tapestry on which History was weaving a further measure of events," but Eleanor thinks only "of the machinery... the black oily wheels; the suffocating atmosphere; the ceaseless din; the weary labour" (*SD* 2:136–37).

Norton's "fish dinners at Greenwich" often took the form of private afternoon meetings with Melbourne at her Storey's Gate home or political suppers, such as that recalled by Fanny Kemble when she shared a sofa with Lord Melbourne and "those three enchanting Sheridan sisters." On another evening, a guest observed that "our little party was very pleasant last night. Miss Kemble came, but was too tired to sing. Mrs. Norton sang comic songs, and was wonderful—splendid; and Lord Melbourne very much in love!"[28] Norton's feelings might be inferred from her spirited singing, but a more accurate measure is found in *Woman's Reward* in the character of William Clavering, which is indebted to Melbourne. A stark contrast to Lionel Dupré, Clavering is the leader of his party and as honorable a man as he is a politician. He "never uttered a sentence, of the truth of which he was not himself thoroughly convinced" (*WWR* 2:4–5). The novel further reveals Norton's feelings in the portrayal of Mary Dupré. Alone and awaiting Melbourne's afternoon visits, Norton must have experienced her protagonist's feeling: "poor Mary, as she sate in the quiet drawing-room,... felt as if a sudden barrier had been placed between her and her lover, so immeasurably great had he become in the eyes of the great world" (*WWR* 2:4–5). Mary expects to fulfill Norton's ideal goal and to receive the wife's portion of "the happiness and security of a career of public usefulness and public elevation" (*WWR* 2:8). A promise to her father, however, prevents her from accepting Clavering's proposal of marriage and providing his domestic retreat:

> Clavering... after the cheers and the murmurs, the struggle and the triumph of a long night's debate, felt as a traveler, who, after long journeying over stony streets and dusty roads, flings himself down on the green turf, and listens to the rippling of a broad and even stream.
>
> (*WWR* 2:8–9)

Norton's Storey's Gate parlor provided such an oasis to Melbourne, that is, until his constant attendance raised the attention of the gossip mongers and the ire of a jealous husband.

The eruption of the Melbourne scandal largely but not entirely ended Norton's influence. Edward Trelawny, for example, encouraged Mary Shelley to seek Norton's help in securing a pension for her stepmother, the widow of William Godwin. Norton wrote to the beleaguered prime minister and lobbied Lord Lansdowne, remembering that Godwin had been her grandfather's friend and one of the few to attend his funeral. She further admired Godwin's political sentiments, having written to Melbourne early in their acquaintance: "I am still enamoured of Caleb Williams. It is one of my manias that the English law does *not* protect the lower orders against the higher" (*LCN* 30). In addition to family loyalty and respect for Godwin, she sympathized with Shelley as a woman who had been shunned by polite society, whose son had been removed from her care, and who struggled to earn a living as an author living under a social cloud. The pension was granted, and Trelawny later observed that the effort "without a doubt . . . would have come to nothing . . . but that I retained on our side the Lady of song and beauty."[29]

Norton had no illusions about the extent of her influence. Her letter advising Shelley acknowledges that petticoat politics is less a matter of power than of weakness (and recalls Lionel's comparison of women to Neapolitan greyhounds):

> As to petitioning, no one dislikes begging more than I do, especially when one begs for what seems mere justice; but I have long observed that though people will resist *claims* (however just), they like to do *favours*. Therefore when *I* beg I am a crawling lizard, a humble toad, a brown snake in cold weather, or any other simile most feebly "*rampante*,"—the reverse of "*rampant*," which would be the natural attitude for petitioning—but which must never be assumed except in poodle-style, standing with one's paws bent to catch the bits of bread on one's nose.[30]

The pun on the English heraldic term and the French adjective for "crawling" captures the essence of chivalric paternalism and expresses her sardonic awareness of women's submissive position.

The trial of Lord Melbourne brought the salon at Storey's Gate to an end. Norton would later claim—though one imagines with tongue in cheek—that their meetings were passed in "reading translations of Aeschylus [and] listening to explanations of the unknown theories of politics" (*ELW* 45). Many others were skeptical of what transpired there. Lord Malmesbury, for instance, noted:

> Mrs. Norton must consider herself very fortunate in being let off so easily. All the Whigs are in raptures, which provoked an old Tory to say that "he really couldn't see why Lord Melbourne should be so triumphant at the verdict given, as it had been proved that he had had more opportunities than any man ever had before, and had made no use of them."[31]

Whatever might be said of Melbourne's near escape, it would be difficult to assert that his alleged lover was as fortunate. Even before the trial, she wrote to Melbourne: "Pray think what it is to *finish all* at seven & twenty, and that on a false & cruel lie" (*LCN* 82). "All" may not in fact have been over, but it was clear that she no longer had a supporting role in "a career of public usefulness and public elevation."

After the trial, Norton was particularly resentful of the double standard that proclaimed the defendant innocent but left his alleged accomplice guilty. When asked if Melbourne should resign, even his political antagonist, the Duke of Wellington, responded: "O Lord, no! Resign? Not a bit of it. I tell you all these things are a nine-days' wonder. . . . [I]t will all blow over, and won't signify a straw."[32] The announcement of Melbourne's acquittal was greeted by cheers in the House, and the Tories were left to disavow accusations of having instigated a groundless scandal. Melbourne returned seamlessly to public office and would soon become Queen Victoria's closest advisor. Norton, by contrast, lost her home and her children, and was sentenced to a lifetime of financial and social woe: nine days' wonder for him, 40 years of hardship for her.

While it is to be expected that a sitting prime minister would detach himself from the woman with whom he had been accused of adultery, Norton was enraged by Melbourne's neglect in the months following the trial. Despite anger and resentment, she maintained the friendship, and their correspondence continued intermittently and increased in the years after he left office. Norton wrote to family and friends, encouraging them to look after the man from whom she had formerly sought favors. Her last letters address her aging friend as "Dearest old boy" (*LCN* 168) and resume a familiar tone. In November 1844, she gently chided him for "turn[ing] such a deaf ear, and such a turned up nose,—to the claims of old Jack Morris? Why don't you help the man that helped your brother at Westminster? in the good old days when *you* wasn't weak & sick, & *he* wasn't faint & starving?" (*LCN* 165). Even to the end and despite altered circumstances, she was coyly "*rampante.*"

THE SECOND TERM: POLITICAL INFLUENCE FROM 1840 TO 1846

Norton's interest in politics did not end with the closing of her Storey's Gate salon. Even in the midst of the troubles of 1836, she wrote to Melbourne: "I have been reading the debate of last night—it is the first thing for *three weeks*, that has made me forget my own affairs for awhile"; furthermore, she clearly had not forgotten the vision of the traveler flinging "himself down on the green turf": "I see you were beat but it will only make the struggle more determined. Let me know that you were not the worse for the fatigue & late hour of breaking up" (*LCN* 107). Of course, Melbourne could no longer avail himself of her solace, and by the time Peel succeeded him in 1841, he was much the worse for fatigue. She, by contrast, was comparatively youthful, still in her early thirties; had survived the wish "from my soul & most earnestly" (*LCN* 100) to be in the grave; and found that both energy and ambition had revived.

After the trial, Norton lived with her bachelor uncle Charles Sheridan, whose companionship added an element of propriety to the anomalous position of a wife separated from her husband. Under greater financial pressure than ever, she pursued literary interests with new urgency and set out to reclaim her social standing. In addition to acting as hostess for the unmarried Samuel Rogers, she entertained for her uncle at Green Street. While Melbourne no longer came, any number of lesser known politicians and literary friends might be found there, including Thomas Talfourd, who helped her with the bill to modify child custody law, and Bulwer Lytton. Just as Disraeli found his way to her salon a decade before, another young and driven politician, Sidney Herbert, discovered that he enjoyed the company gathered around her. After Charles Sheridan's death in 1843, Norton moved into her own house on Bolton Street, where friends continued to congregate, including Hayward, Lockhart, Kinglake, and the Duff Gordons.

Herbert's visits came to rival Melbourne's in frequency and intimacy, but they lacked the condoning presence of a spouse. Even before her uncle's death, rumors abounded concerning their friendship. Norton wrote exasperatedly about the storm of rumor that swirled around her. For example, to Mrs. Gore:

> I write—(not very connectedly because I am ill & feverish)—to *you* ~~*if*~~ (oh! foolish word!) *when* you hear that I have eloped from my Uncle, you will deny it—& when you hear . . . that I have been "honey mooning in a cottage with my love," you will deny it.[33]

She was especially hounded by gossip when she lived alone, prompting this note to Mrs. Hall:

> someone having expressed their doubt as to there being any *rabbit* in the burrow no. 24 of [the] Bolton St. *Warren*—(it never being seen skipping

hopping and nibbling out of its hole, as a true rabbit ought,) I was suddenly greeted with a shower of anxious notes. "*Are* you in town?" I wish I could write a comedy![34]

The situation might have been rendered comically in literature; however, it was anything but laughable in real life. When Locock warned of rumors circulating about her, she replied in frustration:

whereas I was extremely fond of my male friends and glad to welcome them I now receive them with fidgetty suspicion—you have spoilt the honest cordiality of countenance with which I answered their inquiries after my general health. . . . [A] general cold water cure is prescribed for all callers—and I am't near as happy as I was.[35]

Herbert, however, proved impervious to the cold water treatment, and it became widely rumored that they were lovers.[36]

The second son of the Earl of Pembroke, Sidney Herbert found the gossip about his affairs particularly embarrassing in light of his older brother's activities, which included simultaneous affairs with two ballet dancers. The dancers' rivalry spilled spectacularly onto the stage one evening in 1844 when his mistresses began to fight during a performance. Sensing that Melbourne shared the general public's appetite for scandal, Norton reported to her old friend details garnered from Herbert and joked: "*tis* shameful that good dancers should make false steps so often" (*LCN* 166). The risqué humor typifies their correspondence but also betrays blindness to her own missteps. Although resenting her neighbors' insinuating questions, she did not act with discretion. Her boast to the former home secretary almost invites a fall: "My Secretary [the position Herbert held in the Admiralty] is too intellectual to get into those sort of scrapes. Love be damned, as an idle vagabond boy, is our motto, and that is a great satisfaction" (*LCN* 166).

The tenor of Norton's second salon was different from the first. Melbourne, a generation older and vastly more experienced, sought diversion in the company of a youthful, beautiful, and intelligent woman. Herbert, by contrast, was a contemporary who, although a member of the House since 1832, did not receive a cabinet post until 1845. She provided, therefore, not only fish dinners in a grand style (which she could not afford) but also the sage counsel of one who had been a long-term confidante of a prime minister. Norton clearly enjoyed the role of Aspasia to the relative neophyte to whom she referred with fond condescension as "My Secretary."

Herbert, in turn, an ally of Peel and friend of Gladstone, provided her with the conduit to the center of government that had been closed since 1836.

Despite differences in party allegiance, Norton and Herbert shared an innate sympathy for the underprivileged; indeed, it was the keynote of his—as it was of her—political philosophy. A line from one of his speeches serves as the epigraph to *The Child of the Islands*: "There is too little communication between classes in this country. We want, if not the feeling, at least the expression, of more sympathy on the part of the rich towards the poor; and more personal intercourse between them" (*CI* vi). If the *cause célèbre* of the thirties was the Reform Bill, that of the forties was the Corn Laws. Norton and Herbert agreed that high tariffs on imported grain resulted in an economic hardship for the poor; ironically, it was this issue that ended their association. When Peel determined that it was necessary to reverse the government's support of the Corn Laws, he was mortified that the change of policy was announced in the *Times* (December 4, 1846) even before his own party had been fully informed. Almost immediately it was rumored—falsely—that Norton, via Herbert, was responsible for the leak. Falsely accused, as she had been before, she again found herself driven from office. Although her relationship with Herbert was one casualty of the furor, the primary one was the Peel government itself.

Herbert, like Melbourne, escaped the controversy relatively unscathed. He became engaged shortly thereafter, and it was noted that Norton "behaved very well on the occasion and assured him when he married she would never cross his path."[37] He went on to a happy family life and a distinguished public career, although he died at a comparatively young age in 1861. Norton resigned herself to her fate, quietly accepting the end of her second and final term in office. In *The Lady of La Garaye* (1866), she eulogized Herbert in terms that seem better suited to a lost lover than a fallen public servant. She recalls that his eyes were "like stars in darkness":

> Oh! eyes I first knew in our mutual youth.
> So full of limpid earnestness and truth;
> Eyes I saw fading still, as day by day
> The body, not the spirit's strength, gave way;
> Eyes that I last saw lifting their farewell
> To the now darkened windows where I dwell.
> (*LLG* 145–46)

Those darkened windows mark the end of Norton's political career; the house of fiction, by contrast, remained brightly illuminated. Having been long and (in)famously affiliated with prominent politicians of both parties, Norton was an appealing subject to fellow novelists, not as Blessington's "personification of a muse" but as a prominent political hostess.

Fictional Portraits

Although the first salon was more sensational, Norton's connection with Herbert raised greater novelistic interest. Trollope, Disraeli, and Meredith were all drawn to the poignant situation of the modern-day Aspasia. The marital history and truncated political career of Lady Laura Kennedy in *Phineas Finn* (1869) bear significant resemblances to Norton's. Her protégé Phineas serves as an undersecretary in the office in which Herbert served. Unhappily married and supplanted by Madame Max Goesler in Phineas's heart, Lady Laura embodies the loneliness and the bitterness resulting from unfulfilled political and romantic aspirations. *Endymion* (1880) is a roman à clef that freely combines aspects of many figures to capture the tenor of the years leading up to Disraeli's becoming prime minister. Norton's relationships with Melbourne and Herbert are dramatized in Lady Berengaria Montfort's admiration for Lord Roehampton and dedication to Endymion Ferrars. In *Diana of the Crossways*, Meredith uses the Melbourne affair (depicted in Diana's friendship with an aging head of state, Lord Dannisburgh) as a backdrop for the Norton / Herbert relationship (represented by an aspiring young lion, Percy Dacier). Despite differences in emphasis, each novel depicts the strains visited upon the petticoat politician, whose ambition must be simultaneously channeled into the contradictory roles of mother / mentor and wife / lover to her personal Pericles.

Readers of Norton's work encountered in portraits by Maclise, Hayter, Landseer, and Carrick, among others, a woman variously idealized as a supreme beauty and domestic goddess. Readers of fiction about her find an equally beautiful but a more flawed human figure. The literary portraits by Trollope, Disraeli, and Meredith show a woman of ambition and accomplishment, whose missteps and selective blindnesses further compromise an already tenuous position. The complex intersection of sexuality and authorship implicit in the visual images is explored in narratives that foreground the crossways of gender and politics. Love and political advocacy are impossibly complicated by encompassing social and legal contexts.

Laura Kennedy, Berengaria Montfort, and Diana Warwick are Aspasias whose salons become schools for scandal but also provide invaluable tutelage in pragmatic politics. Those who matriculate—Endymion certainly, Dacier probably, and Phineas possibly (once Lady Laura and the taint of scandal have given way to Madame Max and the benefit of money)—are destined for careers of distinction. In two cases, Aspasia is rewarded with marriage; only Trollope accurately depicts the nearly life-long isolation experienced by Norton. In this important regard, although she is the only character not directly based upon Norton, Lady Laura is the most like her.

(i) TROLLOPE'S LAURA KENNEDY

The Nortons have been cited as a possible influence upon *He Knew He Was Right* (1869), but an even stronger case exists for *Phineas Finn* and the marriage of Robert Kennedy and Laura Standish.[38] Lady Laura's inveterate love of politics reflects Norton's, and she, too, finds that intellectual interests and political ambitions are frustrated by an uncongenial husband, sexual scandal, and the hardships visited upon a married woman living alone. Lady Laura's public opinions, especially the lament that women can have no direct role in politics and the complaint that British laws fail to protect married women, directly mirror Norton's. Trollope appears to have drawn upon a familiar public figure in two significant ways: first, the Kennedys' marriage, political jealousies, and legal situation reflect central aspects of the Nortons' history, and, second, Lady Laura's love for "her political godchild" (*PF* 1:248) bears marked similarities to Norton's intimacy with Sidney Herbert. Trollope conflates Norton's two stints as political hostess into a single term, in which the roles of Melbourne, who incites a jealous husband's ire, and Herbert, who elicits a lonely wife's love, are played by a single character, Phineas Finn.

The similarities between the real and the fictional petticoat politicians begin with their manner. Given that Lady Laura is an active woman of pronounced views and independent thought, it is perhaps inevitable that she, like Norton, would be pejoratively described as masculine. With a face lacking "that softness which we all love in women" (*PF* 1:31), she is famous for eyes more challenging than flirtatious: they

> never seemed to quail, never rose and sunk or showed themselves to be afraid of their own power.... She ... would lean forward when sitting, as a man does, and would use her arms in talking, and would put her hand over her face,

and pass her fingers through her hair,—after the fashion of men rather than of women.

(*PF* 1:33)

Red rather than raven hair signals her forays into discursive venues and topics typically restricted to men. Lady Laura "professed to have a care for all the affairs of the world. She loved politics, and could talk of social science, and had broad ideas about religion, and was devoted to certain educational views" (*PF* 1:120). Possessing the conversational manner and interests of men, she readily agrees with Madame Max that the "one great drawback to the life of women is that they cannot act in politics" (*PF* 2:26).

Lady Laura resolves to pursue the next best thing, marrying Robert Kennedy in order to become a powerful political wife. This act suggests that she might not support equality for women, and in this regard she is in accord with Norton: "the cause of the Rights of Women generally was odious to her; but nevertheless, for herself, she delighted in hoping that she too might be useful,—in thinking that she too was perhaps, in some degree, politically powerful" (*PF* 1:89). Norton's motives for marrying remain a matter of speculation, but Lady Laura's choice is guided solely by the desire to make the "half a life" allotted to her as influential as possible. She "looked at the world almost as a man looked at it,—as an oyster to be opened with such weapon as she could find ready to her hand" (*PF* 1:120). Rejecting the impecunious outsider Phineas, she accepts Kennedy, even though she does not love him, because he seems able to place her within the "halo of statecraft" (*PR* 1:358) surrounding the Whig aristocracy. In

marrying Mr. Kennedy she had maintained herself in her high position, among the first of her own people,—among the first socially and among the first politically. But had she married Phineas,—had she become Lady Laura Finn,—there would have been a great descent. She could not have entertained the leading men of her party.

(*PF* 2:157)

Kennedy, however, entirely lacks vision and energy. He, like George Norton, is indolent, maladroit, and indifferent to fame: "He rarely did anything, although he had the means of doing everything. He had very seldom been on his legs in the House though he had sat there for ten years" (*PF* 1:41). These limitations are brought into strong relief as a result of marriage to a socially adept and ambitious woman.

His lack of initiative prompts Phineas to comment, "Great Akinetoses! You know Orion. . . ." (Trollope's ellipsis, *PF* 1:88). In R. H. Horne's *Orion*, Akinetos is "the Great Unmoved," the personification of indolence, as opposed to Orion, who is "ever active and at work,/Honest and skilful."[39] Phineas may or may not be right about the implied comparison between himself and Orion, but he is certainly correct that Kennedy is unlikely to feel the urgency of any political measure. He possesses nothing of the "halo of statecraft" and doggedly follows a course illuminated by his own rather dim interior light. Recognizing that "her intellect was brighter than his," Lady Laura had hoped that "it might be possible for her to lead him" (*PF* 1:209), but his intransigence, uncompromising temper, and cold, imperious will defeat her. Kennedy terminates his wife's fondest hope, forbidding her "to meddle with high politics, to discuss reform bills, to assist in putting up Mr. This and putting down my Lord That" (*PF* 1:209).

Foreclosed from acting through her husband, Lady Laura throws all of her energy into the career of her "Phoebus Apollo" (*PF* 2:66), who willingly accepts the assistance refused by Akinetos. When Kennedy takes offense at her unguarded enthusiasm for the career of her former suitor, she willfully puts the worst interpretation on his objections in order to justify leaving him (*PF* 2:243). In impotent frustration, Kennedy follows the example of George Norton and turns to the press to publicize his grievances. His letter to *The People's Banner* condemns his wife, demands her return, and "expatiate[s] on the absolute and almost divine right which it was intended that a husband should exercise over his wife, and quoted both the Old and New Testament in proof of his assertions" (*PR* 1:199). George's announcement in the newspapers was equally self-righteous but even more venal; he enumerated Caroline's wrongdoings and concluded:

> to protect myself, therefore, against such proceedings, I hereby give notice . . . that I will not be answerable for any debts she may have contracted since the 30th of March, 1836, or hereafter may contract, and that she has no authority to contract debts or deal with any one on my credit.
>
> (*L* 64)

As in *He Knew He Was Right*, the positions of the alienated couple become more firmly entrenched. Lady Laura knows enough to tell her husband, "You have the law on your side" (*PF* 1:113), but she does not realize how completely this is so until after leaving him. There are no children to be sequestered in Scotland, but she discovers that she is little more than chattel: "Is a woman like a head of cattle, that she can be fastened in her crib by force? I will never live with him though all the judges of the land should decide that I must do so" (*PF* 2:303). Remaining in England exposes her "to very disagreeable attempts from Mr. Kennedy to force me to go back again" (*PF* 2:347), so she takes up exile in Europe. Kennedy becomes obsessed with her return, a monomania leading to insanity. While many construed the Greenacre persona and George's erratic behavior after 1836 as signs of insanity, Trollope leaves no ambiguity about Kennedy's descent into madness.

Kennedy's early death means that his widow might return to England and to politics, but she has changed, too. She is no longer as interested in the life that once was everything to her:

> I could go again and sit in that cage in the House of Commons to hear you [Phineas] and other men speak,—as I used to do. I do not believe that any eloquence in the world would make it endurable to me. I hardly care who is in or out.
>
> (*PR* 2:274)

The Cage is the visitors' room open to women, which Norton referred to as "that political pretense, the 'Ladies' Gallery' in the House of Commons" (*LS* 233). The irony of the term is self-evident, and Norton exploited it throughout her career. In *Love in "the World"*, Alice Sinclair visits the Cage: " 'And this is the ventilator!' said our heroine as she entered the large cold and dreary apartment where the wives and sisters of young members may creep unseen, unheard, in breathless anxiety to the eight-inch-square hole where they may hear those dear familiar tones which gladden their homes" (*LW* 2:34–5). "The ventilator" is an ironic name for such a suffocating space, however apt it might be for the speechifying that takes place outside it, but eight square inches accurately conveys the dimensions of the political stage open to women. Madame Max self-consciously invokes the echoing ironies of the term:

> A poor woman, shut up in a cage, feels there more acutely than anywhere else how insignificant a position she fills in the world. . . . Knowing our inferiority I submit without a grumble; but I am not sure that I care to go and listen to the squabbles of my masters. . . . I cannot take so much interest in the proceedings as to spend my time listening where I cannot speak, and in looking when I cannot be seen.
>
> (*PR* 1:288)

In marrying Phineas, Madame Max acquires the only political role open to her, that of political wife and hostess.

The second Nortonesque element in Trollope's portrayal of the political hostess is seen in Lady Laura's political tutelage. A likeable but undistinguished neophyte, Phineas is so much political clay to be shaped by those—primarily women—around him. Lady Laura is responsible for his initial election (*PF* 1:30, 2:293), and when his reelection becomes doubtful, she single-handedly arranges for him to represent the pocket borough controlled by her father. Even after the scandal of her broken marriage, she attempts an epistolary campaign from the Continent to advance his career. Since it is widely believed that she left her husband because she and Phineas were lovers, her patronage is no longer effective or welcome—a bitter circumstance shared with Norton: "Who would care to have me at their houses, or to come to mine? . . . I am as much lost to the people who did know me in London as though I had been buried for a century. A man makes himself really useful, but a woman can never do that" (*PR* 1:103). Phineas's usefulness continues despite the "wretched charge [that] had been made against him which, though wholly untrue, was as it were so strangely connected with the truth, that slanderers might not improbably be able almost to substantiate their calumnies" (*PR* 1:329). His distinguished political career leaves Lady Laura, like Norton before her, resentful of the success to which she contributed, in which she cannot share, and against which her own enforced inactivity stands in marked contrast.

Initially, Phineas willingly embraces the role of Telemachus to Lady Laura's Mentor (*PF* 1:124). As with Norton and Herbert, their ages are actually quite close, but the wise female counselor is more experienced than her protégé. Thus Phineas imagines that she is "somewhat older than himself" (*PF* 1:33), and she herself says: "A mentor ought to be very old, you know, and I am infinitely older than you are" (*PF* 1:74). As feelings of love intertwine with political tutelage, he reconsiders their respective ages and feels "himself to be older than she,—if, indeed, there was any difference in their ages" (*PF* 1:125). In the closing stage of their relation, their relative ages change again: "Lady Laura took upon herself the tone and manners of an elder sister,—of a sister very much older than her brother" (*PR* 1:108). When she returns to England, Phineas is "struck by the great change in her look and manner. She seemed to him to be old and worn, and he judged her to be wretched,—as she was" (*PF* 2:164). They had met only six years before: "Then she had been three-and-twenty, and had not looked to be a day older. Now she might have been taken to be nearly forty, so much had her troubles preyed upon her spirit, and eaten into the vitality of her youth" (*PF* 2:346). She is now almost the age at which Norton, less than a year after the trial, told Melbourne, "I feel as if these few months had turned me into an old woman!" (*LCN* 131). For both perhaps, but certainly for Lady Laura, Mentor is now Sybil—aged, caged, and waiting to die.

In their early thirties, both Lady Laura and Norton felt their lives to be over (*PR* 2:270–71). Both are querulous and melodramatically think of their own deaths. Lady Laura retires to her father's estate to oversee his final days, complaining to Phineas:

> I cannot pretend to say that my bereavements or misfortunes reconcile me to such a fate. I cannot cease to remember my age, my ambition, and I will say, my love. I suppose that everything is over for me—as though I were an old woman, going down into the grave, but at my time of life I find it hard to believe that it must be so. And then the time of waiting may be so long!
>
> (*PR* 2:334–35)

Her words echo Norton's to Melbourne in April 1836:

> I cannot think what spell is on my life that it should *finish* so much sooner than others.... *They* [her siblings] all talk & think of nothing but their future, and I alone stand amongst them, looking back, far back, and thinking that if I could make my peace with God, it would be as well to die *now*, as to wait.
>
> (*LCN* 69)

Readers are not told how long Lady Laura may have waited; for Norton, it would be 40 years until George's death released her from the cage of marriage.

Phineas Redux concludes with a summary of Lady Laura's life that one imagines Trollope intends to be definitive: "Of Lady Laura hardly a word need be said. She lives at Saulsby the life of a recluse" (*PR* 2:360). She is mentioned only once in the final Palliser novels, in the context of a threatened renewal of the old scandal (which for the Nortons occurred after a period of 17 years). She becomes all but invisible, lingering as a spectral reminder of past events that Quintus Slide claims are, "if not . . . criminal, . . . at any rate . . . disgraceful" (*PM* 2:207–8). At this point the similarities between Lady Laura and Norton necessarily end. Lady Laura, like Clara Bellsize, fades out of the picture. Plot lines may come to a clear close, but lives are apt to drag on. Given the Nortons' protracted marital dispute, the recrudescence of the Melbourne scandal in 1853, and the inheritance battle following George's death, one may wonder whether Lady Laura's were not the kinder fate.

(ii) DISRAELI'S BERENGARIA MONTFORT

Disraeli's final novel, *Endymion*, consists of "imaginative recollections" of more than three decades of political life.[40] The work makes no attempt at historical accuracy, but it brilliantly captures the character of mid-Victorian society and politics by freely grafting traits of different historical figures onto single fictional characters. Interspersed throughout are summaries of more than 30 years of British political history. At the end of a long political career and from the perspective of the 1880s, Disraeli surveys the past with equanimity, insight, and an element of nostalgia. Recalling his early years as a silver fork novelist and friend of the Three Graces, he describes post-Regency society in terms that echo Bulwer Lytton and Thackeray:

> The great world then, compared with the huge society of the present period, was limited in its proportions, and composed of elements more refined though far less various.... [T]hose vast and successful invasions of society by new classes which have since occurred, though impending, had not yet commenced.... Conversation was more cultivated; manners, though unconstrained, were more stately; and the world, being limited, knew itself much better. On the other hand, the sympathies of society were more contracted than they are at present. The pressure of population had not opened the heart of man.... They were only half born.
>
> (*E* 1:32–33)

The "great world" is part of a remote and irretrievable past:

> The Government... was not only deemed strong, but eternal. The favour of the Court and the confidence of the country were alike lavished on it. The government of the Duke could only be measured by his life, and his influence was irresistible. It was a dictatorship of patriotism.
>
> (*E* 1:31)

Post-Regency convulsions—"Canadian revolts, Chartist insurrections, squabbles, and mysterious complications in Central Asia" (*E* 1:35)—form the backdrop of the novel, which chronicles the machinations of fictional petticoat politicians from the end of one Tory government, Wellington's, to the beginning of another, that of Disraeli himself.

Endymion Ferrars, like Phineas Finn, has good reason to believe that "everything in this world depends upon woman" (*E* 2:14). His vague aspirations are shaped and actively promoted by Myra, his sister; by Berengaria Montfort, his mentor; and by Adriana Neuchatel, the heiress who finances his first parliamentary election. Myra's observation to her brother—"Women will be your best friends in life" (*E* 2:203)—echoes the situation of Phineas, who "had always gone to some woman—in old days to Lady Laura, or to Violet Effingham, or to Madame Goesler. By them he could endure to be petted, praised, or upon occasion even pitied" (*PR* 1:287). Lady Montfort, who is identified as Norton in the "Key to the Principal Characters," offers a remarkably sensitive portrait of her character, although Disraeli takes great license with the facts of her life. His "Norton" is essentially in the position of Lady Holland, allowing him to combine the temper of his friend with the situation of a powerful Whig hostess. The personal and the political relations of Berengaria and Endymion, however, directly reflect those of Norton and Herbert during the crisis over the repeal of the Corn Laws, although at the end of the novel, the now widowed Berengaria is allowed to marry her protégé.

Berengaria is decisive, independent, and astute, but also flirtatious, outspoken, and unconventional. She possesses a "nature . . . singularly frank and fearless" (*E* 2:34), but also a "passion for admiration" and a "reputation for being capricious" (*E* 2:30, 188)—traits to which Disraeli did not add a masculine inflection. Many of Norton's tics and idiosyncrasies are found in her fictional counterpart, including a reputation for "witty raillery" (*E* 2:29), sometimes at the expense of her husband. For example, sounding rather like Bessie Glenallan, Lady Montfort provocatively professes to "dislike married men. They are very uninteresting" (*E* 2:16). Her forceful opinions and decided delivery lead a friend to protest, "how can you use such strong expressions? . . . Do not say such things" (*E* 2:122–23). She, however, delights in provocative pronouncements and generally shares Norton's disregard for social convention. Late entrances, for instance, which further the objective of being "in every place . . . the cynosure" (*E* 1:319), are a hallmark of both. Each woman "required everybody about her to be gay and diverting," hence Berengaria, with far greater resources than her real-life counterpart, stages "in the evenings a carnival . . . games and dances, and infinite frolic" (*E* 1:332). Disraeli makes the Eglinton Tournament entirely her brainchild, suggesting yet another of Norton's distinguishing attributes, her dynamism: "What was most remarkable, and most interesting, in the character of Berengaria was her energy" (*E* 1:366).

The portrait of Norton's character is remarkably accurate. Although requiring and encouraging "constant admiration," Lady Montfort is "not a heartless coquette. . . . Whenever she made a friend not unworthy of her, she was constant and entirely devoted" (*E* 1:367). Disraeli also recognized that Norton never felt truly loved. Despite her allure and beauty, her high spirits and intellect, Berengaria exhibits the "*sauvagerie*" that Norton had noted in her own character. She consistently feels more loving than loved, and tells Endymion: "I loved your sister, but she did not love me. Nobody that I love ever does love me" (*E* 2:204). Subject to "momentary despondency" and nagging sadness, she laments: "Heigho! I may be the greatest lady of our court, but I am a very unhappy woman" (*E* 2:202, 201).

Her marriage to Lord Montfort is practically motivated and quickly develops into a case of the invisible spouse. After failing to win her husband's love, she remarks with resignation: "At any rate they cannot say my lord and I are separated. We need not live under the same roof, but so long as I live under his roof the world considers us united" (*E* 2:197). As with the Nortons and Kennedys, a determined wife is coupled with a self-involved and indolent man:

> Lady Montfort was a woman of far-reaching ambition. In a certain degree, she had married to secure her lofty aims; and yet it was only by her singular energy, and the playfulness and high spirit of her temperament, that the sacrifice had not proved a failure; her success, however, was limited, for the ally on whom she had counted rarely assisted and never sympathized with her.
>
> (*E* 2:223)

Her husband, like Robert Kennedy, is an Akinetos, whose indolence and egoism are impervious to uxorial influence:

> A man of your position ought to govern the country, and it always was so in old days. Your family were prime ministers; why not you, with as much talent, and much more knowledge?
>
> You would make a very good prime minister, Berengaria.
>
> Ah! You always jest; I am serious.
>
> And so am I.
>
> (*E* 1:338)

Frustrated in her marriage, she sets about fulfilling political ambition in other ways: "For myself, I must have a male friend, and he must be very clever, and thoroughly understand politics" (*E* 2:123).

Endymion proves to be "so agreeable and so intelligent, that at last I . . . found a companion worth helping—and I . . . mean to work hard—until he is Prime Minister" (*E* 2:123). Endymion's passive and indecisive character requires constant prodding, reassurance, and direction. He seems, like the society of his youth, only "half-born" and is very much in need of a mother to complete the process. At one point Berengaria, with a "mixture of surprise, a little disdain, some affection blended with mockery," calls him a "[s]illy boy" (*E* 1:391), and readers are likely to agree. Like Phineas, he is dependent upon the strong women around him: "Lady Montfort . . . could do what she liked with Endymion Ferrars; that was quite certain. Supposed by men to have a strong will and a calm judgment, he was a nose of wax with this woman" (*E* 2:240). Whatever a wax nose might imply for his romantic future, it is a positive political augury. Berengaria is able to guide her "slave" (*E* 2:230) into the House, into a house (which she has purchased and furnished for him, rewriting the Greenacre plot as a quasi-feminist love story), and ultimately into 10 Downing Street.

If Berengaria is Selene to Endymion, she is also Aspasia: "Poor Endymion . . . would do nothing without consulting her, and . . . was moulded, and . . . wished to be moulded, in all his thoughts and feelings, and acts, and conduct, by her inspiring will" (*E* 2:223). She seizes upon the government's reversal on the Corn Laws in 1846 to prod him into action. Although neither Norton nor Berengaria was guilty of betraying secrets on this occasion, it could not be said that either was above trafficking in them. The accusation against Norton was fueled by her reputation for indiscretion. After leaving office in 1841, for example, Melbourne was displeased to learn that her injudicious talk allowed Peel to discover his ongoing correspondence with the Queen.[41] Berengaria is more likely to be indiscreet by calculation rather than carelessness. When she learns that the government is unable to establish a strong trade policy (the issue that led to Melbourne's resignation in 1841) and will in likelihood call for new elections, she immediately takes the intelligence that "nobody knows . . . not five people" (*E* 2:13) to Endymion. He does not recognize his chance to enter the House and must be told: "This is a crisis for our party, but it is something more for you" (*E* 2:14). Privy to gossip and unofficial secrets—"from a high authority, . . . not told me as a real secret" (*E* 2:234)—she considers how they might be put to her advantage. An earlier example is the young Queen's impending marriage (*E* 2:3), "which is not yet Punchinello's secret, though I dare say it will be known when we all return to town. . . . As Lord Roehampton wrote to me this morning, 'Our royal marriage will be much more popular than the Anti-Corn-Law League'" (*E* 2:3). Initially a supporter of the Corn Laws, Berengaria welcomes a distraction from the issue in 1837. Ten years later, tariff reform is an ineluctable movement to be used rather than resisted. Lady Montfort, not Endymion, recognizes the difference, therein confirming Disraeli's sense that "men not measures" or, in the form appropriate to *Endymion*, "women not measures" is the first law of politics.

(iii) MEREDITH'S DIANA WARWICK

Diana of the Crossways is a portrait of a person rather than an age; it lacks, in Jack Lindsay's view, "the deep Meredithian political focus."[42] It is the only one of these novels to follow the outlines of Norton's life carefully, although important elements are left out (the children) or invented (remarriage at a young age) as Meredith attempts to convey the experience of a woman struggling to make her way in mid-Victorian society or to satisfy the tastes of late Victorian readers.[43] It is also the only one of these novels to consider the woman as writer as well as petticoat politician. Meredith's goal is imaginatively to reconstruct the psyche of the person who might have had the experiences that Norton had. His psychological portrait is centered in two contexts, both of which qualify the assertion that the novel is without political focus. On the one hand, Diana's circumstances epitomize the legal and social dilemma of married women in nineteenth-century England. Although she does not take up specific legislative causes, her political philosophy is similar to Norton's and goes well beyond the preoccupation of Berengaria Montfort and Laura Kennedy with parties and power. On the other hand, Diana, as author as well as salonnière, is thoroughly invested in the elegant and witty use of language. Her conversation and socializing enable Meredith to dramatize the literary-political salon of the kind associated with figures like Norton and Blessington.

The salient biographical correspondences in *Diana of the Crossways* are unmistakable: an unhappy marriage, an intimate friendship with an aging but "eminent member of the Cabinet" (*DC* 1:89), and a romantic association with a young Tory politician that is abruptly terminated by the publication of a government secret concerning the Corn Laws. In the manner of an interpretive biographer, Meredith offers psychological explanations for several of Norton's puzzling acts, including her first marriage. Diana selects an unsuccessful attorney, for whom she can muster no more enthusiasm than to describe him as "a gentlemanly official" (*DC* 1:59), because, single and without family, she has been subjected to unwelcome sexual advances. She seeks "a protector, called husband—rashly, past credence, in retrospect; but it had been her propelling motive" (*DC* 1:152–53). Far from defending her, Augustus Warwick publicly and falsely accuses her of adultery. From this point on, "she was in the arena of the savage claws, flung there by the man who of all others should have protected her from them" (*DC* 1:133).

Meredith's primary point is that savagery in modern arenas is both authorized and disguised by chivalric conceptions of marriage. Diana abjures "rosy mediævalism" (*DC* 2:90) in favor of more enlightened values for women: "Liberty to grow: independence is the key of the secret" (*DC* 2:91). She describes her husband as "the average Englishman, excelling as a cavalier, a slayer, and an orderly subject" (*DC* 1:81). English customs and values disguise their violence—just as Meredith embeds the seemingly incongruous "slayer" in the midst of "cavalier" and "orderly subject." Diana discovers that her knight is, at best, a nullity and, at worst, an abusive and controlling man. The concealed connection between average and savage is implied by the pointed comparison of Warwick to "a house locked up and empty:—a London house conventionally furnished and decorated by the upholsterer, and empty of inhabitants" (*DC* 1:83). Her words provide a haunting echo of the Greenacre episode: the description of Warwick's mind uncannily reflects George's choice of meeting place with his estranged wife. Her husband is figuratively, not physically, abusive, but the effect of his behavior is reflected in Diana's novel, *The Cantatrice*, whose protagonist is beaten by her husband/manager (*DC* 1:227).

Meredith employs national stereotypes of garrulity and incommunicativeness to signify the discord between husband and wife (he is English, she Irish). The English

> feel toward the quick-witted of their species as to aliens, having the demerits of aliens—wordiness, vanity, obscurity, shallowness, an empty glitter, the sin of posturing. A quick-witted woman exerting her wit is both a foreigner and potentially a criminal. . . . What is the husband of a vanward woman? The English husband of a voluble woman relapses into a dreary mute.
>
> (*DC* 1:140–41)

Augustus cannot forgive his wife's "sallies" and "trick of 'using men's phrases'" (*DC* 1:178), nor can she hide her disdain of his limitations.

The narrator's summary accurately describes the early years of the Nortons' married life:

> Her dissensions with her husband, their differences of opinion, and puny wranglings, hoistings of two standards, reconciliations for the sake of decency, breaches of the truce, and his detested meanness, the man behind the mask; and glimpses of herself too, the half-known, half-suspected, developing creature claiming to be Diana, and unlike her dreamed Diana, deformed by marriage, irritable, acerb, rebellious, constantly justifiable against him, but not in her own mind, and therefore accusing him of the double crime of provoking her and perverting her.
>
> (*DC* 1:132)

Discovering too late her incompatibility with her husband, Diana finds an outlet in her friendship with the senior Whig statesman, Lord Dannisburgh. His attention excites the political interests of a "young woman of fervid mind, a reader of public speeches and speculator on the tides of politics.... She had been flattered... to believe that she could exercise a judgement in politics—could think, even speak acutely, on public affairs" (*DC* 1:188). He calls her a "crystal spring of wisdom," and after seeing them together, even her level-headed friend Emma Dunstane "could firmly believe in... his winning ideas from the abounding bubbling well" (*DC* 1:90). The flattery is not disingenuous, but it is perhaps taken too much to heart by the youthful enthusiast, who explains to Emma that she does have a role to play in Dannisburgh's career: "I see him almost daily;... as long as he does me the honour to esteem my poor portion of brains by coming to me for what he is good enough to call my counsel, I shall let the world wag its tongue" (*DC* 1:90). If sensible of the dangers of her situation, she is insufficiently attentive to them, thinking that wagging tongues can simply be ignored.

In celebrating her association with Egeria, Diana perhaps does not realize that the young princess was also King Numa's lover. The excitement of having a more significant role than that of providing fish dinners at Greenwich blinds her to the rashness of her behavior: "The moral repute of the great Whig lord and the beauty of the lady composed inflammable material" (*DC* 1:89). The fires of gossip ultimately ignite Augustus's cold jealousy and lead to his unsuccessful divorce action. Despite the verdict, Diana's detractors react just as "bull-dogs are expected to do when they have got a grip of one. It is a point of muscular honour with them never to relax their hold" (*DC* 1:265). When it is subsequently revealed that Dannisburgh has provided for

Diana in his will (as Melbourne had done for Norton), the "social Gods renewed their combat, and the verdict of the jury was again overhauled" (*DC* 1:265). The narrator sarcastically concludes,

> Oh!—the British Lucretia was very properly not legally at home to the masculine world of that day. She plied her distaff in pure seclusion, meditating on her absent lord; or else a fair proportion of the masculine world, which had not yet, has not yet, 'doubled Cape Turk,' approved her condemnation to the sack.
>
> (*DC* 1:265–66)

The reference is to one of Diana's aphorisms, whose truth is painfully borne out in her own case: "*Men may have rounded Seraglio Point: they have not yet doubled Cape Turk*" (*DC* 1:13); that is, the men of England may have made progress on the voyage to civilization and the fair treatment of women, but they have a long way to go.

Diana begins a literary career out of economic necessity, and her success soon brings writers and journalists to her door. The mainstays of her salon are Whitmonby (Samuel Rogers), an editor; Westlake (Alexander Kinglake), "an Oriental traveler" (*DC* 2:76); and Henry Wilmers (Charles Greville), whose diary records many of Diana's epigrams (*DC* 1:12–17). In addition, there are "other gentlemen, literary and military" (*DC* 2:85) and an occasional politician, notably Percy Dacier, Dannisburgh's nephew and a rising figure among the Tories. The swarm of male activity generates the aura of bohemianism conducive to a successful salon but fatal to much that Diana has gained by courting the approval of social matrons following her public disgrace. As she herself observes, her reputation is a kind of scarlet letter, "an immovable patch—attractive to male idiots, I have heard, and a mark of scorn to females. Between the two the remainder of my days will be lively" (*DC* 1:152).

With the mavens of propriety, she curbs her tongue in order to conform to the social dictum that women be "conversationally fair Circassians" (*DC* 1:6):

> Wherever Mrs. Warwick went, her arts of charming were addressed to the women. Men may be counted on for falling bowled over by a handsome face and pointed tongue; women require some wooing from their ensphered and charioted sister, particularly if she is clouded; and old women—excellent

buttresses—must be suavely courted. Now, to woo the swimming matron and court the settled dowager, she had to win forgiveness for her beauty.

(*DC* 1:169)

In the company of male admirers, however, neither beauty nor wit is toned down. These gatherings are devoted to Wildean indulgence in learning and repartee. Rumor of these proceedings leads to indictment on two counts of "criminal conversation": first, speaking freely with men in the absence of her husband (and their wives), and second, professing independent political opinions. Lady Wathin is shocked "that hideous Radical Revolutionary things were openly spoken at Mrs. Warwick's evenings with her friends:—impudently named 'the elect of London' " (*DC* 1:267). Diana may be suspected of being a conversational criminal in the romantic sense, but she is surely one in the social sense. She speaks willingly and well on political topics.

Diana is hardly a rhetorical Jacobin. Like Norton, she is a famous storyteller, but even among men, her narratives are bowdlerized. In recounting a tale about a duel, for instance, she cites the refrain of one of the duelists as, "It's all nonsense," which leads a listener to whisper:

"A lady's way of telling the story!—and excusable to her—she had to *Jonah* the adjective. What the poor fellow said was. . . ." he murmured the sixty-pounder adjective, as in the belly of the whale, to rightly emphasize his noun.

Whitmonby nodded to the superior relish imparted by the vigour of masculine veracity in narration.

(Meredith's ellipsis, *DC* 2:87)

If "bloody" is the weighty word—which Meredith himself Jonahs—it is an aptly ominous one given the likely consequence of a duel. That it can be excusably swallowed by a woman suggests that the male conversationalists share some of the reticences of society at large. In this instance, however, the anecdote leads to a discussion of women's nature, to an appeal for liberty, and finally to Diana's conclusion that the conversation itself is an instance of "the eternal duel between us . . . , and men will protest that they are for civilization. Dear me, I should like to write a sketch of the women of the future—don't be afraid!—the far future. What a different earth you will see!" (*DC* 2:91–92). One imagines that her "Princess" would not be the creation of a group of Oxbridge undergraduates.

That sketch is not written, and she increasingly subordinates her writing career to Dacier's political future. While Norton referred to Herbert as "my Secretary," it was really she who assisted him, as Meredith intuits. Diana makes herself "a kind of secretary to Percy. I labour at making abstracts by day, and at night preside at my supper-table" (*DC* 2:119). He is "a sapling oak—inclined to droop. . . . I begin to perform Mrs. Dr. Pangloss on purpose to brighten him—the mind, the views" (*DC* 1:195). She also offers lessons in and occasions for "conversational gaiety" (*DC* 1:195). Because the guests are invited with political import rather than social comfort in mind, they are not always "perfectly assort[ed]," and she must "strain her adroitness to cover their deficiencies and fuse them. But what other woman could have done it! She led superbly" (*DC* 2:117). Assuming the "loquent lead" (*DC* 1:140), she encourages guests to "toss the ball from hand to hand" (*DC* 1:235), producing "political evenings and . . . social and anecdotal supper-nights" famous for talk that "ran always in perfect accord with [an] ideal of the conversational orchestra: an improvised harmony, unmatched elsewhere" (*DC* 2:116–17).

Conversational competence is only one of Diana's pedagogical objectives; she also provides hard lessons in *realpolitik*. Although she does not advocate sacrificing principles to political advantage, she recognizes that attention must be paid to the business of gaining, maintaining, and wielding political power. Principle holds that "the Repeal of the Corn Laws [is] the simple beginning of the grants due to the people" (*DC* 1:56); pragmatism recognizes that the political climate favoring protectionist tariffs has changed, and she urges Dacier and his party to seize the opportunity. She reasons that reversing the party line satisfies both national and political interests: repeal will not only serve "the inert but suffering majority" (*DC* 2:5) but also solidify the position of the government majority in Parliament. Her acute analysis and astute advice lead Dacier to refer to Diana in exactly the terms used by his uncle: she is "a Lady Egeria, helpful in counsel, prompting, inspiriting, reviving as well-waters, and as temperately cool" (*DC* 1:248–49, also see 2:9–10).

Diana is less clear-sighted—and certainly less cool—with regard to the state of her affections. Sir Lukin Dunstane, a Tory who believes that radicals are pulling down "the Institutions of the Country," singles out Dacier for wavering on the Corn Laws and insinuates that Diana is to blame: "You'll own it was the devil tempted you" (*DC* 2:57). Fearing that he has not made himself clear about the nature of the particular devil, he elaborates: "I was talking about women. They *are* the devil!—or he makes most use of them: and you must learn to see the cloven foot under their petticoats, if you're to escape them" (*DC* 2:58). Lukin, of course, is a foolish man whose nostalgia for the "Institutions of the Country" is unadulterated sentimentality and whose attitude toward women is evidenced by his own philandering—it was his attack that drove Diana to accept Warwick's proposal of marriage. Nevertheless, he articulates a widely held prejudice that invariably compromises even the limited political role open to women: their influence is a matter of cloven hooves rather than clever heads. Lady Wathin, while exempting herself from this account and arrogating to herself the status of "guardian . . . of morality" (*DC* 1:271), corroborates Sir Lukin's view of women's sexual powers and wiles:

> Mrs. Warwick undoubtedly was one of those women (of Satanic construction) who have the art of enslaving the men unhappy enough to cross their path. . . . She had the wiles of a Cleopatra, not without some of the Nilene's experiences. A youthful Antony-Dacier would be little likely to escape her toils.
>
> (*DC* 1:269–70)[44]

One might expect Lady Wathin to say "coils" rather than "toils," and her word choice reveals another of Meredith's points: few recognize the hard and often thankless labor of the political hostess. Diana drives herself to the point of exhaustion and bankruptcy to further Dacier's career. As the hostess, "it was her pride to provide Cleopatra banquets for the lover whose anxieties were soothed by them, and to whom she sacrificed her name willingly" (*DC* 2:117). She strains to manage his social affairs and her own complicated social position. The financial and emotional costs are substantial, but the greatest losses are to her integrity and independence. She plumps for Dacier in the press and mines friends for information that might be valuable to him. She rationalizes her actions by thinking, "Whether anything she wrote was her own, mattered little. . . . Besides she wrote to strengthen him; she naturally laid her friends and the world under contribution" (*DC* 2:107). Even her fiction is compromised by love. Her new novel is easily recognized as an idealized portrait of her protégé:

> THE YOUNG MINISTER OF STATE could be he only who was now at all her parties, always meeting her; had been spied walking with her daily in the park near her house on his march down to Westminster during the session. . . . What effrontery of the authoress, to placard herself with him in a book!
>
> (*DC* 1:270)

Only gradually and painfully does she recognize that the much-cherished independence of thought and circumstance gained by leaving her husband has been compromised by love: "An enamoured Egeria, who is not a princess in her worldy state nor a goddess by origin, has to play one of those parts which strain the woman's faculties past naturalness" (*DC* 2:82). What she has described as being "the busy bee at a window-pane" is more candidly formulated by the narrator: "she had voluntarily, profitlessly, become this man's drudge, and her sprightly fancy, her ready humour and darting look all round in discussion were rather deadened" (*DC* 2:120).

Her circle is broken up by Dacier's desertion following the betrayal of his secret about the government reversal on the Corn Laws. Although she has worked to liberalize his thinking on protective tariffs, the political victory becomes a Pyrrhic one when she sells the story to the *Times*—a betrayal of which Norton was not guilty.[45] While her behavior is culpable, Dacier's reaction proves that he has yet to round Seraglio Point. He refuses to understand or to forgive her action. He creates a tale of "the cloven foot under their petticoats," imagining himself "in the dominion of Love a sultan of the bow-string and chopper period, sovereignly endowed to stretch a finger for the scimitared Mesrour to make the erring woman head and trunk with one blow: and away with those remnants" (*DC* 2:164–65). Diana may not be literally dismembered as was Mrs. Brown, but Dacier's rejection cuts deeply. She describes the end of her second term in this way:

> there are wounds that cut sharp as the enchanter's sword, and we don't know we are in halves till some rough old intimate claps us on the back. . . . I have to join myself together again, as well as I can. It's done . . . but don't notice the cement
>
> (*DC* 2:217)

Despite the bisection, Diana must welcome the end of her salon, since it has exhausted and nearly bankrupted her. The Dacier scandal means that war is "declared against her a second time," and she must once again "go about presenting my face to vindicate my character" (*DC* 2:219, 216). Older, wiser, less sensitive to the world's judgments, she is soon "the brilliant Diana of her nominal luminary issuing from cloud. Face and tongue, she was the same; and once in the stream, she soon gathered its current topics and scattered her arrowy phrases" (*DC* 2:217). Expressly political conversation is reserved for her soul mate, Emma. As young women, they had imagined magically remaking society: with one blow they "cut the knot. . . . [W]e shut our eyes against logic and the vaunted laws of economy. They are the knot we cut; or would cut, had we the sword" (*DC* 1:39). Distaff politicians may lack the weaponry to sever Gordian knots, but there are no restrictions upon wielding "arrowy phrases" in private. Thus the former "democratic rebels" (*DC* 1:39) are "delighted to discover that they were each the rebel of their earlier and less experienced years" (*DC* 2:71). Diana's declaration of independence is not proclaimed in the House; it is not even shared with the men of her salon; only Emma hears her declaim: "Give us the means of independence, and we will gain it, and have a turn at judging you, my lords! You shall behold a world reversed" (*DC* 1:181). Had Diana's rebellion been public, as Norton's was, her readers would have heard the protest reserved for Emma's ears. Thus if not quite the radical feared by Lady Wathin, she is nonetheless a resolute liberal: "In politics I am with the active minority on behalf of the inert but suffering majority. That is my rule" (*DC* 2:5). Her words directly echo Norton's self-described "mania that the English law does *not* protect the lower orders against the higher."[46]

It is significant that both Disraeli and Meredith alter the circumstances of Norton's life to allow the protagonists a second marriage at a young age. As a result, these novels offer a version of the romantic substitution evident in *Bigley* v. *Dupré* and *Angelina* v. *Edwin*. In those breach of promise cases, premarital legal conflicts were resolved by representatives of the legal system acting in a romantic rather than a professional capacity. The new betrothals sidestep the vexed social issues raised by breach of promise and related to the nature of marriage and the status of women. Disraeli and Meredith arrange a more conventional from of romantic substitution. Marital conflict is resolved by the deaths of unsympathetic and apolitical first husbands. The social rebel is then reabsorbed into marriage with a sympathetic partner whose political aspirations can be furthered by his wife. The closure provided by these ideal marriages comes at the cost of implicitly suggesting that women's voices are best heard in the quiet context of influence rather than from the public platforms of power.

Marriage, Disraeli intimates, has a calming effect on Berengaria's restive political energy: "The truth is, her heart was satisfied, and that brought repose. Feelings of affection, long mortified and pent up, were now lavished and concentrated on a husband of her heart and adoration, and she was proud that his success and greatness might be avowed as the objects of her life" (*E* 2:247). Meredith more reluctantly unites Diana and Thomas Redworth in a union that reinscribes previously rejected chivalric values: "A woman of blood and imagination in the warring world, without a mate whom she can revere, subscribes to a likeness with those independent minor realms between greedy mighty neighbours, which conspire and undermine when they do not openly threaten to devour" (*DC* 2:270–71). Meredith implies that women must marry for their protection: they have only to be careful which greedy neighbor they align themselves with. Although Diana chooses more wisely this time, the risks to women remain unchanged. By the end of the novel, the social rebel is silenced. Like Berengaria, Diana immerses herself in the career of her husband: "Either he thought within her thoughts, or his own were at her disposal. Nor was it sufficient for him to be sensible of her influence, to restrain the impetus he took from her. . . . [M]uch that he did, as well as whatever he debated, came of Diana" (*DC* 2:239). In Meredith's ideal marriage, the political wife is not confined to "half a life," and Diana has a reasonable prospect of fulfilling Norton's unrealized goal of having "added so far to the happiness and security of a career of public usefulness and public elevation."

Trollope rejects this romantic/political resolution insofar as he denies Lady Laura a second chance to marry the man she loves. The loss of her lover is fatal to political ambition, and she retires from the fray. *Phineas Finn* nevertheless reinforces the logic of romantic substitution in that Pericles is granted a second marriage to an able Aspasia. With the death of Mary Flood Jones, the innocent Irish bride who is a liability to an aspiring politician in England, Phineas marries the savvy and politically astute widow Maria Goesler, who is able to bankroll his career. In a familiar pattern, love is corrosive for Lady Laura but salvational for Phineas, at least when he finally gets it right. She founders; he undertakes a prosperous romantic and political voyage.

Chapter 6

"Lopsided and Left-Handed Laws": Narratives of Mothers and Wives

She has beauty, Genius, & is not blue! *which I abhor.*[1]

Benjamin Robert Haydon, *Diary*

Mrs. Caroline Norton

I really don't know
Why Miss Martineau
Should pamphleteer so
Against husband and beau.
Let's fill our glasses
My merry-souled lasses!
And drink wedlock's glow
To the spirit of snow,
Whom now we all know
By the name Martineau.[2]

"The Grand Fraserian Festival,"
Fraser's Magazine

Norton might have been excluded from the status of the political wife by virtue of her modest position in "the world," but she did enjoy one privilege denied the Lady Hollands of her day: the possibility of overt political action independent of and in direct opposition to her husband. Two distinct causes provoked the "reluctant rebel" into exercising this independence: maternal custody and uxorial property.[3] In both instances, Norton wrote in support of legislative reforms, abandoning the covert conversation of the hostess for the public pen of the pamphleteer. In the late 1830s she published several treatises: one anonymously, *The Separation of Mother and Child by the Law of "Custody of Infants," Considered* (1838), and another under the nom de guerre Pearce Stevenson, *A Plain Letter to the Lord Chancellor on the Infant Custody Bill* (1839).[4] In the 1850s, she entered the debate on marriage and divorce laws, publishing two long essays under her own name: *English Laws for Women* (1854) and *A Letter to the Queen on Lord Chancellor Cranworth's Marriage and Divorce Bill* (1855).

Coincident with each period of political authorship was a trial in which a tradesman sued George for debts incurred by his wife. In neither was he held liable, and both demonstrated that the Melbourne scandal and Norton's desire for unequivocal legal and public vindication were never far from the surface of her thought and writing. In *Emmott* v. *Norton* (1838), although she was not a party to the suit and could not appear, she hoped to present the defense not offered by Campbell in *Norton* v. *Melbourne.* She convinced John Bayley to introduce letters from George stating that he did not believe that his wife had committed adultery. The judge refused admission on the grounds of relevance, adding to her sense of grievance. Subpoenaed to testify in *Thrupp* v. *Norton* (1853), she could speak in a court of law for the first time and could not resist the chance to make the case not heard either in 1836 or 1838. Thrupp and his unpaid bill receded into the background as the couple rehearsed their longstanding grievances. Whatever rhetorical satisfaction she may have gained was undone by the verdict for the defendant. Having yet again "lost" in court, Norton rededicated her efforts to changing the system that had consistently failed to protect her from her husband's economic violence.

THE POLITICS OF PROTECTION, THE COLORS OF FEMINISM

Although accused of acting out of personal interest rather than concern for the broader issue of women's rights, Norton held coherent and consistent political views. The philosophy called into practical service with regard to child custody and married women's property was rooted in the liberalism of her grandfather, which she maintained throughout her life. A persistent theme in her writing is concern for the suffering majority. Whatever the specific object of consideration, her thought was shaped by the social imperative to alleviate hardship and defend the weak. Norton favored protection rather than empowerment of those who, whether for reasons of gender, class, age, nationality, or race, lived in comparatively vulnerable positions.

This view is unequivocally expressed in "Letters to the Mob," a response to the widespread social upheavals of 1848. Under the pen name Libertas, Norton urges the masses to reject the Chartist dream of equality, which was

> the most cruel of all the temptations with which the mob-traps are baited; for it is at once the most specious and the most false. There can be **no** equality, any more than there can be a sea without a shore! Superiority is not a thing of man's devising, but of God's appointing. Gradation is His law.
>
> ("*LM*" 5)

Norton does not question natural hierarchies; rather, she offers them as the rationale for a social philosophy resembling the revisionist sense of *noblesse oblige* promulgated by Disraeli's Young England movement.[5] "Letters to the Mob" tells its audience that the aristocracy are the "haters of oppression, and honest pioneers of progress. They are workmen of intelligence, as you are the workmen of production" ("*LM*" 15).

This philosophy is evident in less programmatic fashion in Norton's earlier political poetry. A new attention to social and political issues outside "the world" was signaled by the 1836 publication of *A Voice from the Factories.* In a prefatory note to the poem, Norton remarks that "the application of serious poetry to the passing events of the day has fallen into disuse, and is, if not absolutely contemned, at least much discouraged" (*VFF* vi). She suggests that because "poetry is the language of feeling, it should be the language of the multitude" (*VFF* vi). The "passing event" to which she applies this Wordsworthian theory is the abuse of child labor. Her objective is to improve social conditions, not to change the social order:

> There is, among all men, in every clime,
> A difference instinctive and unschooled:
> God made the MIND unequal. From all time
> By fierceness conquered, or by cunning fooled,
> The World hath had its Rulers and its Ruled:—
> Yea—uncompelled—men abdicate free choice,

> Fear their own rashness, and, by thinking cooled,
> Follow the counsel of some trusted voice;—
> A self-elected sway, wherein their souls rejoice.
>
> (*VFF* 37)

Nature may possess two orders, rulers and ruled, but there cannot be "one law for these [the children of the rich],/And one for the pale children of the Poor" (*VFF* 41). The law of charity must ensure that human action compensates for natural inequality and its potential hardships.

In "the language of the multitude," Norton utters a double appeal to rational self-interest: the ruled must accept nature's hierarchy, and the rulers must embrace the principle of social responsibility. The working class has not felt that "self-elected sway," nor has the upper class been swayed by appeals to social justice. She addresses two audiences, warning one against violent social protest and the other against continued neglect. The emphasis here, as opposed to "Letters to the Mob," is upon the failures of politicians and industrialists alike. Her warning is tempered by the conservative fears, first, that "abuses, of such business, must be cautiously dealt with; lest, in eradicating them we shake or disorder the whole fabric," and second, that abuses must be earnestly dealt with lest "[t]he dog that watched and fawned, prepares to bite!" (*VFF* 55). She concludes:

> Therefore should Mercy, gentle and sere,
> Sit by the Ruler's side, and share his Throne:—
> Watch with unerring eye the passing scene,
> And bend her ear to mark the feeblest groan;
> Lest due Authority be overthrown.
>
> (*VFF* 57)

A Voice from the Factories and "Letters to the Mob" constitute a condition-of-England dialogue, or call and response, stretching over more than a decade of increasing social unrest and labor turmoil. If her fears have intensified, Norton's themes nonetheless are consistent: the public must accept "due Authority," and "due Authority" must rectify the neglect and abuse that have exacerbated social injustice during the first decades of Victoria's reign.

The Child of the Islands, begun at the birth of the Prince of Wales, is Norton's longest and most sustained engagement with the condition-of-England question.[6] It consists of four sections, each devoted to a season—a structure that imposes natural order upon social chaos. A prefatory comment announces her intentions in gently optimistic terms:

> It is, on the contrary, a gleam of that union and kindliness of feeling between the Higher and Lower Classes, which it is the main object of the writer of these pages . . . to inculcate; a gleam which may fade into darkness or brighten into sunshine, but which no one who attentively observes the present circumstances of this country, can believe will remain unaltered.
>
> (*CI* xii–xiii)

The point is underscored by an epigraph from Herbert: "If the poor had more justice, they would need less charity" (*CI*). Interspersing narrative comment and sketches of different social and economic groups, Norton pleads for an enlightened and heroic monarch who will address the ills confronting the nation. The symbolic role assigned to the Prince of Wales, juxtaposed with the previous image of the Prince Regent in Norton's silver fork fiction, demonstrates just how far her literary interests have evolved. The foibles of the *haut ton* are of less concern than the oppression of the lower classes. A preoccupation with the manners and mores of the aristocracy has given way to an analysis of their responsibilities. One prince (later George IV), who embodies fashion and corruption, is replaced by another (later Edward VII), who represents hope for social change. By the time of her death in 1877, Norton must have realized that the Prince of Wales was destined to repeat rather than reject the example of his infamous predecessor; nevertheless, she retained the political principles that shaped her life.

Indicative of the political turn in the poetry of the late 1830s and early 1840s is the reappearance in *The Child of the Islands* of a woman preparing for a royal audience. While the earlier fiction satirized the vanity of the jewel-laden coquettes, this topos is now complemented by a sympathetic portrayal of the working classes. Norton juxtaposes the "woman of the world" with the wife of the laborer who makes the cloth for her presentation gown. The former is "[c]areless of all conditions but her own" (*CI* Spring, 25); the latter is a malnourished mother "groaning on her narrow bed" (*CI* Spring, 19). Her husband's work provides a feast for buyers' vanity, but his wages are insufficient to feed his family. The tale of the "pallid weaver at his loom, . . . / In the dull confines of his cheerless room" (*CI* Spring, 17) is drowned out by the convivial hum of the royal presentation:

> That dumb woof tells no story! Silent droops
> The gorgeous train, voluminously wide;

And while the lady's knee stoops
(Mocking her secret heart, which swells with pride,)
No ragged shadow follows at her side
Into that royal presence, where her claim
To be admitted, is to be allied
To wealth, and station, and a titled name,—
No warning voice is heard to supplicate or blame.
(*CI* Spring, 25)

In a satiric barb at her own past preoccupation with royal audiences, Norton uses the unselfconscious voice of this "tinseled, gaudy, selfish fool" to parody the abuses to which the doctrine of natural hierarchy is susceptible. She concludes with a rhetorical question, whose answer has been provided by the litany preceding it:

A life of self-indulgence is for Us,
A life of self-denial is for them:
For Us the streets, broad-built and populous,
For them, unhealthy corners, garrets dim,
And cellars where the water-rat may swim!
For Us, green paths refreshed by frequent rain,
For them, dark alleys where the dust lies grim!
Not doomed by Us to this appointed pain,—
God made us, Rich and Poor—of what do these complain?
(*CI* Spring, 28–29)

The difference between the silver fork and the condition-of-England writing is that aristocratic callousness and cruelty are now pandemic, not simply endemic. She focuses not upon the harm the *haut ton* inflict upon one another but on their criminal insensitivity to those outside "the world."

The Child of the Islands offers a broad survey of the British kingdom, exposing numerous instances of the incongruous existence of the two nations. Another example is found in a haunting picture of the nocturnal dwellers of London's public parks. As the daylight hours wane,

Gaunt, pallid forms
Come, creeping sadly to their hollow hearts,
Seeking frail shelter from the winds and storms,
In broken rest, disturbed by fitful starts;
There, when the chill rain falls, or lightning darts,
Or balmy summer nights are stealing on,
Houseless they slumber, close to wealthy marts

And gilded homes:—there, where the morning sun
That tide of wasteful joy and splendour looked upon!
(*CI* Spring, 43)

The poetic text is annotated with endnotes documenting the described evils. The nighttime habitués of the park are factually discussed in one note (*CI* 220); another responds to a recently published letter in the *Times* signed "Anti-Humbug," whose writer objected both to the presence of the homeless in city parks and to the charity they might receive (*CI* 232–38). These prose commentaries allow Norton to address "passing events of the day" without compromising the dramatic and pictorial quality of the poem itself; they also establish a dialogue of poetry and prose that makes *The Child of the Islands* her most sophisticated essay into socially engaged literature.

Norton extended the principle of natural hierarchy and the concomitant doctrine of protection to the issue of gender. Immediately following *Norton* v. *Melbourne*, when she might have been most likely to question male superiority, she insisted that *The Wife* unequivocally demonstrated her opposition to the doctrine of "sexual equality."[7] Even *English Laws*, despite its withering critique of unjust double standards, overtly disavows equality of the sexes:

> The wild and stupid theories advanced by a few women, of 'equal rights' and 'equal intelligence' are not the opinions of their sex. I, for one (I, with millions more), believe in the natural superiority of man, as I do in the existence of a God.... Masculine superiority is incontestable; and with the superiority should come protections.[8]
>
> (*ELW* 165, also see *PL* 98–99)

The letter to Gladstone, enclosing a copy of *English Laws*, insists that the remedy for cases such as her own lies in statutory safeguards: "Is not the natural answer,...'*if there is no law that can reach it, we will legislate*'.... Do you think women would be less worthy,—if more entirely protected by law?"[9] Norton was a political realist, in Dorothy E. Zaborszky's formulation: "a pragmatist who was not concerned with ideological purity, but very keen on legislative reforms."[10] Pragmatism led to campaigns for legislative protection of women against the abuses of male privilege and authority.

Her refusal to endorse equality and single-minded pursuit of laws that would ameliorate her own situation led some to question Norton's political colors. There can be little doubt that activism was the result of personal circumstance. The silver fork socialite, possessed of an inherent, if abstract, sensitivity to human injustice, was a reluctant activist, "a feminist *malgré lui*," as Joan Huddleston puts it.[11] Norton herself wrote: "it is not from choice that I left poetry and pleasant themes,—for defence of the better part of life."[12] The trial of 1836 and her husband's subsequent behavior compelled her to protest and not merely to endure injustice. The task was unwelcome and onerous; it led to further public exposure and ridicule, but in dedicating her pen to practical legislative objectives Norton discovered

> that my gift of writing was not meant for the purposes to which I have hitherto applied it. It was not intended that I should . . . prove my literary ability, by publishing melodies and songs for young girls and women to sing in happier homes than mine,—or poetry and prose for them to read in leisure hours,—or even please myself by better and more serious attempts to advocate the rights of the people, or the education and interests of the poor. . . . Mr Norton . . . taught me what my gift of writing was worth. . . . It was meant to enable me to rouse the hearts of others to examine into all the gross injustice of these laws.
>
> (*PL* 151–53)

The author of letters encouraging passage of the Reform Bill thus became the primary force behind the Custody of Infants Bill, just as the self-appointed spokeswoman for child workers became an outspoken activist for the rights of married women. The labor of the political writer was less pleasant than that of hostess and much more likely to elicit public condemnation, yet enduring these liabilities was preferable to passive acceptance of wrong.

Despite Haydon's relieved insistence that Norton lacked the blue hue of feminism, she was referred to as "a fashionable 'Bluestocking.' "[13] The chromatic debate was renewed by Harriet Martineau, who felt that Norton was not a true blue because her activism was motivated by self-interest:

> When I see an eloquent writer insinuating to every body who comes across her that she is the victim of her husband's carelessness and cruelty, . . . when I see her violating all good taste by her obtrusiveness in society, and oppressing every body about her by her epicurean selfishness every day, while raising in print an eloquent cry on behalf of the oppressed; I feel, to the bottom of my heart, that she is the worst enemy of the cause she professes to plead.

The best friends of that cause are women who . . . must be clearly seen to speak from conviction of the truth, and not from personal unhappiness.[14]

In response to the accusation of ideological impurity, Norton insisted: "I do not consider this as MY cause: though it is a cause of which . . . I am an illustration. It is the cause of *all* women" (*LQ* 89). Yet even those sympathetic to her situation, as well as her cause, regretted the preponderance of personal grievance in her work. A favorable review of *Letter to the Queen* included this qualification:

But we cannot disguise from Mrs. Norton the fact that the continual repetition of her grievances, however natural, however defensible, will weaken the common cause. She must be careful, that in the minds of men, with less faith in her than ourselves, this common cause, this good woman's cause does not degenerate into "Mrs. Norton's case."[15]

In contrast to Martineau, George Eliot was not troubled by mixed motivation. She commented with regard to *Letter to the Queen* that Norton was no different from Milton in

pleading his own cause as well as urging a general argument. . . . There is much unreasonable prejudice against this blending of personal interest with a general protest. If we waited for the impulse of abstract benevolence or justice, we fear that most reforms would be postponed to the Greek Kalends.[16]

However uncomfortable Eliot was made by some of Norton's public statements, she clearly recognized the pragmatic reasons for, to say nothing of the justice of, her cause.[17]

Norton's pamphlets document that whatever the cause to which her "gift of writing" was dedicated, its defining characteristic is a pronounced narrative flair, the analogue to her performative manner in the salon and drawing room. She is first and foremost a storyteller, and in these works that story is primarily her own. Illustrative narrative and ratiocinative disputation are interwoven in a generic mixture unfamiliar to political pundits and unwelcome to a society squeamish about personal disclosure. When a friend expressed concern about the use of her own exemplary history, Norton replied from the perspective of a novelist and professional author:

nobody would have read my book at all,—had it been grave, dry, and full of legal details from magnificent law books. My first object was to contrive *to be read*.... Depend upon it, therefore, whatever the real faults of the pamphlet may be, it is better *for its purpose* than a better book.[18]

This tack entailed obvious risks, not the least of which was rejection of the position because of its advocate's reputation. Even as an outspoken political activist, Norton encountered the authorial optics and the "feminization" evidenced in her earliest portraits and reviews. Testimony of her physical beauty continued in middle age, to be sure, but even more damaging to the serious political writer than the distraction of beauty was the fear that her prose might serve similarly seductive ends.[19] Reviewers warned of enticing female arguments that disarmed reason and seduced the imagination. Readers were advised that "the charms of her style" were such that "we may be led away by our feelings, and not influenced by our judgment.... We must take some time, as it were to cool."[20] Having already been silenced by English law, Norton must have found it ironic that readers were now advised to fill their ears with wax as a defense against the political Siren. *The Law Review and Quarterly Journal of British and Foreign Jurisprudence* condescendingly noted: "Although her work, being in a great measure personal, is necessarily of a vehement character, we will not forget that she is a woman distinguished for her personal charms, her wit, her literature, her talents, and her industry, and, we may add, her sorrows."[21] As in reviews of *Lost and Saved*, there is a tendency to counterbalance something perceived to be unseemly or indecorous—"the naked deformity" of scenes in a novel, or the "vehement" expression of personal history in an essay—with a reminder of Norton's "personal charms" or her "elevated... social position and literary reputation." Attention is diverted to the author, while the truths of her imagination or the justice of her cause is overlooked, if not deliberately disregarded.

As an activist juggling personal grievance with political objectives, Norton was situated at a literary crossways that threatened to become a *cul de sac*: if too circumspect, she risked not engaging her audience; if too forthcoming, she invariably offended them. Despite this dilemma, like Meredith's protagonist she did "not 'chameleon' her pen from the colour of her audience" (*DC* 1:16). Indeed, she must have felt very much like Diana, who opined:

We women are the verbs passive of the alliance; we have to learn, and if we take to activity, with the best intentions, we conjugate a frightful disturbance. We are to run on lines, like the steam-trains, or we come to no station, dash to fragments. I have the misfortune to know I was born an active. I take my chance.

(*DC* 1:87)

Norton herself put it this way: "When a woman steps out of her domestic tangle to assert, because it *is* a tangle, her rights to partial independence, men sight her for their prey."[22] She complained that her name had become "the watchword of insult and cruel abuse" and felt that public opinion had erected "an imaginary Mrs. Norton, something between a barn-actress and a Mary Wollstonecraft."[23] She may have resisted association with a famous feminist forebear—a comparison also pejoratively made by Martineau—but there are some unexpected parallels.

THE EDUCATION OF WOMEN: WOLLSTONECRAFT, NORTON, AND TENNYSON

Despite dissimilarities in character and circumstance, to say nothing of significant differences in political philosophy, Wollstonecraft and Norton were equally outspoken critics of marriage law.[24] The protagonist of Wollstonecraft's unfinished novel *Maria* (1797) bears uncanny similarities to Norton. Many are sheer coincidence—for example, both women marry second sons named George—but others seem the inevitable consequence of the legal restrictions imposed upon women. It is highly probable that the life of a woman "unfortunately united to an unprincipled man" (*M* 144) would assume the contours imagined by Wollstonecraft and lived by Norton. Indeed, Norton's experience corroborates Wollstonecraft's claim that *Maria* is a "history . . . of woman, [rather] than of the individual" (*M* 59); just as the novel confirms Norton's denial "that this is my personal cause; it is the cause of all the women of England" (*PL* 153). Wollstonecraft's exemplary history and Norton's unhappy life have a single subject, the legal woes awaiting a woman who makes a poor choice of partner, and a single lesson, the importance of educating women about their social status and legal rights.

Maria composes her life story (she is 26 at the time of writing) in the hope that it "might perhaps instruct her daughter, and shield her from the misery, the tyranny, her mother knew not how to avoid" (*M* 66). Norton, beyond the immediate objective of effecting legislative change, intended her writing to educate women about their legal status. She wrote to Shelley at the time her first pamphlet appeared: "I think it is high time that law was *known*, at least among the 'weaker' sex."[25] Like Wollstonecraft, she stressed that the early age at which women were encouraged to marry rendered education all the more urgent. Maria married "when scarcely able to distinguish the nature of the engagement . . . yet submitted to the rigid laws which enslave women" (*M* 142). Norton's experience corroborates this point (George's first proposal came when she was 16), which is also made in *Stuart of Dunleath.* Eleanor recalls that "she was scarcely more than a child when she vowed away her future" (*SD* 3:269). The youthfulness of brides militates against mature choices, and it argues against the wisdom of making such choices virtually irreversible.

The silver fork writing satirized the narrow education given young women as preparation for entering society and marrying advantageously, but it did not make the case for their legal education, as the examples of Eleanor Penrhyn in *Stuart of Dunleath* and Beatrice Brooke in *Lost and Saved* would do. In some instances, characters are more rejected by than rejecting of the gynæceum, either for reasons of race (Milly Nesdale) or disability (Catherine Dalrymple). Women denied access to the finishing school model of education have few alternatives to haphazard instruction by men or lonely autodidacticism. Milly, for instance,

> rather scorned what are termed accomplishments, but she talked well on a variety of subjects; she "read up" in all reviews and papers with sedulous industry for the topics of the day; and she had that puzzling, superficial scholarship common to almost all women who . . . lived very much more among men than women.
>
> (*LS* 230)

Mariana, the protagonist of "The Invalid," observes "that the best of all educations is that which results from a free intercourse with superior and cultivated companions" ("I" 152). She learns widely from the learned conversation of her father and his visitors, and tells her younger sister that, even though "men underrated the capabilities of women," it is possible to become the "match for all your philosophers and sages" ("I" 151–2). These examples suggest that while women might shine with a reflected light, they cannot safely depend upon the beneficent beams shed upon them by men.

Norton did not advocate the founding of a women's university, but her name has been suggested as a model for *The Princess* (1847), Tennyson's medley on this idea.[26] It is possible that Tennyson was influenced by his friend John Kemble, who labeled Norton "a new Bradamante, armed or denuded, *cap-à-pied*, to run a joust or wrestle with any man,—nay, with the whole male sex one after another... in proof of the rights and capacity of women."[27] Kemble linked Norton with Harriet Martineau as "ultra-utopians," whose views were derived from "absurd and suicidal paralogisms" and disseminated in "revolutionary jeremiads."[28] Princess Ida is nothing if not a militant utopian, but neither her realistic goal of a university for women nor her idealistic vision of a female utopia can be traced to Norton. If she contributed to the characterization of Tennyson's "new Bradamante"—the creation, after all, of a group of university students, whose expressed purpose is fabricating "some great Princess, six feet high, / Grand, epic, homicidal" (*P* P:218–19)—it could only be insofar as he associated her name with the general cause of feminism. Apart from having taken offense at her arriving late for dinner and conducting herself with showy garrulity, Tennyson had almost no direct experience of Norton.[29]

If not to the fanciful figure of Ida, however, a claim can be made for a connection between Norton and Lilia Vivian. A modern woman, Lilia is situated between a distant heroic past—the ancestress who "beat her foes with slaughter from her walls" (*P* P:35, 33)—and the visionary future mockingly constructed by her brother and his friends. "Half child half woman as she was" (*P* P:101), Lilia chafes against the restrictions imposed upon her and the seeming inevitability of marriage. When asked where the latter-day "feudal warrior lady-clad" might be found, she asserts that there are thousands

> but convention beats them down:
> It is but bringing up; no more than that:
> You men have done it: how I hate you all!
> Ah, were I something great! I wish I were
> Some mighty poetess, I would shame you then,
> That love to keep us children!
> (*P* P:119, 127–33)

Lilia's youthful enthusiasm, her theatrical gestures (*P* P:100–106), her alternating petulance and self-directed irony (*P* P:152), and even her sarcasm (*P* P:167–69) are reminiscent not only of the youthful Norton but also of the self-dramatizing "mighty poetess" that Tennyson encountered at the home of Samuel Rogers.

Lilia, threatened by the invasive gaze of men, weighs a young woman's dream of accomplishment against the obstacles posed by marriage and family. Whereas the exploits of the students consist of nothing more noble than university pranks, she formulates the heroic ideal of a women's university. This dream is consistent with the teaching of her "maiden Aunt," a bluestocking "crammed with theories out of books," who "preached / an universal culture for the crowd" (*P* P:107–109, C:35). In the mouths of her brother and his friends, however, idealism is diminished to mere "Chimeras, crotchets, Christmas solecisms . . . made to kill / Time by the fire in winter" (*P* P:199–201). Princess Ida may be no more than an undergraduate parody of feminist aspirations, but in the figure of Lilia, Tennyson addresses the concerns of many British women at mid-century, including Norton.

The tale concludes with his own version of the "Anti-Climax Expedition." Princess Ida fails to complete her quest for "equal rights/Against the sons of men, and barbarous laws" (*P* 7:218–19). She laments that "but a girl," she has "made myself a Queen of farce!" (*P* 7:227–28). The Prince suggests that their tale is a romance rather than a farce, insisting that the "woman's cause is the man's"(*P* 7:243). His assurances of paternal protection, spousal harmony, and singleness of purpose uncomfortably echo the rationalizations for the doctrine of coverture. Not surprisingly, his mother the queen exemplifies the virtues he wishes to find in a bride: "Not learned, save in gracious household ways, / Nor perfect, nay, but full of tender wants, / No Angel, but a dearer being, all dipt / In Angel instincts, breathing Paradise" (*P* P:298–301). This domestic ideal is unlikely to be consoling to either Ida or Lilia, and it raises some doubt about the princely promise: "We two . . . / Will clear away the parasitic forms / That seem to keep her up but drag her down" (*P* 7:243, 253–55). With marriage looming and "barbarous laws" still in place, Lilia would do well to listen to her aunt or to Norton, who offered this advice to Gladstone: "*if there is no law that can reach it, we will legislate.*"

Tennyson's "winter's tale" (*P* P:231) does not begin with a prescribed generic objective. It will be "[a]s you will; / Heroic if you will, or what you will" (*P* P:214–16). Nor is its form any more clear at the conclusion. Opinions are split along gender lines, with the men wishing that the seven tales were cast in the mode of "mock-heroic gigantesque" (*P* C:3), while the women

> hated banter, wished for something real,
> A gallant fight, a noble princess—why
> Not make her true-heroic—true-sublime?
> Or all, they said, as earnest as the close?

Which yet with such a framework scarce could be.
Then rose a little feud betwixt the two,
Betwixt the mockers and the realists. . . .
(*P* C:18–24)

The battle between the sexes in the story is reprised by its audience. Norton was clearly on the side of the women. She liked the poem but "object[ed] to [Tennyson's] being playful in that magnificent and magniloquent blank verse."[30] One senses that Norton, along with Ida, Lilia, and her aunt, regrets that the question of women's education unobtrusively disappears in "the gathering darkness" that closes the poem (*P* C:107).

At the end of the tale, Lilia turns to her Aunt Elizabeth for the voice of women's wisdom that neither the undergraduates nor the figures of patriarchy like Sir Walter Vivian, a "great broad-shouldered genial Englishman" (*P* C:85), and Sir Ralph, the famous ancestor who participated in the Crusades, can provide. Aunt Elizabeth "might have told" (*P* C:34), but her words are preempted by the closing of the gates and the conclusion of the festival. Rather than materteral wisdom about "what we are" (*P* C:34), readers hear the conservative voices of the narrator and his "college friend / The Tory member's elder son" (*P* C:49–50), who counsel patience. They imply that radical visions of social change, such as a women's university and gender equality, might have value but cannot be realized in the present. The narrator reaffirms the strength and nobility of English society and counsels prudence and trust in the guiding hand of Providence (*P* C:72–79)—precisely the wisdom offered by Norton in *The Child of the Islands.* Her protest against "parasitic forms" is reserved for the pamphlets on child custody and married women's property.

THE FIRST CAMPAIGN: THE CUSTODY OF INFANTS BILL (1839)

In 1844, upon learning that R. H. Horne's *The Spirit of the Age* would include commentary on her work, Norton wrote to the editor asking "if there is to be any criticism of my writings, to include, not only the trifles published *with* my name, but more serious efforts, published *without it*: and more especially two Pamphlets on the Infant Custody Bill."[31] By this time, she wished to be known not simply as a poet engaged with the serious issues of the day but as an essayist educating women and advancing the cause of equal justice. A letter to Locock sheds some light on her desire:

> I hold Poetry to be as infinitely below prose, as *reason* is below *fancy*. I also hold prose to be a much rarer gift of good writing among women. And I think (as the climax of obstinacy) that prose *on a real subject* must be of higher value than prose for a work of imagination. Infinitely rather would I have written my two pamphlets on the Infant Custody Bill.[32]

Literature might express "opinions," as she explained in *A Voice from the Factories* and in her letter to Gladstone, but the essay is dedicated to knowledge. The custody pamphlets link social narratives about mothers and children to specific legislative goals: the "*real subject*" is new, although the narrative method can be found throughout her poetry and fiction.

Norton penned sentimental portraits of aristocratic mothers ("The English Mother" and "To Lady Graham"); idealized depictions of peasant mothers (*The Child of the Islands*); pathetic tales of children deprived of a mother's love ("The Lament of the Poet Savage" and "The Forsaken Child"); bathetic tales of mothers whose children have died ("The Two Pictures," "The Mother's Last Watch," and "The Young Heir's Death-Bed"); and poetry addressed to her own children ("A Mother's Heart"). The most extended expression of the maternal theme is *The Dream* (1840), written when she had little contact with her children and was actively seeking to change custody statutes. The poem begins with the mother's recollections of her daughter from "snow-white cradle" to "little child at play" to "fairy girl" to "bride betroth'd" (*D* 16–18). It amply documents the point of Chase and Levenson that Norton mastered the "deft rhetoric of motherhood" in service of the "conspicuous political labor of poetic maternity."[33]

The Dream's celebration of maternity is sentimental in the extreme. As in *Maria*, motherhood is idealized, and mothers are beatified. Maternal love is "[t]he *only* love which on this teeming earth / Asks no return from Passion's wayward birth; / The only love that, with a touch divine, / Displaces from the heart's most secret shrine / The idol *SELF*" (*D* 10). Her love might be divine, but the mother's lot is apt to be hellish. The speaker, a world-weary widow, attempts to moderate her child's idealized vision of marriage and expansive hope for the future. She offers a stoic reminder of "the chain / Which knits thy human lot to other's pain" (*D* 45). Her words are close in tone to

Maria's admonitory letter to her daughter. In a long passage reflecting Norton's own unhappy marital history, the mother prays that her child will be spared "the wound [that] rankles on through dreary years" and "the long toil of such unnatural strife" between "those whom man, not God, hath parted" (*D* 54). Unlike Maria, however, she counsels resignation, not rebellion, echoing the familiar theme of woman as helpmeet: "And be not thou cast down, because thy lot / The glory of thy dream resembleth not. / Not for herself was woman first create, / Nor yet to be man's idol, but his mate" (*D* 69). "Mate," however, does not mean "equal," and the expectant bride is warned that she will be "at times deceived, / Outraged, insulted, slander'd, crush'd, and grieved; / Too often made a victim or a toy, / With years of sorrow for an hour of joy" (*D* 69).

The contrast between maternal and conjugal experience is also found in many of the tales. "A Mother," for example, recounts Laura Davenel's leaving her husband and taking the children with her. When informed by her husband's attorney that both the children and her personal property must be returned to their rightful owner, she proclaims: "Sir, you may seize what you please; I have no knowledge of these matters, but for my children, unless they are torn from my arms by force, they remain with me" ("AM"). Shocked to learn that "the law is entirely with the father" ("AM"), Laura offers to abandon legal proceedings in return for allowing the children to live with her, but her husband insists that "the law made him master of his own children . . . he would be accountable to no one for the trust" ("AM"). She is prevented from seeing the children and subsequently discovers that the boys have been sent out of the country and that their sister has been placed in the care of her father's mistress.[34] Laura's suit to have her daughter removed from the care of her husband's paramour is defeated in both the Courts of King's Bench and Chancery.

The pathos of the tale inheres in the alienation of the absent children from their mother. One of Laura's sons writes that the youngest, Willie, "is forgetting your face, Mama, he was so very little when we went away; but I tell him about you every day!" ("AM"). The youngest of Norton's children, William, died in 1842 at age eight while under his father's care. Norton had seen almost nothing of him since 1836. It took this tragedy, as it would the death of Laura's daughter, to sway the fathers to allow the children significant time with their mothers. When reunited with his mother, Laura's oldest acted "gently, courteously, but as to a stranger. His natural timidity had been increased by a residence among those who neither felt nor cared for his infantine joys" ("AM"). The story ends with Laura's impending death and plea to Willie: "do not call me Madam call me *Mother*" ("AM").

This plaintive tone is also found in the commentary that Norton prepared for the privately printed collection of letters concerning custody of her children, *Letters, Etc. Third and Fourth Correspondence with Summary of Facts.* Her editorial voice conveys the pathos of a wronged and forlorn mother. It is strongly colored by the lurid tones of melodrama. The letters themselves record the alternating hope and frustration, along with the growing anger, that characterized negotiations with George over visitation and custody. The first line of her first letter after the trial of 1836 announces what would be, although she could not know it at the time, an oft-repeated theme. She writes as one who assumes that she has been fully exonerated and expresses "deep anxiety to see those children who were so suddenly taken from me, and of whom I have heard so little and so rarely during these three months of painful suspense" (*L* 1:7). The letter concludes with a reference to a mother's obligation to her children—one that is her "solemn duty to perform; . . . they were intrusted to me by a merciful God, to whom I am responsible for the care of their souls and bodies" (*L* 1:8). Four years later, having seen Fletcher, Brinsley, and William briefly on several occasions but not at all for two years, she expresses only anger and despair. All might be well, she suggests, "if I had not borne in deadly agony and at the peril of my life creatures who were hereafter to be claimed by law, or denied by the selfish cold-heartedness of their father" (*L* 4:28).

George was as adept at emotional as physical violence. He repeatedly promised that she would see the children, only to find some new objection or to impose some new condition. They could not return from Scotland in the summer, for instance, because it was too hot in London (May 30, 1837), but then winters in Scotland were much too cold for young children to travel (December 31, 1837). Her letter of May 8, 1840, describes

> *seeing my children for a week or fortnight, maybe, and then having them wrenched away at the instigation of some third party, without even getting a hearing or explanation from* YOU; *being told to get rooms ready for them, and shown your own written recal* [sic] *of them one day; and the next, all broken off and annulled!* I cannot trust to anything from one hour to another.
>
> (*L* 4:24)

A short time later, after another broken promise, she draws a picture of fires burning in empty bedrooms:

I cannot believe, and indeed it is almost incredible that you have once more led me to expect the arrival of my children only to disappoint me. Nevertheless, . . . I am keeping up fires in the rooms I expected them to occupy. . . . The utter carelessness and inhumanity shown me in all this business is so great, that, in an invented story, it would be pronounced unnatural!

(*L* 4:35)

Long after the fires had gone out, resentment still smoldered:

What I suffered on my children's account, none will ever know or measure. . . . The days and nights of tears and anguish, that grew into the struggle of years—it is even *now* a pain to me to look back upon: even *now*, the hot agony of resentment and grief rises in my mind, when I think of the needless tyranny I endured in this respect.

(*ELW* 48)

Letters from attorneys were no more effective in securing the mother's rights. Knowing full well that maternal visitation was not guaranteed by law, Norton's counsel nevertheless wrote to George (November 14, 1836). In a dispassionate and formal tone, he made his view of the circumstances very clear:

Mr Norton will pardon me for saying, that though it is most true he is not amenable to the law, and that his legal rights are undisputed and indisputable, yet there are other tribunals to which a husband may perhaps, consider himself liable to answer, should he deny the natural right of a mother to intercourse with her children, and to the children the benefits to arise to them from the attentions and affections of a mother.

(*L* 1:15)

George apparently did not feel himself accountable to a higher court, leaving his wife with few options. Initially she attempted to circumvent the law, but ultimately she sought the statutory changes that would enable her to confront him in a tribunal on this side of the grave.

For Norton, as well as Wollstonecraft's Maria, maternal deprivation effected what spousal abuse had not: open rebellion against her husband and the law. At the trial of her lover for criminal conversation, Maria arranges to have a statement read in court proclaiming that a woman must be allowed to consult her conscience, and regulate her conduct, in some degree, by her own sense of right. . . . I wish my country to approve of my conduct; but, if laws exist, made by the strong to oppress the weak, I appeal to my own sense of justice.

(*M* 144)

Men and their laws, she writes, make of "many amiable women, the *out-laws* of the world" (*M* 116). Norton, also under the aegis of, and with no other authority than, motherhood, took things into her own hands. Her first "hope was to come peaceably to an agreement. I will not say to *outwit* him [George], but to secure the boys. There is no length of desperation or of meanness that one may not be driven to in my situation."[35] She unsuccessfully attempted to "re-kidnap" her children, an illegal act that in her mind proved nothing so much as her fitness as a mother: "As to my endeavouring to take the children, *I don't deny it*; I should have been a strange sort of mother if I had not" (*L* 4:19). Paternal law meant that any woman might find it necessary to depend more "on wild and romantic expedients, than on the protection afforded them by the . . . rules which govern the community at large" (*SMC* 71).

With the failure of "romantic expedients," Norton resolved to change rather than to elude the law, hence her first foray into the authorship of which she was most proud, "prose *on a real subject.*" *The Separation of Mother and Child* and *A Plain Letter to the Lord Chancellor* were written—the first anonymously, the second pseudonymously—in support of the Infant Custody Bill, first sponsored by Serjeant Talfourd at her request in 1837. Both publications included pertinent legal case histories, but neither referred extensively to her own circumstances, in deference to Lord Melbourne and her own family, all of whom wished the scandal to die down as quickly as possible. The tone of the first is comparatively subdued, and she observed to Shelley: "Perhaps you will not think I have gone *far enough*; I thought it best to have the appearance of calmness and fairness, and I struck out many passages which my sister, Georgina Seymour, called my 'callow-nestling' bits."[36] Both pamphlets demonstrate the "deft rhetoric of motherhood." The conclusion of *The Separation of Mother and Child*, for instance, sounds like a page from Maria's courtroom declamation:

In that unnatural and revolting strife, the father tearing the child from its mother's breast, the mother flying like a hunted hind, and concealing her little ones from the face of him who should be their natural protector, it *may* perhaps occur to the lawgivers of a free country, that it would be more for the peace of society, and the credit of humanity, conditionally to admit the MOTHER'S NATURAL CLAIM.[37]

(*SMC* 30)

Oratorical flourish and melodramatic posturing notwithstanding, these pamphlets consistently demonstrate a mastery of rational argumentation and logical analysis that complement the sentimental ideology of mothers and motherhood—and that led some critics to accuse her, not of masculinity, but of simply reproducing Talfourd's arguments.

A rhetorical question posed at the beginning of *The Separation of Mother and Child* makes Norton's position clear: "Doubtless the claim of a father is sacred and indisputable, but when the mother's claim clashes with it, surely *something* should be accorded to her. There are other laws besides those made by men—what says the holier law, the law of nature?" (*SMC* 9). The sanction for her position may be divine, but her legal reality is of human origin. The law cannot

excuse its non-interference on the plea of the FATHER'S natural right, when it *does* directly interfere with the natural right of the MOTHER, and forces her children from her very breast. Either the right admitted, is NATURAL or ARTIFICIAL; if ARTIFICIAL, the law has the same power to adjudge the custody of infants, that it would have in case of any other artificial right; if NATURAL, the law has no power to order children from their mother, since by nature the rights of both parents are co-equal.

(*SMC* 27)

This argument does not entirely beg the question, but it does assume equal rights: the status quo "is *against nature*, and such a law is not to be borne" (*SMC* 28). This starting point enables the conclusion that exclusive paternal custody is artificially established, therefore liable to revision. The individual who believes otherwise would teach "the fifth commandment, not as written 'Honour your father and mother;' but according to a reading of his own, 'Honour your father and *forget your mother, for she has offended* ME' " (*SMC* 29).

Norton also points to the anomaly that an illegitimate child is held to be the responsibility of the mother, not the father, an inconsistency further underscoring the artificial construction of parental rights. She somewhat maliciously suggests that the status quo might be construed as penalizing a women for marrying her child's father.

She concludes "that if the mothers of BASTARD infants are protected from this misery, *a fortiori* the mothers of LEGITIMATE children should also be protected" (*SMC* 23). To this argument she adds a practical consideration. Mothers, she claims, are better suited than fathers for parenting—a point previously raised by Maria: "The tenderness of a father who knew the world, might be great; but could it equal that of a mother . . . ?" (*M* 94). Norton's impassioned plea anticipates the speaker of "The Dream": "*a mother's love is believed to be the strongest tie of nature, and* HER CARE TO BE ESSENTIAL TO THE WELL-BEING OF HER INFANT CHILDREN" (*SMC* 15). Even were the father required personally to care for his children, there could be no "*substitute* for maternal affection," no replacement for "the halo of a mother's love" (*SMC* 12–13; also see, *PL* 47–48, 103–4). Fathers can claim only "*nominal* custody" of children, as opposed to the mother's "*bona fide* custody" (*SMC* 2). They are obligated to provide for their families but have neither the degree of responsibility nor the level of ability inherently possessed by mothers.

While Norton makes the radical claim of equal rights for mothers, she is nonetheless careful to make this position consistent with the philosophy of protection. *The Separation of Mother and Child* insists that in the final analysis what is being advocated merely corrects an anomaly in current law: "Shall it be said that there is in England a legal protection for *every* right and *every* claim, natural and artificial, except ONE; and that ONE is the tie between mother and child!" (*SMC* 25). Far from threatening male superiority, the proposal assumes it by extending male protection to women as mothers and not simply as wives. Infant custody would be added to the rights guaranteed to women by virtue of marriage, which already include legal separation. Child custody "is a parallel case; it is a case of simple protection of the liberty and rights of the subject, and not of any encroachment on the authority of a father as the master of the house and the head of his family" (*SMC* 7). Although all of her rhetorical powers were dedicated to avoiding alienation of the audience whose concurrence was necessary for passage of the bill, Norton elicited the fierce opposition of John Kemble in *The British and Foreign Review*.

A Plain Letter, published under the nom de plume Pearce Stevenson, responded to this scurrilous attack, which deemed Talfourd's proposal the "Robbery of Fathers' Bill."[38] The American jurist Charles Sumner called *A Plain Letter* "one of the most remarkable things from the pen of a woman. The world here does not suspect her, but supposes that the tract is the production of some grave barrister. It is one of the best discussions on a legislative matter I have ever read."[39] The basic position is familiar: "To say that a wife should be otherwise than dutiful and obedient to her husband, or that she should in any way be independent of him would be absurd.... But there is a very wide difference between being subject to authority and subject to oppression" (*PL* 6–7). What is particularly noteworthy about *A Plain Letter* is its trenchant rebuttal of the objections to the bill proffered in *The British and Foreign Review*:

> I. That it would encourage and increase separations between married couples, by removing the great check which the knowledge of the loss of her children at present imposes on the wife.
>
> II. That it would be impossible to carry such a measure into execution from the difficulty the courts would have in deciding domestic quarrels, and the determined resistance which would be made by fathers to legal interference in such matters.
>
> III. That the result of access (if it could be enforced against the will of the father,) would probably, if not certainly, be the abduction of the children, whom the mother would thus have an opportunity of carrying away.
>
> IV. That ... it would afford a temptation to perjury; and that a woman who was *guilty*, though not *convicted* of misconduct, might obtain access by these affidavits.
>
> V. That it will render reconciliations less probable.
>
> VI. That it will disturb the education of the children under the father's exclusive care.
>
> (*PL* 12–13)

In countermanding these positions, Norton made two general observations: first, that the contentions about wives and mothers might with equal probability be posited of husbands and fathers, and second, that many of the claims either begged the question or expressed prejudices rather than reasonable deductions drawn from common experience.

She also answered each point. Concerning the first, she replied that the alleged "great check" did not exist in practical terms, for, on the one hand, few women were even aware of the legal status quo and, on the other hand, even were they generally known, the obstacles to women who might wish to leave their husbands were formidable and existed "*all on the woman's side*" (*PL* 17, 20). She further reasoned that passage of the bill might dissuade men from leaving their wives by establishing restrictions upon their parental power, therein actually promoting the objective that Kemble alleged it would undermine.

As for the contention about uncooperative fathers, Norton countered that the absence of "legal interference" encouraged a husband's misconduct. The presence even of such modest restraint as proposed in the legislation would moderate behavior: "A man who feels that nothing opposes between his angry will and this object of his anger, will act rashly, suddenly, and probably with great injustice; ... but the man who knows that he is responsible for the manner and measure of his vengeance, will pause" (*PL* 25).

On the third point, the claim that abductions of children would rise, Norton made the obvious counterargument: increased access to children would in all likelihood diminish rather than augment a mother's inclination to steal them. She could, of course, speak from her own experience of "romantic expedients": "The temptation to abduct the children, lies with the woman who is driven to desperation by her inability to see or gain intelligence of them; who is writhing under the infliction of a compulsory separation from them, which the law cannot relieve; who knows *she has but one alternative*" (*PL* 33). A similar logic led her to reject the fifth point, the surmise that reconciliations between alienated spouses would be made less probable by the bill. Norton replied simply that this "is an assertion and nothing more. It is in fact affirming, that a woman is more likely to be soothed into a gentler state of feeling by extreme ill usage, than by obtaining partial justice" (*PL* 45). Both of Kemble's claims were answered with the hypothesis that treating mothers with consideration would generate more and not less cooperation and goodwill.

In response to the fourth point—that the law promoted perjury—Norton simply pointed out that the reason offered for rejecting this law might be applied to any law, and that in no case should the possibility of perjury preclude the pursuit of justice: "*All* these things are possible; and in rare instances it is to be feared that all these things have been done; ... but because they *are* possible, are men to desist from appeals to legal tribunals?" (*PL* 38). This logic also answers Kemble's position on the education of children. The concern that some mothers might attempt to turn children against fathers (something, of course, that fathers might be equally likely to do) should not prevent all mothers from having access to their children. Kemble's contention avoided the key issue by "considering the relief intended for virtuous wives with profligate husbands, as an indulgence invented for profligate and ill-conducted wives with *just* husbands" (*PL* 50). The chance that a profligate wife might attempt to take advantage of the law (or perjure herself) is no reason not to protect "virtuous wives with profligate husbands."

The success of Norton's writing on the subject of a mother's rights must be measured by more than passage of the Infant Custody Bill in 1839. The changes to the law were modest: mothers of good moral character were granted visitation rights to children under the age of seven. The reforms came too late to be of much help to her, and, in any event, George simply eluded its provisions by keeping the children in Scotland. Although relying upon a conservative maternal narrative, Norton's pamphlets represent an important step away from purely sentimental narratives of motherhood and toward the legal construction of maternity and its rights. In that regard, she participates in the general movement, subsequently articulated by Sir Henry Sumner Maine, from status to contract as the foundation of societal relations and structure.[40]

Her writings also illustrate the philosophy of protection applied to the politics of gender. Their combination of rational deduction and rhetorical grace left little room for intelligent disagreement, and they stand as landmarks in the early nineteenth-century debate on women's rights. While feminists may not have entirely agreed with Norton's conservative stance on protection rather than equality, even a severe critic like Martineau acknowledged that the passage of the Infant Custody Bill, which acknowledged the parental rights of wives, was "the first blow struck at the oppression of English legislation in relation to women."[41]

LEGAL FICTIONS AND LICENSE OF THE BAR

Norton's second campaign for legislative reform, marked by the publication of *English Laws for Women* and *A Letter to the Queen*, was in no small part the result of the legal fiction of coverture. A legal fiction in the technical sense is the "assumption or supposition that something which is or may be false is true, or that a state of facts exists which has never really taken place."[42] Blackstone—whose definition this is—was cognizant of the inherent contradiction in admitting falsehoods into a profession presumably dedicated to "the truth, the whole truth, and nothing but the truth," but he defended them on the basis of convenience and usefulness.[43] Convenient and useful to men, perhaps, but to the alienated wife—and one proven to be innocent of adultery in a court of law—legal nonexistence seemed cruel and unusual punishment.

The concept of the legal fiction appears several times in Norton's essays, usually in reference to legal practices or presuppositions that are false either because they create a circumstance that seems unfair (for example, a married woman ceases to have an independent legal existence) or because they assume a circumstance that has no basis in reality (for example, the presumption that husbands' possession of rights invariably leads to the performance of the duties attendant upon them). Norton included in her sense of legal fiction the practice generally referred to as "license of the bar," that is, the use of hypothetical narratives, typically by defense attorneys, to cast doubt upon the accusations against their clients. These suppositional tales need not be proven; their sole purpose is to suggest plausible alternatives to the facts alleged by the prosecution. She cites, for example, the trial of a man charged with burglary whose attorney, in offering an explanation of his client's presence on the premises, suggested that he "might perhaps have had a love-appointment with the lady of the house! This extraordinary insult being complained of the barrister pleaded 'license of the bar' " (*ELW* 92).

Letter to the Queen describes license of the bar as the professional privilege "to assert that which is untrue with impunity" (*LQ* 84), which is exercised in *Bigley* v. *Dupré* and more damningly in *Norton* v. *Melbourne*, when both Follett and Campbell made free use of largely fictive accounts of events under consideration. In *Emmott* v. *Norton*, Sir Fitzroy Kelly claimed that the truly guilty party was not George, but his wife, because she willfully intended Emmott's suit—and the others that he was certain would follow—"to ruin Mr. N. and drive him out of the country" (*LQ* 68). In this version of things, the defendant was "a high-minded and excellent man" whose legal defeat (in *Norton* v. *Melbourne*) had left him with "a wife utterly unworthy" but who nevertheless "vainly strove, with mingled economy and generosity, to provide for her and his children" (*ELW* 132). Coverture may have meant that Mrs. Norton could not be held liable for her unpaid bills, but it also meant that she could not rebut the fictions of her husband's attorney: "nothing was published but a feeble anonymous denial, in a morning paper, of the general thread of Sir Fitzroy Kelly's remarks" (*ELW* 135). After *Thrupp* v. *Norton*, she reported that the defense counsel, Mr. Needham, "tendered me a sort of apology, saying that 'however impertinent I might consider his questions, they were within the limit of his legal instructions' " (*ELW* 92). "Legal instructions" should not include mendacity. While Kelly and Needham would surely have insisted that they were merely doing the best for their client, Norton labeled their tactic "the Romance of the Bar" (*ELW* 92), therein associating the attorneys with the most fanciful practices of novelists. She protested, by contrast, that "*my* history *is real.* I know there is no poetry in it to attract you" (*ELW* 166).

Anything might be said of her in court and out (because a married woman could not initiate an action for libel) with neither the burden of proof imposed upon the accuser nor the possibility of defense offered to the accused. Fifteen years as an undivorced wife had made Norton a staunch opponent of coverture. In *Letter to the Queen*, she wrote: "A married woman in England has *no legal existence*: her being is absorbed in that of her husband. Years of separation or desertion cannot alter this position. . . . [T]he legal fiction holds her to be '*one*' with her husband, even though she may never see or hear of him" (*LQ* 8).[44] The bitter significance of "Romance of the Bar" might be retrospectively applied to "Curious Customs in the County of Middlesex." At the time of formulating the mathematics of marriage, Norton could not have fully understood the legal calculus of coverture. She could not have known, for instance, that marriage for a woman was a form of legal suicide in which two were reduced to one. Her pamphlets of the 1850s, in contrast to the bemused irony of the earlier tale, are angry and direct; the case is made largely without "poetry in it to attract you." The figurative language is strained, for example, in this reference to alienated couples who "are about as much 'one' as those ingenious twisted groups of animal death we sometimes see in sculpture; one creature wild to resist, and the other fierce to destroy" (*LQ* 28). "Ingenious twisted groups of animal death" may be catachrestic—it is certainly melodramatic—but Norton insists that her marriage offers just such a picture of contorted combat. *English Laws* presents her situation more prosaically as a "divorce-less separation," in which "every human circumstance, except death" divides spouses but "does not affect the legal fiction which assumes that a married couple are *one*" (*ELW* 156).

The narrator of "Curious Customs in the County of Middlesex" draws a distinction to which Norton returns when criticizing the patriarchal calculus of English marriage law. Carleton never seriously entertains the idea that spousal invisibility might be a good thing; he never even considers the issue of divorce. He does, however, differentiate three orders of law in terms consistent with Norton's political writing, especially the child custody pamphlets. He maintains that the

> divine law says that man and wife are one, the English law says that all property (with exceptions, for which I refer my readers to Blackstone,) is the husband's; but who does not know that the law of custom is stronger than either the divine law or the laws of Great Britain?
>
> (*KB* 1:146)

His sympathies, like Norton's, are with the first code; his antipathies, again like Norton's, are reserved for the last; and he speaks authorially when posing the rhetorical question: "There are laws besides the laws of fashion, there is a tribunal beyond that of 'the world.' What if they should differ? What if it should be found after the glitter hath passed away, and the shadow of death is come and gone, that 'God judgeth not as man judgeth?'" (*KB* 1:152). *English Laws* sustains this critique of law and enlists it in support of legal reform: "We have an idol; our idol is traditionary custom; and great is that Diana of the Britons!" (*ELW* 142). The final pamphlets make the case that Norton had not when simply mocking the rule of fashion: she proposes a new marital equation that only seems tautological: 1 + 1=1 + 1. A husband and wife, no less than a man and a woman, should be equally visible in the eyes of the law. Norton never felt that Emmott or Thrupp—or any of the more than 20 tradesmen whom George claimed had threatened him with legal action—should be cheated of payment for services they had rendered. A wife separated from her husband "*should* be responsible to the law, and liable to a civil action" (*ELW* 157). The difference between the two sides of this marital equation inheres in the protections and rights that should naturally accompany love but that must invariably be guaranteed by law.

The threatening implications of Norton's challenge to the customary privilege of British husbands were evident from Kemble's attack on the "Robbery of Fathers' Bill." He singles out "Curious Customs," along with works by Lady Charlotte Bury and the Countess of Blessington, as proof of the dangerous influence of literature upon established institutions. Addressing the House of Lords, which had yet to act on Talfourd's bill, Kemble writes, "We refer them to the sensual state of literature; . . . we ask them to look at the state of married life among the aristocracy of this country as described by those who have lived in it."[45] He identifies Norton and Martineau as "renowned agitatrices,"[46] perhaps not understanding that the latter is ironically invoked in the tale. Carleton only pretends to be "neither condemning, nor . . . eulogising the custom of keeping asunder those whom God hath joined" (*KB* 1:149) when in a mock serious tone, he asks for Martineau's help in understanding modern mores:

To you, dear madam, with your clear head and feeling heart, I leave these puzzling points, while simply keeping to my own subject, I affirm, that whatever may be the cause of interested marriages, it is, because they *are* made that the invisibility of London husbands is become the law of custom.

(*KB* 1:151)

He solicits Martineau's help only because he does not need it—knowing full well that commercial rather than companionate marriages are to blame for London mores. By interposing a naive but astute narrator between herself and readers, Norton manages to baffle at least one of them: Kemble himself. Far from exemplifying sensual literature, "Curious Customs" critiques modern marriage and distances Norton from the very person with whom Kemble associates her.

No such distance was required in the case of Eliza Lynn Linton's "One of Our Legal Fictions" (1854), allegedly the "true story" of Charlotte and Robert Desborough but in actuality a virtual history of the Nortons.[47] Readers of *Household Words* would have readily recognized the "conte à clef," since the Nortons' private history had been widely publicized in a series of letters to the *Times* in August and September of 1853 and since Linton changed almost nothing except names. The husband is "a man of violent temper, [who] held supreme views of marital privileges"; his wife is "young, impassioned, beautiful, and clever" ("OLF" 258). Eventually "high words" lead to "rough deeds," and the result is a "sad, unhinged" family ("OLF" 258). An unsuccessful adultery action means that the couple cannot divorce, and the wife is deprived "of even the small amount of protection afforded by the law to English wives of the nineteenth century" ("OLF" 258). Imprisoned by "the iron bars of the law" ("OLF" 259), they battle over children and money: "Years trailed wearily on. . . . But the criminal law swept on the beaten track, and no one stopped to ask over whose heart this great car of our Juggernaut passed" ("OLF" 259).

Linton's title documents her greater concern with the political significance than the narrative interest of her tale. While the unsuccessful plaintiff retained full legal powers, his estranged wife could do nothing because of the "legal poetic fiction 'that, by law, man and wife were one' " ("OLF" 260). Linton inserted "poetic" into this phrase—as Norton had changed "license" to "romance" of the bar—in order to emphasize the fictitiousness of the concept and to underscore its origins in an idealized and imaginative construct:

Yet what can be more beautiful than the ideal of an English marriage! This strict union of interests—although it does mean the absorption of the woman's whole life in that of the man's—although it does mean the entire annihilation of all her rights, individuality, legal existence, and his sole recognition by the law—yet how beautiful it is in the ideal!

("OLF" 257)

Linton suggests that the "marriage idyl" ("OLF" 260) for couples like the Nortons becomes "a dirge for ruined hopes and wasted youth, for a heart made desolate, and a home destroyed; a dirge for the shattered household gods and the fleeting of the fond visions of her heart" ("OLF" 259). Whatever Norton's hopes for marriage in 1827, a quarter century of strife had long since extinguished them; nevertheless, she refused Linton's funereal tone and resigned attitude. In the mid-1850s she set about improving the legal status of married women.

THE SECOND CAMPAIGN: THE MARRIAGE AND DIVORCE BILL (1855)

Norton decided to use *English Laws for Women* to tell her side of a nearly three-decade marital history, having resolved never again to feel, as she had with her first pamphlet, that she had not gone far enough:

And if it be asked why, having spared him so long, I expose him now,—I answer that *I* am the judge,—not others,—where endurance merged in exasperation: and the boundary line was reached, the day Mr Norton met me in the County Court; the day that to evade a just claim, he unburied all the falsehoods of the past; endeavoured to disgrace (in 1853, as he had done in 1836) for the sake of money; and in cold blood re-published, to the grieving of my grown-up sons, the slanders which had blighted my youth in their infancy.

(*ELW* 71)

Arthur Arnold, in an article published shortly after her death, defends the vehement tone and personal preoccupation of Norton's late political writing:

Her style was not employed in its perfection to protest against any other wrongs or to depict other sorrows than those which had pierced her own heart. This is not an imputation of selfishness; it is merely an illustration of the fact that the highest and most successful efforts of genius are those which have their inspiration from the deepest feelings.[48]

Although *English Laws* begins with the claim that "it is of more importance that the law should be altered, than that I should be approved"

(*ELW* 2), the emphasis gradually shifts to the injustices of her own situation and the outrage of *Thrupp* v. *Norton*. The interweaving of personal grievance with the greater cause of suffering women and broken families was not, however, an ineffective strategy. As Elaine Hadley has shown, "By affiliating her own story of domestic cruelty with the suffering of the poor, by pleading for a protector for them both, Norton universalizes (in a pose she had adopted in her earlier poetry) her particular narrative into an emblematic melodrama of nationwide familial estrangement."[49]

Letter to the Queen, written the following year, while it does rehearse personal history, is more directly focused on the specific objective of legislative reform. Given her "opinion" on the morality of divorce, Norton faces a considerable rhetorical challenge in presenting her "case" and the case for divorce in this pamphlet (to use the terms of her letter to Gladstone). The argument is altered slightly from that offered for unhappy mothers, whose rights as parents are divinely sanctioned but violated by British law. In the case of unhappy wives, she urges the active intervention of human law to curb those who ignore divinely sanctioned principles and to protect their victims. She does not disagree that "the husband is the administrator and exponent of the law, for he stands in his natural capacity of protector of his wife" (*ELW* 161), but

> that married persons should be still considered *one*, without the possibility of interference on the part of justice when living alienated and in a state of separation—is unjust, unfit, and unnatural; and can be productive only of social disorder and scandalous struggle. . . . [The husband] is no longer the administrator and exponent of the law, but its direct opponent; (for the *intention* of the law certainly is, that the woman shall be protected; and that he shall be her protector.)
>
> (*ELW* 161)

The political philosophy underlying this position is consistent with that applied to child custody: spouses no less than parents are deserving of equal protection. She explicitly connects the two efforts: "There was not law then to help the mother, as there is no law now to help the wife. . . . The father possessed precisely the right the husband still possesses—namely, to do exactly what he pleased" (*LQ* 64). Having helped to curb the power of fathers to do what they wished with their children, she hopes to restrict husbands' power over wives. The rationale now as then was that "women are not appealing *for an exceptional law in their favour*; on the contrary, they are appealing not to be made an exception from the general protection of the laws" (*LQ* 106). She cites three ways in which divorce laws are unfair. The primary inequity is that women need several grounds upon which to seek divorce, while men require only one, adultery. In effect, the "marriage ceremony is a civil bond for him,—and an indissoluble sacrament for her; and the rights of mutual property which that ceremony is ignorantly supposed to confer, are made absolute for him, and null for her" (*LQ* 13).[50] Men, furthermore, are able to sue for a divorce (*à vinculo*), enabling both parties to remarry; whereas, women could initiate only a separation (*à mensa et thoro*) allowing spouses to live apart but not to remarry. The second inequitable circumstance, also noted by Dickens in *Hard Times* (1854), is that the civil bond/sacrament distinction applies to class as well as gender. Divorce is a realistic option only for the wealthy. Her third objection recalls Eleanor's position in *Stuart of Dunleath*: "It is not fit there should be one law one for the poor and another for the rich,—one law for the weak, and another for the strong,—one law for England, and another for Scotland" (*LQ* 128–29, also see 59). Apart from its inherent unfairness, "this confusion" creates "scandal, outrage, and fraud; and an impossibility of carrying out the ends of justice" (*LQ* 129).

Norton argues that the incentives against divorce are and should be great but asks "in *un*usual cases—in cases of the dreary, stormy, deserted life—where profligacy, personal violence, insult, and oppression, fill up the measure of the wrong which pardon cannot reach,—why is there to be no rescue for the woman?" (*LQ* 37). Those cases may be few, but they demonstrate the potential fate of any British woman as a result of the "grotesque anomaly which ordains that married women shall be 'non-existent' in a country governed by a female Sovereign" (*LQ* 5). *Letter to the Queen* retains the rhetoric of maternity from the previous campaign and fully exploits the rhetorical advantage of linking women's rights to the presence of a female monarch. Victoria figured consistently and prominently in Norton's imagination, to say nothing of the national consciousness. One of her most endearing personae was as a prolific and devoted parent. In "The Queen," Norton takes royal fecundity as a harbinger of national prosperity: "Her own and England's hopes renewed, / In many a stately boy:— / All holy ties of Life complete, / A Woman,—though a Queen, / So, may Victoria's reign surpass, / The glories that have been!" (*FDS 47*:6).[51] In invoking the name of the Queen, however, Norton had to be careful to balance criticism with commendation, a point made clear by the flattering preface to the often critical *The Child of the Islands*:

In the brief space of time since this poem was commenced, there has been great evidence of increasing attention to the sufferings, and to the endurance, of the lower classes. Much has been said—and something has been done. . . . [T]he reign of Victoria bids fair to claim a more hallowed glory than that which encircled the "Golden Age" of Elizabeth.

(*CI* x–xi)

Letter to the Queen implies that as a mother Victoria will be more sympathetic to women's causes than her female predecessors: "Not lone and vainglorious, like the virgin Queen Elizabeth,—nor childless, like the hypochondriac Mary,—nor heirless, like the feeble-minded Anne,—more of 'the beauty of womanhood' adorns the destiny of Queen Victoria, than has belonged to the barren reigns of former English Queens; and the link to all the interests of woman's life should be greater" (*LQ* 133). By excluding comparison to English kings, Norton intimates that by virtue of gender alone Victoria will be sensitive to the hardships visited upon women.

Just as she had pointed out the anomalous circumstance in which unwed mothers possessed rights that married women did not, Norton now argues that in some respects the cast-off but virtuous wife would have been better off had she committed adultery. She could then be legally divorced, own property in her own name, and generally assume the status of feme sole. Norton posits the hypothetical case of a woman who thinks:

"*Would I had been indeed a sinner and divorced, rather than live this life of torment, injustice, and mockery!*" Wild words: terrible sinful words: are they not? A bad, shocking woman to say so. . . . But also a bad law I think. A bad, wicked law, which makes it utterly indifferent whether she can or can not claim to be an innocent woman: and whether her husband is or is not a bad worthless man.

(*LQ* 59)

These "wild words" were not to be taken seriously, but Norton did want readers to recognize the penalty indiscriminately imposed upon unsinning, undivorced women. She had been exonerated; her husband had admitted that his accusations were not justified; yet she remained without legal recognition or individual rights:

I am, as regards my husband, in a worse position than if I had been divorced. . . . I am *not* divorced, and I cannot divorce my husband; yet I can establish no legal claim upon him, nor upon any living human being! . . . I cannot release myself. I exist and I suffer; but the law denies my existence.

(*LQ* 96)

Norton drew barbed conclusions about the reasons for these inequities. She suggested, for example, that passage of a partial reform measure, which left the double standard intact, would have the effect of "*legalis[ing]* a special indulgence for the animal passions of men" (*LQ* 22). She satirically hypothesized that the chief "obstacle to this legal reform must be, that men fear to curb the license of their own pleasures" (*LQ* 150). In answer to the charge that establishing uniform grounds for divorce would promote female infidelity, she invited readers to examine the situation in Scotland, where women could obtain a divorce solely on grounds of adultery (*LQ* 16). She derided the view that England would become "a hot-bed of vice" by fancifully imagining cold Caledonia as

a land dedicated to Cupid. Statues of Venus are set up in all the principal squares of Edinburgh. The marriage-tie is a mere true lover's knot. The ladies who present themselves at Holyrood are triumphant Messalinas. And on the decks of the emigrant vessels which crowd the harbour of Leith, groups of melancholy cast-off husbands may be seen, bidding reproachful farewell to that inhospitable country where they only exist to be repudiated!

(*LQ* 20–21)

The farcical tone carries a serious message concerning the sexual double standard: male power and privilege are the principal reasons for the unequal divorce and property laws.

Norton further recognized that "England's merchant spirit" contributes to the legal status quo: "property, not morality, being the thing held sacred . . . the wife's adultery may give the husband a spurious son to inherit!" (*ELW* 152). George had doubted the paternity of his second son (*LCN* 108), and Follett introduced the fear that a man's property might not be inherited by his lawful issue into *Norton* v. *Melbourne*. Setting aside the issue of damages, Norton bitterly observed that "although *women* are not protected in England *property* is guarded by the most stringent rules" (*LQ* 45). Meredith, too, comments on this "merchant spirit." Contemplating a married woman's legal dependence, Diana says, "Whenever I am distracted by existing circumstances, I lay my finger on the material conditions, and I touch the secret. Individually, it *may* be moral with us; collectively, it is material—gross wrongs, gross hungers. I am a married rebel, and thereof comes the social rebel" (*DC* 1:181).[52]

Following Wollstonecraft in proclaiming women the world's outlaws, Norton noted that "sneerers" may declare hers to be "the mere rebellion of a clever woman against the authority of her natural lord and master," but "in families, as in nations, Rebellion is a disease that springs from the *malaria* of bad government. WRONGS make REBELS. Those who would dwell submissive in the wholesome atmosphere of authority, revolt in the jail fever of tyranny" (*LQ* 123–24). *Letter to the Queen* ends with a resounding proclamation:

> For *this*, I believe, God gave me the power of writing. To this I devote that power. I abjure all other writing, till I see these laws altered. I care not what ridicule or abuse may be the result of that declaration. They who cannot bear ridicule and abuse, are unfit and unable to advance *any* cause; and once more I deny that this is my personal cause; it is the cause of all the women of England. If *I* could be justified and happy tomorrow, I would still strive and labour in it; and if I were to die tomorrow, it would still be a satisfaction to me that I had so striven. Meanwhile, my husband has a legal lien (as he has publicly proved), on the copyright of my works. Let him claim the copyright of THIS.
>
> (*LQ* 151–53)

Her protest recalls Maria's statement at Darnford's trial, and its force explains why hers was an important voice in support of the rights of married women.

Letter to the Queen revived in one reviewer's mind the familiar image of Bradamante: "she has charged and overthrown those Rodomonts and Sacripants of modern days, commonly known to fame as the Law Lords."[53] Norton's pamphlets did, in fact, contribute to changes in the legislation eventually passed by Parliament, even if the "Giants of the Law" were not entirely vanquished and thorough reform of property law and equal protection under marriage laws would not come for many years.[54] Lord Lyndhurst quoted Norton extensively during the debate of the measure—introducing several amendments along lines that she recommended—and even her old nemesis on child custody, Lord Brougham, noted: "It is as clever a thing as ever was written, and it has produced great good. I feel certain that the Law of Divorce will be much amended, and she has greatly contributed to it."[55]

After the passage of the Divorce Act of 1857, Norton devoted little time to political writing. She did circulate a small number of copies of "Taxation by an Irresponsible Taxpayer" in 1874—"irresponsible" referring to herself and reminding readers of her rebel status. The irritation that occasioned this tract was the rising tax rate, combined with decreasing municipal services and a Byzantine metropolitan bureaucracy. Her complaints focused on "the ill-managed parish of St. George's, Hanover Square . . . where I have the misfortune to be a nominal 'householder' " ("T" 6)—"nominal" for purposes of ownership, "real" for purposes of taxation. Public injustice invariably reminded her of private wrongs and led, in turn, to long-standing personal grievances. Well after *Letter to the Queen*, she was galled to find herself still "[n]on-existent for protection, but not non-existent for extortion. . . . Liable as a 'female occupier' to pay taxes, but not able as a 'female occupier' to hold my house except through trustees, or to compel by any process of law the payment of an agreed income" ("T" 17).

Self-interest rather than social activism, however, is the stronger note here. The tone is querulous rather than idealistic, mean spirited rather than public spirited. In *A Voice from the Factories*, for example, she had commented on "[t]he boy-Italian's voice, so soft and deep, / Asks alms for his poor marmoset asleep: They fill our hearts with pitying regret / Those little vagrants doomed so soon to weep" (*VFF* 8). Thirty-eight years later, however, she complains of "the live-stock of organ-grinders . . . who pasture in those purlieus" and have so befouled her street that its name should be changed to "OOZY LANE" ("T" 10). She seems especially curmudgeonly on this subject, citing the "vagabond foreigners, both men and women, [who] lounge through our streets incessantly turning the handle of a toy instrument" ("T" 10). It is she who comes off as the crank, sounding more like "Anti-Humbug" than a rebel.

In *The Child of the Islands*, Norton recalled visiting Parkhurst, a prison for boys, and seeing the "[g]erms of men" locked up there:

And though 'tis mournful, in their prison garb,
To see them trooping to their silent mean;
And though, among them, many brows reveal
Sorrow too bitter for such childish hearts;
Yet the most pitiful (if just) must feel
(E'en while the tear of forced compassion starts)
That blessed is the hope their suffering imparts!
(*CI* 40)

If punishment is necessary, it is regrettable, and its effects are mitigated by hope for the boys' future. By 1874, however, her expression is terse, and the emphasis is upon condign punishment. She writes that children " 'found begging' or 'sleeping under archways' are (very properly) packed off to schools and reformatories to learn more regular habits of life" ("T" 10). "Very properly" echoes but darkens the parenthetical "(if just)" in the earlier work. Norton seems not to consider that the reformatory might not be either an adequate or a just response to childhood poverty. The eponymous prince of *The Child of the Islands* did not, of course, mature to fulfill the hope that Norton placed in him, but even more significantly her own ongoing struggles and disappointments diminished her faith in the hope borne of suffering.

The comparatively stable and secure life in Chesterfield Street could not obscure the insult (and injury) of being no more than a "female occupier" after all the years of writing and fighting. Lady Margaret Fordyce's long meditation on changing times—delivered in 1851 to her protégé, Elizabeth Penrhyn—turns out to be sadly proleptic. After light-heartedly speculating on modern "improvements," such as chalk replacing coal in stoves and fireplaces, she says:

> Conceive our old familiar friend the coal-scuttle, wearing a new face, and dismally presenting itself to notice, with half a bushel of white, ghastly, cheerless lumps, for all the world like the ghosts of the coals we burned in our childhood! "Old King *Coal* was a jolly old soul," his successor is a horror. All the pretty little endearing ways, all the playful fancies of our fires are extinguished for ever. None of the flickering and flaming bursts of gas and tar, mute brilliancies that were to us, as we sate alone, what jests and repartees are in conversation; but a dull smouldering, prosaic, detestable way of warming oneself. Even Mrs. Ellis will never teach the women of England to make their firesides pleasant under such circumstances. The fire is put out, and so are we; we cannot accustom our minds to the new embarrassment. What are we to do with our old tropes, similes, and metaphors? What will be the use of talking of the flame of love, to a generation who burn red hot chalk?
>
> (*SD* 1:187–89)

The mock rebel railing against the indignities of chalk evinces the scintillating wit that sparkled and not infrequently singed its object. By the end of her career, however, "playful fancies" and passionate protests alike have died out, and words themselves have turned to chalk.

Afterword

"Such Is the Tale They Tell!": The Narratives of Caroline Norton

It is impossible not to be haunted *by experiences of real life when one is writing,—as painters and all artists are obviously haunted by certain types of humanity they have seen with their bodily eyes; but it is an unconscious, and* general *copy:—the realization of a* type *and not of an* individual.[1]

Caroline Norton, Letter to Miss Dempster

I am no-where!*—My history is too long & doleful to write.*[2]

Caroline Norton, Letter to Helen Blackwood

As the author of popular literature and polemical pamphlets, Norton encountered various "optical" obstacles: for women, a visible presence in the competitive worlds of commercial publication or political disputation necessarily entailed criticism and controversy. The gendered values of modesty, reticence, and privacy conflicted with the self-advertisement associated with publication, a dilemma only partially mitigated by anonymous or pseudonymous authorship. To be a woman and a writer was to be doubly but dichotomously visible. Literary success might be pejoratively attributed to feminine beauty or wiles, on the one hand, or taken as unflattering evidence of a masculine nature, on the other. In either case, the woman writer was seen as a discredit to her sex, and the writings themselves were often not seen at all.

The beauty that eased Norton's access to silver fork society also cast a shadow over her literary reputation. Dickens, Thackeray, and others insinuated that a "superb lump of flesh" could hardly be a writer—or a suffragette—of significance. Nor were the efforts of Bulwer Lytton and others to apostrophize her as the "queenly Spirit of a Star" likely to promote success in the rough and tumble of the literary marketplace and the political arena. Other factors further distracted readers from Norton's poetry and fiction, including the protracted public scandal surrounding her marriage, her role as political hostess, and her reputation as a "renown agitatrix." Thus it is not entirely surprising that following the publication of her last two novels in the 1860s and after almost 40 years in the public eye, the literary light of "the Byron of modern poetesses" dimmed to the point of disappearance from the pantheon of literary luminaries.

The publication of three biographies in the twentieth century demonstrates that interest in the "scandalous woman" persists, even as her writing is underappreciated. The correlation between personal visibility and professional invisibility is documented by *The French Lieutenant's Woman.* Fowles's narrator refers to "Sheridan's granddaughter" and to "Melbourne's mistress," while dismissively observing, "You may think that Mrs. Norton was a mere insipid poetastrix of the age. Insipid her verse is . . . but she was a far from insipid person."[3] While feminist scholars have questioned this critical assessment, attention to her work has largely been limited to the polemical writing and an occasional poem, with scant attention paid to the fiction and no attempt to assess the lifetime of accomplishment of "that remarkable woman." Thus the legal nonexistence that lasted virtually all of her life has had an unfortunate critical corollary.

This critical aporia has a curious parallel in Norton's own work, which, despite being described as autobiographical, includes few writers. When the subject of authorship appears in her correspondence, it is usually in the context of anxieties concerning finances and publication deadlines. Writing is considered a business, a matter of economic necessity rather than aesthetic inspiration. Indeed, her request of Peel in 1843 that she be named poet laureate was undisguisedly based upon need rather than merit: "No doubt hundreds more worthy, & of great abilities, may be named; but it might not be the same object to them as to me, to whom it would at once be a great assistance as to income and a mark of favor."[4] Although personal experience strongly influenced her writing in other ways, Norton did not tend to write about the prosaic profession of authorship. Her fiction contains a wide range of literary allusions, testifying to the breadth of her reading, but it is not populated by authors.

Those who do appear are typically diarists or amateur poetesses expressing private sorrow without expectation of publication. Their efforts, often in the form of a private lament or prayer, are evidence of poetry's power to console and, in so doing, to exhaust the impetus to write. One example is the "sickly, deformed, and dwarfish" (*WWR* 3:54) sister of the heroine in *The Wife*. Catherine Dalrymple vents resentment at her lot in life in verse of the "most unfeminine intenseness of expression" (*WWR* 3:55). In "Lines on a Picture at Moorfields Park," she writes of her profound loneliness and exclusion: "That thirst returns— / That first deep quenchless thirst—companionship— / Which smote sad Adam in *thy* garden bowers, / Lost Eden, and made Paradise imperfect!" (*WWR* 3:155). Similar verse is penned by Eleanor Penrhyn after the deaths of her children. Separated by marriage from the man she truly loves and alienated from her husband, she turns to poetry to express bereavement and unhappiness. Just as Catherine prayed "against that very madness—*hate*" and "for a more Christian spirit—a more patient heart—and prayed in vain" (*WWR* 3:115), Eleanor counsels herself to "hush this vain lamenting; / Earth's anguish will not alter Heaven's decree" (*SD* 3:274).[5] Versification assuages but cannot eliminate the anguish of unhappily (un)married women.

Women poets—as opposed to poetical women like Catherine and Eleanor—are found in several poems. The best known among them is described by Norton as "an ode to myself."[6] "The Picture of Sappho" resembles "The Lady of Shalott" in raising the possibility that art and life, or at least art and love, are irreconcilable pursuits for women. While Tennyson's protagonist dies after abandoning her island tower for Camelot and Lancelot, Sappho, according to the legend invoked by Norton, despairs of her lover's return and commits suicide by leaping into the sea. The forlorn Sappho, the opposite of the amateur poet in whom unhappiness inspires poetry, loses all interest in art: "Thy harp neglected by thee idly lying" (*D* 203), and all desire for poetic success: "With Fame's cold light around thee vainly shining" (*D* 202). The final stanza indicates that artistic success is no consolation for human suffering:

> *FAME*, to thy breaking heart
> No comfort could impart,
> In vain thy brow the laurel wreath was wearing;
> One grief and one alone
> Could bow thy bright head down—
> Thou wert a *WOMAN*, and wert left despairing!
> (*D* 205)

"The Picture of Sappho" suggests that a woman's melancholy is inimical to poetic expression and accomplishment, if not to life itself. As an "an ode to myself," it further intimates Norton's attitude toward her own tumultuous life and poetic accomplishment.

If suffering is unfavorable to art, then it is no less the case that literary fame can be injurious to the individual. Success might obscure and, therefore, exacerbate the reality of suffering: the human being is lost behind a mask of authorial success. In the case of Sappho, there has been a triple occlusion of the "*WOMAN*" by her "*FAME*": the first is of the individual by the legend, the second is of the experience of melancholy by the reputation for artistic genius, and the third takes place in the minds of onlookers for whom "many a wandering thought / Thy loveliness hath brought, / Warming the heart with its imagined glory" (*D* 202). "Imagined" need not, of course, mean "false," but Norton surely implies that audiences' warm hearts, no less than "Fame's cold light," have obscured the suffering individual.

While addressed to Sappho, the poem is less about her than pictures of her, that is, representations of the woman "whose impassion'd face / The Painter loves to trace, / Theme of the Sculptor's art and Poet's story" (*D* 202). It returns us, therefore, to the images of Caroline Norton with which this study began. The speaker poses six questions in succession concerning the accuracy of the "old traditions" about Sappho, for example: "Yet, was it History's truth, / That tale of wasted youth, / Of endless grief, and Love Forsaken pining?" (*D* 202). The speaker's relentless questioning (stanzas 2–7) insinuates that the old traditions—the "Poet's story" and "History's truth"—mask rather than reveal their subject. These narratives disclose more of those who perpetuate them than of Sappho herself. In that regard, "The Picture of Sappho" might suggestively be read as "A Narrative of Caroline Norton."

The relentless inquiry into the old traditions amplifies the legend that the speaker appears to doubt. Was Sappho really "anxious, nerveless, dejected"; were her days actually passed in "languid lone despair" (*D* 203)? The answers come in the final three stanzas (8–10), in which question marks are replaced by exclamation points, and they can be expressed in a single word: "Yea." Peace is found only in death:

> Thy heart at length found rest!
> The ever-moving waves above thee closing—
> The winds, whose ruffling sigh
> Swept the blue waters by,
> Disturb'd thee not!—thou were in peace reposing.
>
> (*D* 204)

Norton's "ode to myself," published when she was in her early thirties, resonates with the anguish of her suffering heroines. "The Picture of Sappho" features not the beautiful woman known for feminist protest, poetry, and music but the suffering woman who finds in death the calm that eluded her in life.[7] The legend of Sappho—the woman who died for love—lives on, while her literary reputation depends upon a few surviving poetic fragments. Later in her life, Norton must have felt that "The Picture of Sappho" ironically confirmed Haydon's posing her as Cassandra. The poem issues a dark warning about her own future, one that perhaps even she did not believe: "Such is the tale they tell! / Vain was thy beauty's spell— / Vain all the praise thy song could still inspire" (*D* 205).

While "The Picture of Sappho" employs what Yopie Prins identifies as the "rhetoric of dispossessed womanhood" to underscore the fate of the woman poet, several of the other works in *The Dream and Other Poems* take up the related question of literary reputation.[8] These poems are also elegiac in tone. "The Winter's Walk" recalls the example of her grandfather, which taught "what Fame meant, or Slander's fabled dart!" (*D* 182). Norton praises Samuel Rogers's loyalty to Sheridan and recalls Rogers's own youthful "fever-dreams / Of Fame and Glory" (*D* 181). These hopes, which have been only partially achieved, are complemented by his generosity to younger poets, to "some poor struggling Son of Genius . . . / And measuring not how much beneath thine own / Is the sick mind thus pining to be known, / But only what a wealth of hope lies hushed / As in a grave,—when men like these are crushed!" (*D* 181–82). "Winter's Walk" counsels satisfaction with the "daylight qualities," that is, the "unseen records of more gentle deeds" (*D* 181). Significant poetic accomplishment need not mean lasting literary fame, and literary fame is not a reliable measure of artistic—and certainly not of human—accomplishment.

Appreciation of enduring human virtues is also the keynote of "The Poet's Choice," which concerns an aspiring writer who abandons poetic fancy to look "on earthly things / With a calm content" (*D* 155–56). Norton herself appears to have understood but never fully to have realized this wisdom. After finally completing *The Child of the Islands* in 1845, she considered a new long poem on the subject of British missionaries:

> I think my heart would warm to it, and that I could do it justice; and I would *like that task*. But it cannot be *yet*. In the first place it is a subject which would require a good deal of reading up, before I commenced writing . . . (I do not

> follow the rule laid down by a poetess friend of mine, who said she never read for fear of destroying her originality of thought.) In the second place, I must knock off the stocks such small craft, as lie there now with naked ribs & rough keels, hastily tacked together,—before I build *another great ship*. I have several things half completed: I do not expect you to look on them so kindly & approvingly as my Child of the Islands,—I mean they have not as much thought & purpose in them, as I desired to put in that. Still, there they are, and you must not forget that literature (even this slight walk in literature that I follow) is a sort of *half profession* to me.[9]

The missionary project was never undertaken, although Norton did go on to write the long work dismissed by Fowles (*The Lady of La Garaye*), three novels, and several political pamphlets. Her remark confirms that writing was always a profession for her, always labor completed for payment, whatever "fever-dreams of fame" she may have once harbored. And necessarily, writing was never more than "a sort of half profession" because she was also a wife, a single parent, a political hostess, and an activist. After laboring for seven years to secure the children's return, she devoted herself to her two surviving sons. Fletcher's tenuous health required considerable care (he died in 1859), and Brinsley's impractical marriage—and character—meant that she assumed care and financial responsibility for her two grandchildren. Missionary labor was one casualty of these efforts; nevertheless, other "great ships" and numerous "small craft" survived the Scylla and Charybdis of parenting, politicking, and publishing.

Several poems about Hagar provide an important narrative complement to Sappho. The mother, banished to the desert accompanied by her child, finds that her "busy thought, which none forbid to roam, / Unexiled,—wanders back, to the cool palm-shadowed home. / Past hours return, (return! ah, changed and sad they seem!) / And the present fades away, like a broken bitter dream" ("The Departure of Hagar," *FDS 47*:11).[10] Norton also felt herself to be a social exile and addressed the "broken bitter dream" of the present in an 1843 letter to Shelley:

> I declare to you, and *you* will not think it affected, —that the habit of *expecting ill news*, and, '*papers*', is still so strong upon me, that often in houses where I am a stranger, and a visitor, —if a servant suddenly enters with a salver on which letter and notes are brought in, the old sickness comes over my heart, and I could not rise from my chair, or stand, if I tried. And then comes a sort of thankfulness that I am not in *my own house*, that I am not where any event *can* concern me—and *last of all* the full knowledge that the past *is* past! These are the small shadows which shew how people become mad.[11]

The past, however, was never irrevocably past; the battles of the 1850s and the lingering resentments of the 1860s demonstrate that "the old sickness" was both chronic and incurable. A few years before her death, Norton sent a copy of *The Child of the Islands* to an acquaintance with this note: "You must remember that it was written when I was still young and eager. It is more than thirty years ago. . . . I have not altered my views—but altered perhaps my belief in the power of *poetry* to disseminate and urge their value."[12] After a lifetime of struggle, Norton anticipated Auden's aperçu: "poetry makes nothing happen."[13] The pessimism of her later life should not obscure the accomplishments of 50 years of labor.

Woman and writer, mother and political hostess, socialite and feminist—Norton experienced and might be said to embody the contrary forces exerted upon women in the nineteenth century. She stands today at yet another crossway—an intersection of critical recognition. Through the work of the many scholars cited in this study, the invisible wife and all-too-visible woman is finally emerging from "the old traditions" to find her rightful place on the map of Victorian social, political, and literary history.

NOTES

FOREWORD

1. Aeschylus, *Agamemnon*, trans., Herbert Weir Smyth (Cambridge: Harvard University Press, 1926), 1192. http://www.perseus.tufts.edu.
2. Nina Auerbach, *Private Theatricals: The Lives of the Victorians* (Cambridge: Harvard University Press, 1990), 4.
3. Benjamin Robert Haydon, *The Diary of Benjamin Robert Haydon*, ed. Willard Bissell Pope (Cambridge: Harvard University Press, 1963), 4:56; also see 4:97, 4:110–11. Also see Clarke Olney, *Benjamin Robert Haydon: Historical Painter* (Athens: University of Georgia Press, 1952). In a letter of September 28, 1837, Fanny Allen notes: "Mrs N. is very beautiful—the countenance of a Sybil." Henrietta Litchfield, ed., *Emma Darwin: A Century of Family Letters, 1792–1896* (London: John Murray, 1915), 1:283. Lady St. Helier commented that Norton "had a most perfect Grecian profile and head, and such wonderfully lustrous soft brown eyes." *Memories of Fifty Years* (London: Edward Arnold, 1909), 89.
4. The anonymous contumely is assumed to have come from John Kemble. It appears in "Custody of Infants' Bill," *The British and Foreign Review; or European Quarterly Journal*, 7 (July–October 1838), 407.
5. Percy Fitzgerald, *The Lives of the Sheridans* (London: Richard Bentley and Son, 1886), 2:436.
6. Benjamin Robert Haydon Papers, Houghton Library, Harvard University, MS Eng 1331.
7. Beinecke Rare Book and Manuscript Collection, GEN MSS 260, Folder 77.

INTRODUCTION: "THE CAUDINE FORKS" AND THE OPTICS OF AUTHORSHIP

1. Frances Ann Kemble, *Records of a Girlhood*, 2nd ed. (New York: Henry Holt, 1879), 176. Also see her poem, "To Mrs. Norton."
2. William Maginn, " 'The Gallery of Illustrious Literary Characters.' No. X. Mrs. Norton," *Fraser's Magazine* (March 1831), 222. Another of Bulwer's poems, "Almacks, A Satiric Sketch," includes a reference to the Sheridan beauty. *Weeds and Wildflowers* (Paris: not published, 1826), 54.

3. Caroline Norton, "Books of Gossip: Sheridan and his Biographers," *Macmillan's Magazine* (January 3, 1861), 174.
4. Juliet Barker, ed., *The Brontës: A Life in Letters* (London: Viking, 1997), 166–67. Wilfred S. Dowden, ed., *The Letters of Thomas Moore: 1818–1847* (Oxford: Clarendon, 1964), 2:695. Lord Lamington offered Caroline and her sisters as "the brightest proofs of the transmission of hereditary qualities." *In the Days of the Dandies* (London: Eveleigh Nash, 1906), 88.
5. "Hon. Mrs. Norton's 'Undying One,'" *Fraser's Magazine* (September 1830), 180.
6. Linda M. Shires, "The Author as Spectacle and Commodity: Elizabeth Barrett Browning and Thomas Hardy," in *Victorian Literature and the Victorian Visual Imagination*, ed. Carol T. Christ and John O. Jordon (Berkeley: University of California Press, 1995), 199. Also see Dorothy Mermin, *Godiva's Ride: Women of Letters in England: 1830–1880* (Bloomington: Indiana University Press, 1993), 43–59.
7. Alice Adburgham, *Women in Print: Writing Women and Women's Magazines from the Restoration to the Accession of Victoria* (London: George Allen and Unwin, 1972), 253. Also see Margaret Beetham, *A Magazine of Her Own? Domesticity and Desire in the Woman's Magazine, 1800–1914* (London and New York: Routledge, 1996).
8. Hartley Coleridge, "Modern English Poetesses," *Quarterly Review* 66 (September 1840), 375. This essay has also been attributed to John Lockhart.
9. R. H. Horne, *A New Spirit of the Age* (London: Smith, Elder and Co, 1844), V. 1:136, 139.
10. Eric S. Robertson, *English Poetesses: A Series of Critical Biographies, with Illustrative Extracts* (London: Cassell and Company, 1883), 244.
11. This is Charlotte Brontë's comment on the sisters' use of pseudonyms. "Biographical Sketch of Ellis and Acton Bell," *Wuthering Heights* (Harmondsworth: Penguin, 1965), 31. For more on actresses and social standing, see Michael R. Booth, *Theatre in the Victorian Age* (Cambridge: Cambridge University Press, 1991), 112–14, and Tracy C. Davis, *Actresses as Working Women: Their Social Identity in Victorian Culture* (London: Routledge, 1991), 69–101.
12. Kemble, *Records of a Girlhood*, 175. Fanny Allen's letter of September 28, 1837 expressed a common reaction to Norton's demonstrative social manner: "Mrs Norton is a very fine actress, scarcely inferior to Grisi, I think. Her manner is very striking." Henrietta Litchfield, *Emma Darwin: A Century of Family Letters, 1792–1896* (London: John Murray, 1915), 1:283. Also see Charles Eastlake Smith, ed., *Journals and Correspondence of Lady Eastlake* (London: John Murray, 1895), 1:257 and 2:21.
13. Benjamin Robert Haydon, *The Diary of Benjamin Robert Haydon*, ed. Willard Bissell Pope (Cambridge: Harvard University Press, 1963), 4: 210. Also see Lord David Cecil, *Melbourne* (Indianapolis and New York: Bobbs-Merrill, 1962), 225.

14. Mary Shelley, *The Letters of Mary Wollstonecraft Shelley*, ed. Betty T. Bennett (Baltimore: Johns Hopkins University Press, 1988), 2:256.
15. Mabell, Countess of Airlie, *Lady Palmerston and Her Times* (London, New York [etc.] Hodder and Stoughton, 1922), 1:137–38.
16. Kemble, *Records of a Girlhood*, 173; André Maurois, *Disraeli: A Picture of the Victorian Age*, trans. Hamish Miles (New York: Random House, 1928), 357.
17. Henry E. Carlisle, ed., *A Selection from the Correspondence of Abraham Hayward, Q.C.*, (New York: Scribner and Welford, 1887), 2:24–25. The letter is dated January 27, 1859.
18. Alan Chedzoy, *A Scandalous Woman: The Story of Caroline Norton* (London: Allison and Busby, 1992). The others are Alice Acland, *Caroline Norton* (London: Constable, 1948) and Jane Grey Perkins, *The Life of the Honourable Mrs. Norton* (New York: Henry Holt, 1909).
19. "Living Literary Characters, No. 11. The Honourable Mrs. Norton." *New Monthly Magazine* 31:3 (February 1831), 180.
20. Ibid., 181.
21. Ibid., 181, 183.
22. Ibid., 180.
23. Cited by Perkins, *Mrs. Norton*, 156.
24. Maginn, *Fraser's Magazine* 3 (March 1831), 222. For a study of this series, see Judith L. Fisher, "'In the Present Famine of Anything Substantial': *Fraser's* 'Portraits' and the Construction of Literary Celebrity; or, 'Personality, Personality Is the Appetite of the Age,'" *Victorian Periodicals Review* 39, no. 2 (Summer 2006): 97–135.
25. William Bates, *The Maclise Portrait Gallery of Illustrious Literary Characters* (London: Chatto and Windus, 1898), 355. The expanded 1836 text includes prurient references to Actæon, Clodius, and Peeping Tom.
26. Maginn, *Fraser's*, 222. See Fisher, "Present Famine," 117.
27. Kieran Dolan insightfully discusses Maclise's drawing along with other portraits in "The Transfigurations of Caroline Norton," *Victorian Literature and Culture* 30, no. 2 (September 2002), 503–27.
28. Maclise reprised this setting in 1836 when *Fraser's* published "Regina's Maids of Honour," an essay on nine contemporary women writers. The writers, "every one a lovely she," are "very busy taking tea, or coffee, as the chance may be." Bates, *Maclise*, 355.
29. Maginn, *Fraser's*, 222.
30. Ibid., 222.
31. Ibid., 222.
32. Ibid., 222. Maginn, an alcoholic, may have been thinking of himself.
33. Ibid., 222.
34. Ibid., 222.
35. Bates, *Maclise*, 53–54. Dante Gabriel Rosetti found Maclise's portrait of Caroline Norton "whimsical as in the spirit of the series—yet truly appreciative,—of that noble beauty which in Caroline Norton inspired the best genius of her long summer-day" (53).

36. See William St Clair, *Trelawny: The Incurable Romancer* (London: John Murray, 1977), 177–78; Eric George, *The Life and Death of Benjamin Robert Haydon, Historical Painter: 1786–1846*, second edition with additions by Dorothy George (Oxford: Clarendon, 1967); and Alethea Hayter, *A Sultry Month: Scenes of London Literary Life in 1846* (London: Faber and Faber, 1965), 99–100.
37. Dickens is imagining which of his female acquaintances is "more kissable." Edgar Johnson, *Charles Dickens: His Tragedy and Triumph*, revised and abridged (New York: Viking, 1977), 237, 204. His fantasy is less salacious than Haydon's: "Mrs. Norton's grand majesty of beauty is sublime, but her mouth is not sufficiently voluptuous to kiss with *inside* lip" (4:57). Norton inspired other gratuitous osculatory comments, even from confirmed bachelors like Samuel Rogers. See Carlisle, *A Selection from the Correspondence of Abraham Hayward, Q.C.*, 2:8. William Makepeace Thackeray, *The Letters and Private Papers of William Makepeace Thackeray*, ed. Gordon N. Ray (Cambridge: Harvard Univ. Press, 1946), 2:373 n. 93.
38. Coleridge, "Modern English Poetesses," 375, 376. This significance of the comparison is discussed by Elaine Hadley in *Melodramatic Tactics: Theatricalized Dissent in the English Marketplace, 1800–1885* (Stanford: Stanford University Press, 1995), 146–47.
39. Coleridge, "Modern English Poetesses," 374–75.
40. Winthrop Mackworth Praed, *The Poetical Works of Winthrop Mackworth Praed*, Vol. 1 (New York: Redfield, 1860).
41. Frances A. Gerard, *Some Fair Hibernians. Being a Supplementary Volume to "Some Celebrated Irish Beauties of the Last Century"* (London: Ward and Downey, 1897), 232.
42. Letter of April 21, 1833. Benjamin Disraeli, *Benjamin Disraeli Letters: 1815–1834*, Vol. 1, ed. J. A. W. Gunn, John Matthews, Donald M. Schurman, and M. G. Wiebe (Toronto: University of Toronto Press, 1982), 1:350.
43. William Makepeace Thackeray, "A Grumble about the Christmas-Books," *Fraser's Magazine* (January 1847), 123.
44. Thackeray, "A Grumble," 123.
45. Thackeray, *Letters*, 2:264.
46. Thackeray, "A Grumble," 123, 124.
47. Ibid., 123.
48. Ibid., 124.
49. Ibid.
50. Horne, *A New Spirit of the Age*, 136. Janet Ross's comment about G. F. Watts's 1848 portrait confirms this opinion: "If the reader will hide the frill, and sloping shoulders—so unlike Mrs. Norton's—with a piece of paper, he will see how far finer the head looks." *The Fourth Generation* (London: Constable, 1912), 202.
51. Earl of Malmesbury, James Howard Harris, *Memoirs of an Ex-Minister: An Autobiography* (London: Longmans, Green, and Co, 1885), 50–51.

52. Malmesbury, *Memoirs of an Ex-Minister*, 173. L. G. Mitchell speculates that Melbourne was peculiarly attracted to masculine women. *Lord Melbourne: 1779–1848* (Oxford: Oxford University Press, 1997), 91–92.
53. Harold Nicholson, *Helen's Tower* (New York: Harcourt, Brace and Company, 1938), 53. Mermin similarly "confines" Norton to Byronic dimensions, noting that "[i]n the 1820s and '30s Letitia Landon and Caroline Norton made poetic careers mostly with quasi-Byronic narratives" (8).
54. Coleridge, "Modern English Poetesses," 376.
55. Ibid., 378, 379.
56. Ibid., 382.
57. Percy Fitzgerald, *Lives of the Sheridans* (London: Richard Bentley and Son, 1886), 2:372–73.
58. "Stanzas from the Grande Chartreuse," *Matthew Arnold: Selected Poems* (Harmondsworth: Penguin, 1994), 113.
59. Edward Bulwer Lytton, *England and the English*, ed. and intro. by Standish Meacham (Chicago: University of Chicago Press, 1970), 318–19.
60. Coleridge, "Modern English Poetesses," 382.
61. "Custody of Infants' Bill," *The British and Foreign Review; or European Quarterly Journal* 7 (July-October 1838), 377–78. Mermin notes: "Like Byron, she made her notorious marital misfortunes the thinly disguised subject of verse, and her attacks on the legal system that empowered her husband exposed her, like Byron, to additional obloquy on the score of her personal life" (12).
62. Mary Poovey, *Uneven Developments: The Ideological Work of Gender in Mid-Victorian England* (Chicago: University of Chicago Press, 1988), 65. Also see Hadley, 158.
63. Virginia Surtees, ed., *A Second Self: The Letters of Harriet Granville, 1810–1845* (Salisbury: Michael Russell, 1990), 266.

1 "The World" and "The (Sm)all Great": Silver Fork Narratives

1. Fitzgerald, *The Lives of the Sheridans*, 2:427–28.
2. Thackeray, *Letters*, 2:373–74.
3. This setting features prominently in *Love in "the World."* When Colonel Maurer learns that Alice "had never been to Almacks" he stops talking to her "as Alice thought from having nothing more to say—as Col. Maurer himself thought from her not being worthy to hear" (*LW* 109). Beinecke Rare Book and Manuscript Library, GEN MSS 260. For more on the haut ton, see Alison Adburgham, *Silver Fork Society: Fashionable Life and Literature from 1814 to 1840* (London: Constable, 1983), 102–10.
4. The migration is described in *Stuart of Dunleath*: "the London season was over, and the flock of lions was quietly dispersing, and going to prowl

singly or in lesser groups in the country" (*SD* 2:246). A more cutting account is found in Disraeli's *Endymion* (1:291).

5. This phrase describes the "venerable inhabitants of that venerable pile" (Hampton Court), whom Dickens also calls "the gipsies of gentility." *Little Dorrit* (Harmondsworth: Penguin, 1998), 331. Acland, *Caroline Norton*, 24.
6. Bulwer Lytton, *England and the English*, 85–86.
7. *England and the English*, 85. William Hazlitt, "The Dandy School," *The Complete Works of William Hazlitt*. Centenary Edition, ed. A. P. P. Howe (London: J. M. Dent and Sons, 1934), 20:143–49.
8. See Matthew Whiting Rosa, *The Silver-Fork School: Novels of Fashion Preceding Vanity Fair* (Port Washington, NY: Kenikat Press, 1964; New York: Columbia University Press, 1936). Also see Sally Mitchell, *The Fallen Angel: Chastity, Class and Women's Reading, 1835–1880* (Bowling Green: Bowling Green University Popular Press, 1981), 59–66.
9. On the occasion, she was August in a quadrille dedicated to the 12 months. Wilfred S. Dowden, ed., *The Journal of Thomas Moore: 1826–1830* (Newark: University of Delaware Press, 1986), 3:932–33. See Alan Horsman, *The Victorian Novel* (Oxford: Clarendon, 1990), 31.
10. Kemble, *Records of a Girlhood*, 47.
11. Fisher, "Present Famine," 98.
12. George Eliot, *Middlemarch* (Harmondsworth: Penguin, 1994), 268. See Harriet Devine Jump, " 'The False Prudery of Public Taste': Scandalous Women and the Annuals, 1820–1850," in *Feminist Readings of Victorian Popular Texts*, ed. Emma Liggins and Daniel Duffy (Aldershot: Ashgate, 2001), 1–17.
13. Fitzgerald, *Lives of the Sheridans*, 2:370–72.
14. James Pope-Hennessy, *Monckton Milnes: The Years of Promise 1809–1851* (New York: Farrar, Straus & Cudahy, 1955), 111.
15. An annotation on the cover of *Love in "the World"* accounts for why it was never published: "Prosy, foolish little book written partly as a girl and [?] after my marriage—am quite surprised at its stupidity." On the first page of the second volume, Norton repeats the disclaimer: "Novel when I was yet 'in my teens.' " Beinecke Rare Book and Manuscript Library, GEN MSS 260.
16. She wrote, "I have been, and am, very busy with the somewhat tiresome task of 'The Scrap Book.' Thirty-six prints to be married to an equal number of copies of verses is a task which ought to admit of the employment of curates and deputies, but I do not find many willing to do duty." Gertrude Lyster, ed., *A Family Chronicle: Derived from Notes and Letters Selected by Barbarina, the Hon. Lady Grey* (London: John Murray, 1908), 248.
17. Hazlitt, "The Dandy School," 146.
18. Winifred Hughes, "Mindless Millinery: Catherine Gore and the Silver Fork Heroine," *Dickens Studies Annual*, 25 (New York: AMS Press, 1996), 167.

19. Carlisle, Correspondence of Abraham Hayward, Q.C., 1:287.
20. Winifred Hughes, "Silver Fork Writers and Readers: Social Contexts of a Best Seller," *Novel* 25, 3 (Spring 1992): 328–48. http://80-weblinks1.epnet.com.silver.ulib.
albany.edu, 2.
21. All quotations from *The Dandies' Rout* are courtesy of The Lilly Library, Indiana University, Bloomington, Indiana. Dickens employs exactly the same terms, tropes, and figures in his sketch of "dandy fashion" in *Bleak House* (*BH* 144).
22. William Makepeace Thackeray, *The Four Georges, Sketches of Manners, Morals, Court, and Town Life* (Garden City: Doubleday, n.d.), 108.
23. A complete and comic taxonomy of old maids appears in *Stuart of Dunleath* (2:59–61).
24. She disqualifies herself as a silver fork heroine, as Adburgham points out: "To run away for good, to elope with a lover, was social suicide. It was something never done by the heroine of a fashionable novel, although sometimes by a secondary character who is doomed to be deserted" (Silver Fork Society, 119).
25. For another poetic treatment of this theme, see "I Was Not False to Thee" (*UO*).
26. Of George Norton it was said: "he swallows the lovers or not according to their rank and position. Lord Melbourne yes, Captain Trelawny no." Virginia Surtees, ed., *A Second Self: The Letters of Harriet Granville, 1810–1845* (Salisbury: Michael Russell, 1990), 268.
27. Cited by R. Glynn Grylls, *Mary Shelley: A Biography* (London: Oxford University Press, 1938), 198.
28. Hazlitt, "The Dandy School," 144.
29. Jane Austen, *Persuasion* (Peterborough, Ontario: Broadview, 1998), 186.
30. Karen Chase and Michael Levenson, *The Spectacle of Intimacy: A Public Life for the Victorian Family* (Princeton: Princeton University Press, 2000), 28. For a refinement of this thesis in relation to empire, see Muireann O' Cinnéide, *Public Grandeur & Private Discomfort: Aristocratic Identity in the Works of Rosina Bulwer Lytton, Emily Eden and Caroline Norton* (Diss. Oxford University, 2004).
31. Fitzgerald, *Lives of the Sheridans*, 2:439.
32. *The Norton Shakespeare*, ed. Stephen Greenblatt, Walter Cohen, Jean E. Howard, Katharine Eisaman Maus (New York: Norton, 1997), 1962.
33. Thackeray, *The Four Georges*, 107–08.
34. Thackeray, *Letters*, 2:229.
35. Ibid., 1:197.
36. Gordon N. Ray, *Thackeray: The Age of Wisdom, 1847–1863* (New York: McGraw-Hill, 1958), 53.
37. Micael M. Clarke, *Thackeray and Women* (DeKalb: Northern Illinois University Press, 1995), 74. Clarke argues that Norton is "the 'original' for Lady Lyndon, Becky Sharp, and Clara Pulleyn Newcome."

38. Clarke, 77. Invisible husbands, Carleton points out, risk instilling in their wives "that emptiness of heart which makes any excitement seem happiness, like the visions of an opium eater" (*KB* 1:150–51).
39. *Melbourne*, 224, 229.
40. Acland, *Caroline Norton*, 127.
41. Her first royal presentation was to King William IV and Queen Adelaide on April 26, 1831, and "her splendid beauty made something of a sensation." Perkins, *Mrs. Norton*, 37, 178.
42. Lady Elizabeth Holland, *Elizabeth, Lady Holland to Her Son: 1821–1845*, ed. The Earl of Ilchester (London: John Murray, 1946), 187–88.
43. This is a frequent theme in the poems collected in *The Sorrows of Rosalie* ("As When from Dreams Awaking," "Old Friends," and "The Bride") and *Kate Bouverie* ("On Reading an Old Letter" and "The Friend of Our Early Days"). This theme also runs throughout *The Dream*.
44. Barbara Leckie, *Culture and Adultery: The Novel, the Newspaper, and the Law, 1857–1914* (Philadelphia: University of Pennsylvania Press, 1999), 126.

2 "Strange Unstable World": Structure and Synthesis in the Final Narratives

1. "Our Female Sensation Novelists," *Littell's Living Age* 78:1003 (August 23, 1863), 352.
2. Anna Jameson, *Sacred and Legendary Art* (London: Longmans, Green, and Co., 1866), 343.
3. "The Popular Novels of the Year," *Fraser's Magazine* 68:404 (August 1863), 262–63.
4. On the eve of her elopement, Rosalie dreams of her father and decides not to go, although in the morning this resolve dissolves (*SR* 16; also see 21–22). Beatrice invokes the name of her father in an unsuccessful attempt to dissuade Montagu from eloping (*LS* 95).
5. It is not simply a matter of women's victimization at the hands of men, however; women are also guilty of enforcing unjust social prejudice. When no longer able to pay her rent, Rosalie is forced out onto the street "beneath the inclement sky— / Woman to woman did this deed of cruelty" (*SR* 63). Women's inhumanity to women is a recurring theme in *Lost and Saved*. Maurice Llewellyn asks of his aunt: "Do such women ever care? Do they know the value of the words right and wrong? Not if weighed against invitation-cards and diamonds—certainly not" (*LS* 314–15; also see 357).
6. Barabara Z. Thaden discusses Frank's ambiguous legal status in *The Maternal Voice in Victorian Fiction* (New York and London: Garland, 1997), 80.

7. On seamstresses and lace menders, see Helena Michie, *The Flesh Made Word: Female Figures and Women's Bodies* (New York: Oxford University Press, 1987), 56, and Deborah Anna Logan, *Fallenness in Victorian Women's Writing: Marry, Stitch, Die, or Do Worse* (Columbia: University of Missouri Press, 1998), 32–35.
8. "Our Female Sensation Novelists," 354.
9. Ibid., 362.
10. "Current Literature," *Illustrated News*, May 30, 1863, 590.
11. James Fitzjames Stephen, "Anti-Respectability," *The Cornhill Magazine* 8 (September 1863), 282.
12. Beinecke Rare Book and Manuscript Library, GEN MSS 260, Folder 15.
13. Stephen, "Anti-Respectability," 285.
14. Norton's heroine can be linked to Magdalene Vanstone in Wilkie Collins's *No Name*. See Winfred Hughes, *The Maniac in the Cellar: Sensation Novels of the 1860s* (Princeton: Princeton University Press, 1980), 30–31.
15. *Extraordinary Trial! Norton* v. *Viscount Melbourne, for Crim. Con. Damages laid at $10,000!!!* (London: William Marshall, n.d.), 25.
16. Jameson, *Sacred and Legendary Art*, 380.
17. Ibid., 344, 345.
18. *Illustrated News*, 590.
19. Ibid.
20. Jameson, *Sacred and Legendary Art*, 393–94.
21. Letter of December 5, 1848, *Anna Jameson: Letters and Friendships (1812–1860)*, ed. Mrs. Stuart Erskine (New York: E. P. Dutton, 1915), 238.
22. Jameson, *Sacred and Legendary Art*, 381–82.
23. See Jennifer DeVere Brody, *Impossible Purities: Blackness, Femininity, and Victorian Culture* (Durham and London: Duke University Press, 1998), 27–45.
24. "Our Female Sensation Novelists," 350; H. L. Manse, "Sensation Novels," *Quarterly Review* 113:226 (April 1863), 482–514. http://gaslight.mtroyal.ab.ca/sensnovl.htm, 6, 12.
25. Norton shared the view of Tennyson's speaker about Nicholas I. See Otto Hans Rauchbauer, "Some Unrecorded Letters by Caroline Norton," *Notes and Queries* 17 (September 1970), 338.

3 "The Brethren of the Long Robe": Legal Satire and Courtroom Humor

1. "Cromwell and the Lawyers," *Fisher's Drawing Room Scrap-Book, 1849*, 73.
2. W. S. Gilbert, *Utopia Limited*, *The Complete Annotated Gilbert and Sullivan*, ed. Ian Bradley (Oxford: Oxford University Press, 1996), 1029.

3. Sheridan Family Papers (bMS Eng 1276), Houghton Library, Harvard University. For an early portrait of an attorney who describes himself as "monster of cruelty and meanness" (55), see "Leaves of a Life; or, the Templar's Tale," *La Belle Assemblée, or Court and Fashionable Magazine* (1832).
4. Chedzoy, *A Scandalous Woman*, 115.
5. *Times* (London), June 23, 1836, 2.
6. Ibid. George expressed concern about the paternity of his second son (*LCN* 108).
7. *Extraordinary Trial!*, 13.
8. *Extraordinary Trial!*, 12, 15.
9. Chedzoy, *A Scandalous Woman*, 12.
10. Christine L. Krueger, "Witnessing Women: Trial Testimony in Novels by Tonna, Gaskell, and Eliot," in *Representing Women: Law, Literature, and Feminism*, ed. Susan Sage Heinzelman and Zipporah Batshaw Wiseman (Durham: Duke University Press, 1994), 340.
11. *Times*, June 23, 1836, 5.
12. Ibid., 4.
13. Ibid., 2.
14. Ibid.
15. Ibid., 3.
16. Ibid.
17. Ibid., 2.
18. Ibid., 5.
19. Ibid. In a letter to the *Times* of August 24, 1853, George offered a different explanation: "the impropriety of her conduct and total disregard of outward appearances, by which alone society can form its opinion, no one who moved in our circles could doubt" (7). He then provided this example: "On one occasion I had seen her arm round his neck, and when I remonstrated with her she said, 'Well, and what if I had my Melly round the neck—what was it' " (7).
20. *Times*, June 23, 1836, 5.
21. Ibid.
22. Ibid.
23. *Extraordinary Trial!*, 36.
24. One exception occurred in closing remarks, when Campbell stated "that his client solemnly and upon his honor declared his innocence." Defendants were not allowed to speak on their own behalf, and this maneuver was criticized in Ballantine's *Some Experiences of a Barrister's Life* (New York: Henry Holt, 1882), 121–22.
25. Fitzgerald, *The Lives of the Sheridans*, 2:421. Norton prepared a point-for-point rebuttal of Follett's case, which she sent to her brother immediately after the trial. British Library, Sheridan Papers, Add. 42767, f. 8.
26. British Library, Sheridan Papers, Add. 42767, f. 8.

27. See Percy Fitzgerald, *Bardell* v. *Pickwick* (London: Elliot Stock, 1902), as well as Randall Craig, *Promising Language: Betrothal in Victorian Law and Fiction* (Albany: SUNY Press, 2000).
28. *Times*, June 23, 1836, 2.
29. Ibid.
30. *Extraordinary Trial!*, 31.
31. Ibid., 35.
32. *Times*, June 23, 1836, 5.
33. Ibid., 3.
34. Ibid., 5.
35. *Extraordinary Trial!*, 33.
36. *Times*, June 24, 1836, 3.
37. Ibid., June 25, 1836, 5.
38. Ibid., August 24, 1853, 7.
39. British Library, Sheridan Papers, Add. 42767, f. 87.
40. *Times*, June 23, 1836, 2, 5.
41. *Extraordinary Trial!*, 28.
42. *Times*, June 23, 1836, 5.
43. Ibid.
44. See Charles J. MacColla, *Breach of Promise: Its History and Social Considerations* (London: Pickering, 1879).
45. In *Bigley* v. *Dupré*, the "legal" narrative is articulated by the litigants' attorneys; the "natural" narrative is supplied by the narrator.
46. See Alan Fischler, *Modified Rapture: Comedy in W. S. Gilbert's Savoy Operas* (Charlottesville: University Press of Virginia, 1991), 56.
47. *Times*, June 23, 1836, 2.

4 "INK STANDS AND LAW BOOKS": DOMESTIC AND LEGAL VIOLENCE

1. George Eliot, *Daniel Deronda* (Harmondsworth: Penguin, 1995), 353.
2. Haydon, *Diary*, 4:215.
3. Chedzoy, *A Scandalous Woman*, 102.
4. Chase and Levenson call Lionel a "transparent counterpart to her husband." Karen Chase and Michael Levenson, *The Spectacle of Intimacy: A Public Life for the Victorian Family* (Princeton: Princeton University Press, 2000), 31. Melbourne himself saw something of George in Lionel (*ELW* 69–70).
5. Poovey, *Uneven Developments*, 87.
6. "By marriage, the husband and wife are one person in law: that is, the very being or legal existence of the woman is suspended during the marriage, or at least is incorporated and consolidated into that of her husband: under whose wing, protection, *cover*, she performs everything." William Blackstone, *Commentaries on the Laws of England*, ed. Thomas Lee, 18th ed. (London: Strahan, 1809), 1:441–42.

7. Maeve E. Doggett, *Marriage, Wife-Beating and the Law in Victorian England* (London: Weidenfeld and Nicolson, 1992), 35.
8. Beinecke Rare Book and Manuscript Library, GEN MSS 260, Folder 55.
9. British Library, Add. 44379, f. 12.
10. British Library, Add. 44379, f. 12. The distinction between opinion, which she holds appropriate to literature, and fact, which is the province of nonfiction, is also expressed in the preface to *A Voice from the Factories.*
11. British Library, Add. 44379, f. 118.
12. Kate Lawson and Lynn Shakinovsky, *The Marked Body: Domestic Violence in Mid-Nineteenth-Century Literature* (Albany: SUNY Press, 2002), 16. For a discussion of divorce court journalism, see Leckie, 62–111.
13. Thackeray, *Letters*, 3: 428.
14. In "The Forsaken Child," Madeline Marchmont's situation resembles Clara's. She leaves her husband and son for a man with whom she has two children. Madeline ill-advisedly attempts to unite the children of her two marriages: "Woe for that day! woe for the attempt to bind together, in that strange and unnatural alliance, the children of her who had broken her first natural ties" (*KB* 2:92). A mother may see no difference between her children, irrespective of their fathers, but society does not think in these terms.

5 "Half a Life": Narratives of Women and Politics

1. Fitzgerald, *Lives of the Sheridans*, 2:436.
2. Anthony Trollope, *Phineas Finn* (Oxford: Oxford University Press, 1982), 1:58.
3. K. D. Reynolds, *Aristocratic Women and Political Society in Victorian Britain* (Oxford: Clarendon Press, 1998), 158. Justin McCarthy cites Lady Palmerston as epitomizing the lamentable influence of women in politics. "The Petticoat in the Politics of England," in *Victorian Women's Magazines: An Anthology*, ed. Margaret Beetham and Kay Boardman (Manchester: Manchester University Press, 2001), 155. Also see Dorothy Stetson, *A Woman's Issue: The Politics of Family Law Reform in England* (Westport, CT: Greenwood, 1982).
4. *Lady Palmerston and Her Times*, 2:180. Hoge and Olney note that after the trial, Lady Cowper "took an exceedingly dim view of her brother's association with Mrs. Norton. . . . Like most of his family, Melbourne's sister was more concerned with protecting his future than with assuaging Mrs. Norton's distress" (*LCN* 129).
5. George Eliot, *Felix Holt, the Radical* (Harmondsworth: Penguin, 1995), 328.
6. See Michael Sadleir, *The Strange Life of Lady Blessington* (New York: Farrar, Straus and Company, 1947).
7. *Reynolds's Miscellany* 1:15 (February 13, 1847), 233.
8. Sadleir, *Lady Blessington*, 323.

9. Reynolds, *Aristocratic Women*, 158.
10. Haydon, 4:271.
11. Lady Marguerite Blessington, *The Repealers. The Works of Lady Blessington* (Philadelphia: E. L. Carey and A. Hart, 1838), 1:249.
12. Sadleir, *Lady Blessington*, 323.
13. Blessington, *The Repealers*, 1:249.
14. Charles C. F. Greville. *The Greville Memoirs: A Journal of the Reigns of King George IV and King William IV* (London: Longmans, Green, and Co, 1874), 3:349.
15. Reynolds, *Aristocratic Women*, 158.
16. Kathryn Gleadle and Sarah Richardson point out that the petticoat was "used to depict female influence in the realm, as well as women's dominance within the home. It would be wrong to assume, however, that these portrayals of female power were invariably and simplistically misogynist." *Women in British Politics, 1760–1860* (London: Macmillan, 2000), 1.
17. Barbara Leah Harman, *The Feminine Political Novel in Victorian England* (Charlottesville: University Press of Virginia, 1998), 6.
18. Lyster, *A Family Chronicle*, 69.
19. Greville, cited by Reynolds, *Aristocratic Women*, 156.
20. See W. M. Torrens, *Memoirs of the Right Honourable William Second Viscount Melbourne* (London: Macmillan, 1878).
21. Torrens, *Memoirs*, 1:138–39.
22. Hoge and Olney, (*LCN* 7).
23. Chedzoy, *A Scandalous Woman, 78.*
24. André Maurois, *Disraeli: A Picture of the Victorian Age*, trans. Hamish Miles (New York: D. Appleton, 1928), 95–96.
25. Benjamin Disraeli, *Benjamin Disraeli Letters: 1835–1837*, Vol.2, ed. J. A. W. Gunn, John Matthews, Donald M. Schurman, and M. G. Wiebe (Toronto: University of Toronto Pres, 1982), 2:425.
26. Maurois, *Picture of the Victorian Age*, 73.
27. Disraeli, *Letters*, 1:350.
28. Lyster, *A Family Chronicle*, 72.
29. Edward John Trelawny, *Letters of Edward John Trelawny*, ed. H. Buxton Forman, C.B. (New York: AMS, 1973), 199.
30. Cited by Fitzgerald, *Lives of the Sheridans*, 398–99.
31. Malmesbury, *Memoirs of an Ex-Minister*, 53–54.
32. Greville, *Greville Memoirs*, 3:349. Melbourne used the same expression with Norton (*ELW* 71).
33. Beinecke Rare Book and Manuscript Library, GEN MSS 260, Folder 50.
34. Greville, *Greville Memoirs*, 3:349; Beinecke Rare Book and Manuscript Library, GEN MSS 260, Folder 36.
35. Beinecke Rare Book and Manuscript Library, GEN MSS 260, Folder 15.
36. Both Acland and Chedzoy assume this circumstance. Acland further contends that passages in the novels can be construed as signs that Norton

experienced an unwise love and that its object was Herbert (*Caroline Norton*, 166–67).

37. Alice Acland, *Caroline Norton* (London: Constable, 1948), 170–71.
38. R. C. Terry notes that "highly visible signs of victimized wives deprived of their children," such as Caroline Norton and Rosina Bulwer, "possibly coloured the Trevelyans' marriage break-up in *He Knew He Was Right*." R. C. Terry, ed., *Oxford Reader's Companion to Trollope* (Oxford: Oxford University Press, 1999), 395.
39. R. H. Horne, *Orion: An Epic Poem*, ll. 239, 277–78, http://www.bartleby.com/246/77.html.
40. Richard A. Levine, *Benjamin Disraeli* (New York: Twayne, 1968), 146.
41. See John Raymond, *Queen Victoria's Early Letters* (London: Batsford, 1963), 71–72.
42. Jack Lindsay, *George Meredith: His Life and Work* (London: Bodley Head, 1956), 163.
43. S. M. Ellis, *George Meredith: His Life and Friends in Relation to His Work* (London: Grant Richards, 1919), 331.
44. Norton herself had grown used to such comparisons, exemplified by the comment of Mrs. Frederick Sullivan: "Mrs. Norton, too splendidly, magnificently, furiously beautiful. . . . She had a Cleopatra head! I never saw anything so tormentingly beautiful"—an intimation of exotic excess echoed by Anne Thackeray, who remarked that her father's acquaintance was "a beautiful slow sphinx" (Lyster, *A Family Chronicle*, 69). Hester Thackeray Ritchie, ed., *Thackeray and His Daughter: The Letters and Journals of Anne Thackeray Ritchie, with Many Letters of William Makepeace Thackeray* (New York: Harper and Brothers, 1924), 151.
45. Upon learning that Norton was not responsible for leaking the secret, Meredith inserted this retraction into the novel: "A lady of high distinction for wit and beauty, the daughter of an illustrious Irish House, came under the shadow of a calumny. It has latterly been examined and exposed as baseless. The story of 'Diana of the Crossways' is to be read as fiction."
46. Neil Roberts finds Meredith misrepresents Norton's "authentic political activity" and calls his aesthetic choices "provoking." *Meredith and the Novel* (London: Macmillan, 1997), 206.

6 "LOPSIDED AND LEFT-HANDED LAWS": NARRATIVES OF MOTHERS AND WIVES

1. Haydon, *Diary*, 4:112.
2. "The Grand Fraserian Festival," *Fraser's Magazine*, (January 1836), 78.
3. Katherine Moore, *Victorian Wives* (London: Allison and Busby, 1974), 53.
4. *The Separation of Mother and Child* exists in an earlier version, *Observations on the Natural Claim of the Mother to the Custody of Her Infant*

Children as Affected by the Common Law Right of the Father (London: James Ridgway and Sons, 1837). Perkins reports that Norton was working on this document immediately after her separation from her husband (Mrs. Norton, 130).

5. See, for example, Egremont's speech on the People in *Sybil* (Oxford and New York: Oxford University Press, 1981), 276–77.
6. One reviewer praised the poem for what is, in effect, the essence of Norton's philosophy and expression: "the writer's catholic bredth of sympathy with all weakness and all misfortune, and at the same time the searching anatomy of... hard-hearted vice." "*The Child of the Islands*," *The Quarterly Review* 76:151 (June 1845), 8. One of the epigraphs in *Mary Barton* comes from the poem. For more on the relation of Norton and Gaskell, see Shirley Foster, *Elizabeth Gaskell: A Literary Life* (New York: Palgrave Macmillan, 2002), 75–77. Also see Michael Young, "The Writer as Reader in *Mary Barton*," *Durham University Journal* 67 (December 1974), 92–102.
7. Letter to Editor, *Examiner*, August 26, 1836. This view is upheld in *Lost and Saved* (433–36).
8. Norton's name was invoked in support of this position by Wendell Phillips at the Women's Rights Convention of 1851. Elizabeth Cady Stanton, Susan B. Anthony, and Matilda Joslyn Gage, ed., *History of Woman Suffrage*, Vol. 1, (New York: Arno and the New York Times, 1969), 228. It has been suggested that Norton's stance is a pragmatic compromise. See Kathryn Caras, *Public Complaint and Private Sorrow: The Feminism of Caroline Norton* (Diss. Indiana University, 1984), 27, 45–46; and Stetson, *A Woman's Issue*, 47–50.
9. British Library, Add 44379, f. 12.
10. Dorothy E. Zaborszky, "'Domestic Anarchy and the Destruction of the Family': Caroline Norton and the Custody of Infants Bill," *International Journal of Women's Studies* 7, no. 5 (November/December 1984), 397.
11. Joan Huddleston, "Introduction," *Caroline Norton's Defense* (Chicago: Academy Chicago, 1982), ii. Margaret Forster writes: "Her particular brand of feminism began as naïve and romantic but ended as something much more daring and closer to the ideas of those 'strong minded women' she so abhorred." *Significant Sisters: The Grassroots of Active Feminism, 1839–1939* (London: Secker and Warburg, 1984), 16.
12. Beinecke Rare Book and Manuscript Library, GEN MSS 260, Folder 81.
13. Chedzoy, *A Scandalous Woman*, 119.
14. Harriet Martineau, *Harriet Martineau's Autobiography*, ed. Maria Weston Chapman (Boston: J. R. Osgood, 1877), 302.
15. "The Non-Existence of Women. Letter to the Queen on Lord Chancellor Cranworth's Marriage and Divorce Bill," *The North British Review* 23 (May-August 1855), 560.

16. George Eliot, "Life and Opinions of Milton," *Essays of George Eliot*, ed. Thomas Pinney (New York: Columbia University Press, 1963), 156.
17. Eliot, for example, disapproved of Norton's public feud with Ellen Wood. *The Letters of George Eliot*, ed. Gordon S. Haight (New Haven: Yale University Press, 1955), 5:208.
18. Beinecke Rare Book and Manuscript Library, GEN MSS 260.
19. Meeting Norton in 1858, John Lothrop Motley wrote that her beauty and demeanor "twisted men's heads off and hearts out." George William Curtis, ed., *The Correspondence of John Lothrop Motley* (New York: Harper and Brothers, 1889), 242.
20. "Woman's Law.—Mrs. Norton's Letter to the Queen," *The Law Review and Quarterly Journal of British and Foreign Jurisprudence* 22 (1855), 334.
21. "The Laws Relating to Women," *The Law Review and Quarterly Journal of British and Foreign Jurisprudence* 20 (1854), 27–28. Also see, "The Non-Existence of Women," 536.
22. Cited by Moore, *Victorian Wives*, 49.
23. Letter to John Murray, cited by Perkins, *Mrs. Norton*, 151. Also see Barbara Caine, *English Feminism 1780–1980* (Oxford: Oxford University Press, 1997), 93–102.
24. James O. Hoge and Jane Marcus note that Norton was less romantic and radical than Wollstonecraft, but that as writers and women of influence in nineteenth-century England they had much in common. "Introduction," *Selected Writings of Caroline Norton* (Delmar, NY: Scholars' Facsimiles and Reprints, 1978), vii–viii.
25. Fitzgerald, *Lives of the Sheridans*, 432.
26. John Kilham, *Tennyson and The Princess: Reflections of an Age* (London: Athlone Press, 1958), 142–69. For more on Norton and Tennyson, see: Thomas Sadler, ed., *Diary, Reminiscences, and Correspondence of Henry Crabb Robinson* (Boston: Fields, Osgood, and Co., 1869), 2:335; Lord Hallam Tennyson, ed., *Tennyson and His Friends* (London: Macmillan, 1911), 41; and Robert Martin, *Tennyson: The Unquiet Heart* (London: Faber and Faber, 1983), 284.
27. John Kemble, "Custody of Infants' Bill," *The British and Foreign Review; or, European Quarterly Journal* 7 (July—October, 1838): 395.
28. Kemble, "Custody of Infants' Bill," 397, 402, 410. Other derogative terms include: "she-fire-brand" (404), "she-*misanthrope*—man-hateress" (405), and "social Ate" (405). This author also refers to Norton's "well-known, though perhaps *non-convicted* gallantries" in connection with the alleged affair with Lord Melbourne (407). Norton was defended by Nathaniel Ogle in *Fraser's Magazine* (February 19, 1839), 210.
29. See Martin, *Tennyson*, 284.
30. Lyster, *A Family Chronicle*, 244.
31. Beinecke Rare Book and Manuscript Library, GEN MSS 260.
32. Ibid.

33. Karen Chase and Michael Levenson, *The Spectacle of Intimacy*, 43, 45. Poovey, *Uneven Developments*, 83–84.
34. For the biographical basis of the tale, see Fitzgerald, 2:430.
35. Ibid., 429.
36. Ibid., 2:433.
37. The trope of a child torn from the mother's breast occurs several times in Wollstonecraft and Norton (*M* 61, 139; *PL* 3, 69, 104).
38. Kemble, "Custody of Infants' Bill," 309. Norton responded directly in a letter to the *Times* (August 29, 1838), noteworthy for its acknowledgement of women's inferiority.
39. Perkins, *Mrs. Norton*, 155.
40. Sir Henry Sumner Maine, *Ancient Law* (London: Oxford University Press, 1959).
41. Harriet Martineau, *A History of Thirty Years Peace* (London: 1878), 4:10.
42. Bryan A. Garner, ed., *Black's Law Dictionary*, 6th ed. (St. Paul, MN: West Publishing, 1990), 623.
43. He observes: "these fictions of law, although at first they may startle the student, he will find upon further consideration to be highly beneficial and useful." *Commentaries on the Laws of England* (Oxford: Clarendon, 1765), 3:43.
44. For a discussion of this principle as well as of the events leading to the Divorce Act of 1857, see Mary Lyndon Shanley, *Feminism, Marriage, and the Law in Victorian England* (Princeton: Princeton University Press, 1989).
45. Kemble, "Custody of Infants' Bill," 386–90.
46. Ibid., 407.
47. Eliza Lynn Linton, "One of Our Legal Fictions," *Household Words* 9 (April 1854), 260.
48. Arthur Arnold, *The Hon. Mrs. Norton and Married Women* (Manchester: A. Ireland, 1878), 3.
49. Hadley, *Melodramatic Tactics*, 162.
50. Lynda Nead argues that "although Norton played a central role in the campaign for *married women's* rights, her demands remained within the parameters of an uncritical acceptance of marriage and the ideology of female sexual passivity." *Myths of Sexuality* (London: Basil Blackwell, 1988), 54.
51. For a discussion of maternity and maternal plots in Norton and others, see Elisabeth Rose Gruner, "Plotting the Mother: Caroline Norton, Helen Huntingdon, and Isabel Vane," *Tulsa Studies in Women's Literature* 16:2 (Fall 1997), 303–25.
52. Her formula exactly defines the situation of Caroline Norton, described by one biographer as that of a "reluctant rebel." Moore, *Victorian Wives*, 53.
53. *Remarks upon the Law of Marriage and Divorce; Suggested by The Hon. Mrs. Norton's Letter to the Queen* (London: James Ridgway, 1855), 3.

54. *Remarks upon the Law of Marriage and Divorce*, 3.
55. Cited by Perkins, 254.

AFTERWORD: "SUCH IS THE TALE THEY TELL!": THE NARRATIVES OF CAROLINE NORTON

1. Beinecke Rare Book and Manuscript Library, GEN MSS 260, Folder 56.
2. Sheridan Family Papers, Houghton Library, Harvard University, (bMS 1276).
3. John Fowles, *The French Lieutenant's Woman* (New York: New American Library, 1969), 95.
4. British Library, Sheridan Papers, Add. 40526, f. 312.
5. Norton herself turns such feelings into poems like "May-Day, 1837" and "The Fever-Dream" (*D* 216–22), both written after her children were removed from her care.
6. British Library, Sheridan Papers, Add 42767, f. 97.
7. Patricia Pulham notes that for Hemans and Norton "Sappho as art object merges with their identities." " 'Jewels—delights—perfect loves': Victorian Women Poets and the Annuals," in *Essays and Studies 2003*, ed. Alison Chapman (Cambridge: D. S. Brewer, 2003), 28.
8. Yopie Prins, "Personifying the Poetess: Caroline Norton, 'The Picture of Sappho,' " in *Women's Poetry, Late Romantic to Late Victorian: Gender and Genre, 1830–1900*, ed. Isobel Armstrong and Virginia Blain (New York: St. Martin's, 1999), 61.
9. Beinecke Rare Book and Manuscript Library, GEN MSS 260, Folder 29.
10. Beatrice Brooke is also compared to a "young Hagar" (*LS* 336).
11. Beinecke Rare Book and Manuscript Library, GEN MSS 260, Folder 70.
12. Beinecke Rare Book and Manuscript Library, GEN MSS 260, Folder 72.
13. "In Memory of W. B. Yeats," in *W. H. Auden: Selected Poems*, ed. Edward Mendelson (New York: Random House, 1979), 82.

Bibliography

Abramowicz, Sarah. "English Child Custody Law, 1660–1839: The Origins of Judicial Intervention in Paternal Custody." *Columbia Law Review* 99:5 (June 1999): 1344–91.

Acland, Alice. *Caroline Norton*. London: Constable, 1948.

Adburgham, Alison. *Silver Fork Society: Fashionable Life and Literature from 1814 to 1840*. London: Constable, 1983.

——. *Women in Print: Writing Women and Women's Magazines from the Restoration to the Accession of Victoria*. London: George Allen and Unwin, 1972.

Airlie, Mabell, "Countess of." *Lady Palmerston and Her Times*. 2 Vols. London, New York [etc.]: Hodder and Stoughton, 1922.

Alexander, Annie Hector. "Mrs. Norton." In *Women Novelists of Queen Victoria's Reign: A Book of Appreciations*. London: Hurst and Blackett, 1897.

Arnold, Arthur. *The Hon. Mrs. Norton and Married Women*. Manchester: A. Ireland, 1878.

Auerbach, Nina. *Private Theatricals: The Lives of the Victorians*. Cambridge: Harvard University Press, 1990.

Austen, Jane. *Persuasion*. Peterborough, Ontario: Broadview, 1998.

Ballantine, Serjeant. *Some Experiences of a Barrister's Life*. New York: Henry Holt, 1882.

Barker, Juliet, ed. *The Brontës: A Life in Letters*. London: Viking, 1997.

Bates, William. *The Maclise Portrait Gallery of Illustrious Literary Characters*. London: Chatto and Windus, 1898.

Beetham, Margaret. *A Magazine of Her Own? Domesticity and Desire in the Woman's Magazine, 1800–1914*. London and New York: Routledge, 1996.

Bennett, Regina J. *Naming the Violence: Women's Domestic Violence Narratives*. Diss. University of Oklahoma, 1998.

Blackstone, William. *Commentaries on the Laws of England*. 4 Vols, 18th ed. Ed. Thomas Lee. London: Strahan, 1809.

Blake, Robert. *Disraeli*. London: Eyre and Spottiswoode, 1966.

Blessington, Lady Marguerite. *The Repealers. The Works of Lady Blessington*. 2 Vols. Philadelphia: E. L. Carey and A. Hart, 1838.

Booth, Michael R. *Theatre in the Victorian Age*. Cambridge: Cambridge University Press, 1991.

Boumehla, Penny. " 'The Rattling of Her Discourse and the Flapping of Her Dress': Meredith Writing the 'Women of the Future.' " In *Feminist Critics: Theory and Practice*. Ed. Susan Sellers. Toronto: Toronto University Press, 1991.

Braun, Thom. *Disraeli the Novelist*. London: George Allen and Unwin, 1981.

Brody, Jennifer DeVere. *Impossible Purities: Blackness, Femininity, and Victorian Culture*. Durham and London: Duke University Press, 1998.

Brontë, Charlotte. "Biographical Notice of Ellis and Acton Bell," Rpt. *Wuthering Heights*. Harmondsworth: Penguin, 1965.

——. *Jane Eyre*. Peterborough, Ontario: Broadview, 1999.

Bulwer Lytton, Edward. *England and the English*. Ed. and intro. Standish Meacham. Chicago: University of Chicago Press, 1970.

Caine, Barbara. *English Feminism 1780–1980*. Oxford: Oxford University Press, 1997.

Campbell, James L., Sr. *Edward Bulwer-Lytton*. Boston: Twayne, 1986.

Caras, Kathryn. *"Public Complaint and Private Sorrow": The Feminism of Caroline Norton*. Diss. Indiana University, 1984.

Carlisle, Henry E., ed. *A Selection from the Correspondence of Abraham Hayward, Q.C.* 2 Vols. New York: Scribner and Welford, 1887.

Cecil, Lord David. *Melbourne*. Indianapolis and New York: Bobbs-Merrill, 1962.

Chase, Karen and Michael Levenson. *The Spectacle of Intimacy: A Public Life for the Victorian Family*. Princeton: Princeton University Press, 2000.

Chedzoy, Alan. *A Scandalous Woman: The Story of Caroline Norton*. London: Allison and Busby, 1992.

"*The Child of the Islands*," *The Quarterly Review* 76:151 (June 1845): 1–11.

Clarke, Micael M. *Thackeray and Women*. DeKalb: Northern Illinois University Press, 1995.

Coleridge, Hartley. "Modern English Poetesses." *Quarterly Review* 66 (September 1840): 374–418.

Coolidge, Bertha, ed. *Some Unrecorded Letters of Caroline Norton in the Altschul Collections of the Yale University Library*. Boston: privately printed, 1934.

Courtney, Janet E. *The Adventurous Thirties: A Chapter in the Women's Movement*. London: Oxford University Press, 1933.

Craig, Randall. *Promising Language: Betrothal in Victorian Law and Fiction*. Albany: SUNY Press, 2000.

——. *The Tragicomic Novel: Studies in a Fictional Mode from Meredith to Joyce*. Newark: University of Delaware Press, 1989.

Cunningham, Valentine. *In the Reading Gaol: Postmodernity, Texts, and History*. Oxford: Blackwell, 1994.

Curtis, George William, ed. *The Correspondence of John Lothrop Motley*. New York: Harper and Brothers, 1889.

"Custody of Infants' Bill." *The British and Foreign Review; or European Quarterly Journal* 7 (July–October 1838): 269–411.

"The Custody of Infants' Bill." *Fraser's* (February 19, 1839): 205–14.

Davis, Tracy C. *Actresses as Working Women: Their Social Identity in Victorian Culture.* London: Routledge, 1991.

Dent, Alan. *Preludes & Studies.* New York: Kennikat Press, 1970.

Dibello, Catherine. *Every Woman's Secret: Subversion and Accommodation in Women's Sensation Novels.* Diss. Indiana University. September 1983.

Dickens, Charles. *Bleak House.* Ed. George Ford and Sylvère Monod. New York: Norton, 1977.

——. *Great Expectations.* Ed. Graham Law and Adrian J. Pinnington. Peterborough, Ontario: Broadview Literary Texts, 1998.

——. *Hard Times.* Ed. Graham Law. Peterborough, Ontario: Broadview Literary Texts, 1996.

——. *The Letters of Charles Dickens.* Vol. 5. Ed. Kathleen Tillotson. Oxford: Clarendon, 1977.

——. *Little Dorritt.* Harmondsworth: Penguin, 2003.

——. *Oliver Twist.* Peterborough, Ontario: Broadview Encore Editions, 2005.

——. *The Pickwick Papers.* Harmondsworth: Penguin, 1972.

Disraeli, Benjamin. *Benjamin Disraeli Letters.* 7 Vols. Ed. J. A. W. Gunn et al. Toronto: University of Toronto Press, 1982–2004.

——. *Endymion. The Works of Benjamin Disraeli.* Vols 19–20. London and New York: M. W. Dunne, 1904–05.

Doggett, Maeve E. *Marriage, Wife-Beating and the Law in Victorian England.* London: Weidenfeld and Nicolson, 1992.

Dolan, Kieran. "The Transfigurations of Caroline Norton." *Victorian Literature and Culture* 30:2 (September 2002): 503–27.

——. "A Woman's Pleading: Caroline Norton's Pamphlets on Laws for Women in Nineteenth-Century England." *The Australian Feminist Law Journal* 10 (1998): 51–59.

Dowden, Wilfred S., ed. *The Journal of Thomas Moore: 1826–1830.* 4 Vols. Newark: University of Delaware Press, 1986.

——. *The Letters of Thomas Moore: 1818–1847.* 2 Vols. Oxford: Clarendon, 1964.

Dufferin, Lady Helen. *Songs, Poems, & Verses.* Ed. The Marquess of Dufferin and Ava. London: John Murray, 1895.

Dussol, Elizabeth. *"The legal axiom is, that sin is not sin in a man, if it be against a woman": Caroline Norton's Fight Against Injustice.* M.A. Thesis. University of St. Thomas, 1999.

Elam, Diane. " 'We Pray to Be Defended From Her Cleverness': Conjugating Romance in George Meredith's *Diana of the Crossways.*" *Genre* 21:2 (Summer 1988): 179–201.

Eliot, George. *Daniel Deronda.* Harmondsworth: Penguin, 1986.

——. *Felix Holt, the Radical.* Harmondsworth: Penguin, 1995.

——. *The Letters of George Eliot: 1869–1872.* Vol. 5. Ed. Gordon S. Haight. New Haven: Yale University Press, 1955.

——. "Life and Opinions of Milton." *Essays of George Eliot*, 154–57. Ed. Thomas Pinney. New York: Columbia University Press, 1963.

——. *The Mill on the Floss.* Harmondsworth: Penguin, 1985.

Ellis, S. M. *George Meredith: His Life and Friends in Relation to His Work.* London: Grant Richards, 1919.

Extraordinary Trial! Norton v. *Viscount Melbourne, for Crim. Con. Damages laid at £10,000!!!* London: William Marshall, n.d.

Fisher, Judith L. "'In the Present Famine of Anything Substantial': *Fraser's* 'Portraits' and the Construction of Literary Celebrity; or, 'Personality, Personality Is the Appetite of the Age.'" *Victorian Periodicals Review* 39:2 (Summer 2006): 97–135.

Fitzgerald, Percy. *Bardell* v. *Pickwick.* London: Elliot Stock, 1902.

——. *The Lives of the Sheridans.* 2 Vols. London: Richard Bentley and Son, 1886.

Forster, Margaret. *Significant Sisters: The Grassroots of Active Feminism, 1839–1939.* London: Secker and Warburg, 1984.

Foster, Shirley. *Elizabeth Gaskell: A Literary Life.* New York: Palgrave Macmillan, 2002.

Fowles, John. *The French Lieutenant's Woman.* New York: New American Library, 1969.

Fraser, Hilary. *The Victorians and Renaissance Italy.* Oxford: Blackwell, 1992.

Gallagher, Catherine. *Nobody's Story: The Vanishing Acts of Women Writers in the Marketplace, 1670–1820.* Oxford: Oxford University Press, 1994.

Garnett, Richard. *The Life of W. J. Fox.* London: John Lane, 1946.

George, Eric. *The Life and Death of Benjamin Robert Haydon, Historical Painter: 1786–1846.* 2nd ed., with additions by Dorothy George. Oxford: Clarendon, 1967.

Gerard, Frances A. *Some Fair Hibernians. Being a Supplementary Volume to "Some Celebrated Irish Beauties of the Last Century".* London: Ward and Downey, 1897.

Gilbert, W. S., and Arthur Sullivan. *Trial by Jury. The Complete Annotated Gilbert and Sullivan.* Intr. and Ed. Ian Bradley. Oxford: Oxford University Press, 1996.

Gleadle, Kathryn and Sarah Richardson, eds. "Introduction: The Petticoat in Politics: Women and Authority." In *Women in British Politics, 1760–1860*, 1–18. London: Macmillan, 2000.

Goodman, Andrew. *Gilbert and Sullivan at Law.* Rutherford, Madison, Teaneck, NJ: Fairleigh Dickinson University Press, 1983.

Gordon, Jan B. "Diana of the Crossways: Internal History and the Brainstuff of Fiction." In *Meredith Now.* Ed. Ian Fletcher. London: Routledge and Kegan Paul, 1971.

Greville, Charles C. F. *The Greville Memoirs: A Journal of the Reigns of King George IV and King William IV.* 3 Vols. London: Longmans, Green, and Co, 1874.

Grosvenor, Caroline, and Charles Beilby, Lord Stuart of Wortley. *The First Lady Wharncliffe and Her Family (1779–1856)*. 2 Vols. London: William Heinemann, 1927.

Gruner, Elisabeth Rose. "Plotting the Mother: Caroline Norton, Helen Huntingdon, and Isabel Vane." *Tulsa Studies in Women's Literature* 16:2 (Fall 1997): 303–25.

Grylls, R. Glynn. *Mary Shelley: A Biography*. London: Oxford University Press, 1938.

Hadley, Elaine. *Melodramatic Tactics: Theatricalized Dissent in the English Marketplace, 1800–1885*. Stanford: Stanford University Press, 1995.

Halperin, John. *Trollope and Politics: A Study of the Pallisers and Others*. New York: Barnes and Noble, 1977.

Hardy, Thomas. *Tess of the D'Urbervilles*. Harmondsworth: Penguin, 1978.

Harman, Barbara Leah. *The Feminine Political Novel in Victorian England*. Charlottesville: University Press of Virginia, 1998.

Haydon, Benjamin Robert. *The Diary of Benjamin Robert Haydon*. 5 Vols. Ed. Willard Bissell Pope. Cambridge: Harvard University Press, 1963.

Hayter, Alethea. *A Sultry Month: Scenes of London Literary Life in 1846*. London: Faber and Faber, 1965.

Hazlitt, William. "The Dandy School." In *The Complete Works of William Hazlitt*. Centenary Edition. 21 Vols. Ed. P. P. Howe. London: J. M. Dent and Sons, 1934.

Helsinger, Elizabeth K., Robin Lauterbach Sheets, and William Veeder. *The Woman Question: Society and Literature in Britain and America, 1837–1883*. Vol. 2. New York and London: Garland, 1983.

Hoge, James O. and Jane Marcus, eds. "Introduction." In *Selected Writings of Caroline Norton*, vii-xvii. Delmar, NY: Scholars' Facsimiles & Reprints, 1978.

Hoge, James O. and Clarke Olney, eds. *The Letters of Caroline Norton to Lord Melbourne*. Columbus: Ohio State University Press, 1974.

Holcombe, Lee. *Wives and Property: Reform of the Married Women's Property Law in Nineteenth-Century England*. Toronto: University of Toronto, 1983.

Holland, Lady Elizabeth. *Elizabeth, Lady Holland to Her Son: 1821–1845*. Ed. The Earl of Ilchester. London: John Murray, 1946.

Horne, R. H. *A New Spirit of the Age*. 2 Vols. London: Smith, Elder and Co., 1844; New York: Garland, 1986.

——. *Orion: An Epic Poem*. http://www.bartleby.com/246/77.html.

Horsman, Alan. *The Victorian Novel*. Oxford: Clarendon, 1990.

——. *Victorian Divorce*. London: Croom Helm, 1985.

Hughes, Winifred. *The Maniac in the Cellar: Sensation Novels of the 1860s*. Princeton: Princeton University Press, 1980. "Mindless Millinery: Catherine Gore and the Silver Fork Heroine." In *Dickens Studies Annual* 25:159–76. New York: AMS Press, 1996.

Huxley, Leonard, ed. *Jane Welsh Carlyle: Letters to Her Family, 1839–1863.* Garden City, NY: Doubleday, 1924.

Ilchester, The Earl of, ed. *The Journal of the Hon. Henry Edward Fox, 1818–1830.* London: Thornton Butterworth Limited, 1923.

Iremonger, Lucille. *And His Charming Lady.* London: Secker and Warburg, 1961.

Jameson, Anna. *Sacred and Legendary Art.* 2 Vols. London: Longmans, Green, and Co., 1866.

Johnson, Edgar. *Charles Dickens: His Tragedy and Triumph.* Revised and abridged. New York: Viking, 1977.

Johnston, Judith. *Anna Jameson: Victorian, Feminist, Woman of Letters.* Aldershot, England: Scolar Press, 1997.

Jump, Harriet Devine. "'The False Prudery of Public Taste': Scandalous Women and the Annuals, 1820–1850." In *Feminist Readings of Victorian Popular Texts: Divergent Femininities*, 1–17. Ed. Emma Liggins and Daniel Duffy. Aldershot, Hampshire: Ashgate Publishing, 2001.

Kemble, Frances Ann. *Records of a Girlhood.* New York: Henry Holt, 1879.

Kemble, John. "Custody of Infants' Bill," *The British and Foreign Review; or, European Quarterly Journal.* 7 (July–October, 1838): 269–411.

Krueger, Christine L. "Witnessing Women: Trial Testimony in Novels by Tonna, Gaskell, and Eliot." In *Representing Women: Law, Literature, and Feminism*, 337–55. Ed. Susan Sage Heinzelman and Zipporah Batshaw Wiseman. Durham: Duke University Press, 1994.

"Lady Blessington, Miss Eliza Cook, and the Hon. Mrs. Norton." *Reynolds's Miscellany* 1:15 (February 13, 1847): 233.

Lamington, Lord Alexander. *In the Days of the Dandies.* London: Eveleigh Nash, 1906.

Latané, David E., Jr. "Two Letters from Caroline Norton to Charles Molloy Westmacott." *Notes and Queries* 52:1 (March 2005): 65–68.

"The Laws Relating to Women." *The Law Review and Quarterly Journal of British and Foreign Jurisprudence* 20 (1854): 1–34.

Lawson, Kate and Lynn Shakinovsky. *The Marked Body: Domestic Violence in Mid-Nineteenth-Century Literature.* Albany: SUNY Press, 2002.

Leckie, Barbara. *Culture and Adultery: The Novel, the Newspaper, and the Law, 1857–1914.* Philadelphia: University of Pennsylvania Press, 1999.

Levine, Richard A. *Benjamin Disraeli.* New York: Twayne, 1968.

Lindsay, Jack. *George Meredith: His Life and Work.* London: Bodley Head, 1956.

Linton, Eliza Lynn. "One of Our Legal Fictions." *Household Words* 9 (April 1854): 257–69.

Litchfield, Henrietta, ed. *Emma Darwin: A Century of Family Letters, 1792–1896.* 2 Vols. London: John Murray, 1915.

"Living Literary Characters, No. 11. The Honourable Mrs. Norton." *New Monthly Magazine* 31:3 (February 1831): 180–83.

Lodge, David. *The Novelist at the Crossroads*. Ithaca: Cornell University Press, 1971.

Logan, Deborah Anna. *Fallenness in Victorian Women's Writing: Marry, Stitch, Die, or Do Worse*. Columbia: University of Missouri Press, 1998.

Lyster, Gertrude, ed. *A Family Chronicle Derived from Notes and Letters Selected by Barbarina, the Hon. Lady Grey*. London: John Murray, 1908.

Lytton, Earl of. *The Life of Edward Bulwer, First Lord Lytton*. 2 Vols. London: Macmillan, 1913.

Maginn, William. "'The Gallery of Illustrious Literary Characters.' No. X. Mrs. Norton," *Fraser's Magazine* (March 1831): 222.

Maine, Sir Henry Sumner. *Ancient Law*. London: Oxford University Press, 1959.

Malmesbury, James Howard Harris, Earl of. *Memoirs of an Ex-Minister: An Autobiography*. London: Longman's Green, and Co, 1885.

Manse, H. L. "Sensation Novels." *Quarterly Review* 113:226 (April 1863): 482–514. http://gaslight.mtroyal.ab.ca/sensnovl.htm.

Martin, Robert. *Tennyson: The Unquiet Heart*. London: Faber and Faber, 1983.

Martineau, Harriet. *Harriet Martineau's Autobiography*. Ed. Maria Weston Chapman. Boston: J. R. Osgood, 1877.

——. *The History of England during the Thirty Years Peace*. 2 Vols. London: C. Knight, 1849–50.

Masefield, Muriel. *Peacocks and Primroses: A Survey of Disraeli's Novels*. London: Geoffrey Bles, 1953; rpt. Millwood, NY: Kraus Reprint Co., 1973.

Maurois, André. *Disraeli: A Picture of the Victorian Age*. Trans. Hamish Miles. New York: Random House, 1928.

McCarthy, Justin. "Novels with a Purpose." *The Westminster Review* 82 (July 1864): 24–49.

McDowell, Paula. "Consuming Women: The Life of the 'Literary Lady' as Popular Culture in Eighteenth-Century England." *Genre* 26 (Summer/Fall 1993): 219–52.

McGlamery, Gayla. "In His Beginnings, His Ends: The 'Preface' to Meredith's *Diana of the Crossways*." *Studies in the Novel* 23 (1991): 470–89.

McMaster, R. D. *Thackeray's Cultural Frame of Reference*. Montreal and Kingston: McGill–Queen's University Press, 1991.

Meredith, George. *Diana of the Crossways. The Works of George Meredith*. Vols 17 and 18. London: Archibald Constable and Co., 1897.

Mermin, Dorothy. *Godiva's Ride: Women of Letters in England: 1830–1880*. Bloomington: Indiana University Press, 1993.

Michie, Helena. *The Flesh Made Word: Female Figures and Women's Bodies*. New York: Oxford University Press, 1987.

Mitchell, L. G. *Lord Melbourne: 1779–1848*. Oxford: Oxford University Press, 1997.

Mitchell, Sally. *The Fallen Angel: Chastity, Class and Women's Reading, 1835–1880*. Bowling Green: Bowling Green University Popular Press, 1981.

"Modern English Poetesses." *Quarterly Review* 66 (September 1840): 374–418.

Monsarrat, Ann. *An Uneasy Victorian: Thackeray the Man, 1811–1863.* New York: Dodd, Mead and Company, 1980.

Moore, Katherine. *Victorian Wives.* New York: St. Martin's, 1974.

Morely, John. *The Life of Richard Cobden.* Boston: Roberts Brothers, 1881.

Motley, John Lothrop. *The Correspondence of John Lothrop Motley.* 2 Vols. Ed. George William Curtis. New York: Harper and Brothers, 1889.

Nead, Lynda. *Myths of Sexuality.* London: Basil Blackwell, 1988.

Nicholson, Harold. *Helen's Tower.* New York: Harcourt, Brace and Company, 1938.

"The Non-Existence of Women. Letter to the Queen on Lord Chancellor Cranworth's Marriage and Divorce Bill." *The North British Review* 23 (May–August 1855): 536–62.

Norton, Caroline. "Books of Gossip: Sheridan and his Biographers." *Macmillan's Magazine* (January 3, 1861): 173–79.

——. *The Child of the Islands.* 2nd ed. London: Chapman and Hall, 1846.

——. *The Dandies' Rout.* London: John Marshall, 1820.

——. *The Dream.* London: Henry Colburn, 1840.

——. "*English Laws for Women.*" In *Caroline Norton's Defense.* Intro. Joan Huddleston. Chicago: Academy Chicago, 1982.

——, ed. *Fisher's Drawing Room Scrap-Book, 1847.* London: Fisher, Son, and Co., 1846.

——, ed. *Fisher's Drawing Room Scrap-Book, 1849.* London: Peter Jackson. Late Fisher, Son, and Co., 1849.

——. *Kate Bouverie, and Other Tales and Sketches, in Prose and Verse.* 2 Vols. Philadelphia: E. L. Carey and A. Hart, 1835.

——. *The Lady La Garaye.* London: Macmillan, 1866.

——. *A Letter to the Queen on Lord Chancellor Cranworth's Marriage and Divorce Bill.* London: Longman, Brown, Green and Longmans, 1855. http://www.indiana.edu/~letrs/vwwp/.

——. *Letters, etc. third and fourth correspondence with summary of facts.* London: Privately printed, 1841?.

——. *Letters to the Mob.* London: Thomas Bosworth, 1848.

——. *Lost and Saved.* Intro. and Notes S. Bailey Shurbutt. Delmar, NY: Scholars' Facsimiles and Reprints, 1988.

——. "Love in 'the World.'" Rare Book and Manuscript Collection, Yale University.

——. "A Mother." Beinecke Rare Book and Manuscript Collection, Yale University.

——. *Old Sir Douglas.* 2 Vols. Leipzig: Bernhard Tauchnitz, 1867.

——. *A Plain Letter to the Lord Chancellor on the Infant Custody Bill.* London: James Ridgway, 1839. http://www.indiana.edu/~letrs/vwwp/.

——. *Selected Writings of Caroline Norton.* Intro. and Notes James O. Hoge and Jane Marcus. Delmar, NY: Scholars' Facsimiles and Reprints, 1978.

——. *The Separation of Mother and Child by the Law of "Custody of Infants," Considered*. London: Roake and Varty, 1838.

——. *The Sorrows of Rosalie, A Tale with Other Poems*. London: John Ebors, and Co., 1829.

——. *Stuart of Dunleath: A Story of Modern Times*. 3 Vols. London: Colburn and Co., 1851.

——. *Taxation. By an Irresponsible Taxpayer*. Beinecke Rare Book and Manuscript Collection, Yale University.

——. *The Undying One and Other Poems*. London: H. Colburn and R. Bentley, 1830.

——. *A Voice From the Factories*. London: John Murray, 1836.

——. *The Wife and Woman's Reward*. 3 Vols. London: Saunders and Otley, 1835.

Obermueller, Erin V. "The Artist's Model in Mid-Victorian Women's Fiction." *Women's Writing* 11:1 (2004): 55–72.

O' Cinnéide, Muireann. *Public Grandeur & Private Discomfort: Aristocratic Identity in the Works of Rosina Bulwer Lytton, Emily Eden and Caroline Norton*. Diss. Oxford University, 2004.

Ogle, Nathaniel. "The Custody of Infants Bill." *Fraser's Magazine* (February 19, 1839): 205–14.

Olney, Clarke. *Benjamin Robert Haydon: Historical Painter*. Athens: University of Georgia, 1952.

——. "Caroline Norton and Lord Melbourne." *Victorian Studies* 8:3 (March 1965): 255–62.

Orr, Clarissa Campbell. *Wollstonecraft's Daughters: Womanhood in England and France, 1780–1920*. Manchester and New York: Manchester University Press, 1996.

"Our Female Sensation Novelists." Rpt. *Littell's Living Age*. Third Series. Vol. 22 (August 23, 1863): 352–69.

Pellum, Frederick James, Jr. *The Case of Norton Versus Lord Melbourne*. M.A. Thesis. University of Florida, 1968.

Perkins, Jane Grey. *The Life of the Honourable Mrs. Norton*. New York: Henry Holt, 1909.

Poovey, Mary. *Uneven Developments: The Ideological Work of Gender in Mid-Victorian England*. Chicago: University of Chicago Press, 1988.

Pope-Hennessy, James. *Monckton Milnes*. 2 Vols. New York: Farrar, Straus and Cudahy, 1955.

"The Popular Novels of the Year," *Fraser's Magazine* 68:404 (August 1863): 253–69.

Praed, Winthrop Mackworth. *The Poetical Works of Winthrop Mackworth Praed*. 2 Vols. New York: Redfield, 1860.

Prins, Yopie. "Personifying the Poetess: Caroline Norton, 'The Picture of Sappho.'" In *Women's Poetry, Late Romantic to Late Victorian: Gender and Genre, 1830–1900*, 50–67. Ed. Isobel Armstrong and Virginia Blain. New York: St. Martin's, 1999.

Pulham, Patricia. " 'Jewels—delights—perfect loves': Victorian Women Poets and the Annuals." In *Essays and Studies 2003*, 9–32. Ed. Alison Chapman. Cambridge: D. S. Brewer, 2003.

Rauchbauer, Otto Hans. "Some Unrecorded Letters by Caroline Norton." *Notes and Queries* 17 (September 1970): 335–39.

Ray, Gordon N. *Thackeray: The Age of Wisdom, 1847–1863.* New York: McGraw-Hill, 1958.

Remarks upon the Law of Marriage and Divorce; suggested by the Hon. Mrs. Norton's Letter to the Queen. London: James Ridgway, 1855.

Reynolds, K. D. *Aristocratic Women and Political Society in Victorian Britain.* Oxford: Clarendon Press, 1998.

Reynolds, Margaret. " 'I lived for art, I lived for love': The Woman Poet Sings Sappho's Last Song." In *Victorian Woman Poets: A Critical Reader*, 277–306. Ed. Angela Leighton. Oxford: Blackwell, 1996.

Ritchie, Hester Thackeray, ed. *Thackeray and His Daughter: The Letters and Journals of Anne Thackeray Ritchie, with Many Letters of William Makepeace Thackeray.* New York: Harper and Brothers, 1924.

Roberts, Neil. *Meredith and the Novel.* London: Macmillan, 1997.

Robertson, Eric S. *English Poetesses: A Series of Critical Biographies, with Illustrative Extracts.* London: Cassell and Company, 1883.

Rosa, Matthew Whiting. *The Silver Fork School: Novels of Fashion Preceding Vanity Fair.* Port Washington, NY: Kennikat Press, 1964.

Ross, Janet. *Three Generations of English Women: Memoirs and Correspondence of Susannah Taylor, Sarah Austin, and Lady Duff Gordon.* London: T. Fisher, Unwin, 1912.

——. *The Fourth Generation.* London: Constable, 1912.

Sadleir, Michael. *Bulwer: A Panorama.* Vol. 1. Boston: Little, Brown, and Company, 1931.

——. *The Strange Life of Lady Blessington.* New York: Farrar, Straus and Company, 1947.

Sadler, Thomas. ed. *Diary, Reminiscences, and Correspondence of Henry Crabb Robinson.* 2 Vols. Boston: Fields, Osgood, and Co., 1869.

Shanley, Mary Lyndon. *Feminism, Marriage, and the Law in Victorian England.* Princeton: Princeton University Press, 1989.

Shelley, Mary. *The Letters of Mary Wollstonecraft Shelley.* 3 Vols. Ed. Betty T. Bennett. Baltimore : Johns Hopkins University Press, 1988.

Shires, Linda M. "The Author as Spectacle and Commodity: Elizabeth Barrett Browning and Thomas Hardy." In *Victorian Literature and the Victorian Visual Imagination*, 198–212. Ed. Carol T. Christ and John O. Jordon. Berkeley: University of California Press, 1995.

Shurbutt, Sylvia Bailey. "The Popular Fiction of Caroline Sheridan Norton: The Woman Question and the Theme of Manipulation." *Studies in Popular Culture* 9:2 (1986): 24–40.

Smith, Charles Eastlake, ed. *Journals and Correspondence of Lady Eastlake.* 2 Vols. London: John Murray, 1895.

St. Clair, William. *Trelawny: The Incurable Romancer.* London: John Murray, 1977.

St. Helier, Lady. *Memories of Fifty Years.* London: Edward Arnold, 1909.

Stanton, Elizabeth Cady, Susan B. Anthony, and Matilda Joslyn Gage, eds. *History of Woman Suffrage.* Vol. 1. New York: Arno and the New York Times, 1969.

Stephen, James Fitzjames. "Anti-Respectability." *The Cornhill Magazine* (September 18, 1863): 282–92.

Stetson, Dorothy M. *A Woman's Issue: The Politics of Family Law Reform in England.* Westport, CT: Greenwood, 1982.

Stone, Lawrence. *The Family, Sex and Marriage in England: 1500–1800.* New York: Harper and Row, 1977.

——. *The Road to Divorce.* Oxford: Oxford University Press, 1990.

Surtees, Virginia, ed. *A Second Self: The Letters of Harriet Granville, 1810–1845.* Salisbury: Michael Russell, 1990.

Tennyson, Lord Alfred. "Maud." *Alfred Tennyson.* Ed. Adam Roberts. Oxford: Oxford University Press, 2000.

Terry, R. C., ed. *Oxford Reader's Companion to Trollope.* Oxford: Oxford University Press, 1999.

Thackeray, William Makepeace. *The Four Georges, Sketches of Manners, Morals, Court, and Town Life.* Garden City: Doubleday, n.d.

——. "A Grumble about the Christmas-Books." *Fraser's Magazine* (January 1847): 111–26.

——. *The Letters and Private Papers of William Makepeace Thackeray.* 4 Vols. Ed. Gordon N. Ray. Cambridge: Harvard University Press, 1946.

——. *The Newcomes: Memoirs of a Most Respectable Family.* London: J. M. Dent, 1994.

——. *Pendennis.* Oxford: Oxford University Press, 1994.

——. *Vanity Fair.* Harmondsworth: Penguin, 1985.

Thaden, Barbara Z. *The Maternal Voice in Victorian Fiction.* New York and London: Garland, 1997.

Thomas, Deborah A. *Thackeray and Slavery.* Athens: Ohio University Press, 1993.

Torrens, W. M. *Memoirs of the Right Honourable William Second Viscount Melbourne.* 2 Vols. London: Macmillan, 1878.

Toynbee, William, ed. *The Diaries of William Charles Macready, 1833–1851.* 2 Vols. New York: Benjamin Blom, 1912.

Trelawny, Edward John. *Letters of Edward John Trelwany.* Ed. H. Buxton Forman. New York: AMS Press, 1973; first published, London: Oxford University Press, 1910.

Trollope, Anthony. *Phineas Finn: The Irish Member.* Oxford: Oxford University Press, 1991.

——. *Phineas Redux.* Oxford: Oxford University Press, 1991.

Wheeler, Michael D. "The Writer as Reader in *Mary Barton,*" *Durham University Journal* 67 (December 1967): 92–102.

Williams, David. *George Meredith: His Life and Lost Love.* London: Hamish Hamilton, 1977.

Wilt, Judith. *The Readable People of George Meredith.* Princeton: Princeton University Press, 1975.

Wollstonecraft, Mary. *Mary* and *Maria*. Harmondsworth: Penguin, 1991.

"Woman's Law.—Mrs. Norton's Letter to the Queen." *The Law Review and Quarterly Journal of British and Foreign Jurisprudence* 22 (1855): 334–45.

Wordsworth, Jonathan. "Ann Yearsley to Caroline Norton: Women Poets of the Romantic Period." *The Wordsworth Circle* 26:3 (Summer 1995): 114–24.

Wyndham, Maud Mary, Baroness Leconfield, ed. *Three Howard Sisters: Selections from the Writings of Lady Caroline Lascelles, Lady Dover and Countess Gower, 1825–1833.* London: John Murray, 1955.

Zaborszky, Dorothy E. " 'Domestic Anarchy and the Destruction of the Family': Caroline Norton and the Custody of Infants Bill." *International Journal of Women's Studies* 7:5 (November–December): 397–411.

Ziegler, Philip. *Melbourne: A Biography of William Lamb 2nd Viscount Melbourne.* London: Collins, 1976.

INDEX

Note: The letter 'n' denotes note numbers